MASTER OF PAXWAX

Phillip Mann established himself as an exciting new talent with his first novel, *The Eye of the Queen*, acclaimed as one of the most convincing portrayals of an alien species ever written. Now he returns with the first part of a sweeping far-future epic, a compelling example of science fiction on the grand scale. The human race dominates the galaxy, having ruthlessly established superiority over a whole variety of intelligent aliens during the period of history known as the Great Push. Their society is autocratic, dynastic and decadent, dominated by the Eleven: old-established families, each of which controls an empire. Unknown to any of them, under the barren surface of the apparently dead world of Sanctum the aliens wait and watch, preparing for the time when they will strike back. Now they have found the man whom they will manipulate to bring about the fall of the human empire. His name is Pawl Paxwax, second son of the Fifth Family, who finds himself thrust unexpectedly into power – and into a deadly crisis – when his elder brother and his father die in rapid succession.

Master of Paxwax is a remarkable book, effortlessly blending drama and philosophy, and introducing a large and memorable cast of humans and aliens. A sequel, *The Fall of the Families*, concluding the story of Pawl Paxwax, will be published early next year.

MASTER OF PAXWAX

Book One of the story of
Pawl Paxwax, the Gardener

by

PHILLIP MANN

LONDON
VICTOR GOLLANCZ LTD
1986

First published in Great Britain 1986
by Victor Gollancz Ltd,
14 Henrietta Street, London WC2E 8QJ

British Library Cataloguing in Publication Data
Mann, Phillip
Master of Paxwax: book one of the story
of Pawl Paxwax, the gardener.
I. Title
823'.914[F]   PR9639.3.M256

ISBN 0-575-03807-1

Typeset in Great Britain by Centracet
and printed by St Edmundsbury Press,
Bury St Edmunds, Suffolk

TO MY DAUGHTER,
DELIA MANN

We affirm our superiority to mere existence because we dare to create. Creation is the extension of consciousness itself, the conquest of new areas of awareness.

HERBERT READ

1

ON SANCTUM

We will begin on the dead and almost invisible planet called Sanctum.

Sanctum has the face of a dead world. It glimmers a dull and muddy red in the light of its dying sun. It has no bright dawns or blazing sunsets, just a creeping redness followed, hours later, by a creeping darkness. Where once there were seas of tumbling green water, there are now only dusty cracked plateaux. The wide meanderings and bird's-foot deltas which once marked the passage of great rivers have now almost completely disappeared, choked. High cliffs of rubble and rounded hills are all that remain to show where continents and mountains once stood.

There is no atmosphere on Sanctum. No movement. No life.

Occasionally a meteorite, hurtling in from the blackness, raises a brief incandescent storm. But this quickly subsides leaving a puddle of dull congealing lava and yet another high-rimmed crater to scar the world's surface. There are many such craters: so many indeed that they link together, like petrified rain drops, patterning the surface of the dead planet.

And if you arrived above Sanctum and looked down on its frigid plains you would say, "How dreary. How dead and uninviting. Nothing can live here." And you would move on in search of a green and blue world.

That of course is part of the great plan, for the psychosphere of Sanctum is tuned to repel the casual visitor.

But as with most things concerning the Inner Circle, appearances are deceptive. If you were to dig under the surface, like a child plunging its hands into the wet sand by the sea shore, you would quickly discover life.

Tunnels lined with blue fluorescent tiles burrow through this world. They dip and loop and join all of Sanctum like a vast vascular system. There are giant echoing chambers which enclose tepid subterranean seas. Pale artificial suns dangle over faded green plains and scraggly forests. Great funnels, quarried from the bedrock of the planet, crawl with life. There are many habitats on Sanctum, for Sanctum is one of the last holds of alien life.

Deep inside the planet, and the focus of many tunnels, is a cavern which stretches from the deepest level of rivers up to the topmost layer of rock. Living here is a silver tree. It juts up from the soft loam around its base and soars upwards while its trunk narrows until it spreads in a wide white canopy. Silver and grey branches support the canopy, which has the greasy appearance of polished ivory or an exposed brain. This tree is the guiding intelligence of Sanctum.

The Tree is an alien among aliens. Its thought radiates out through the planet. It is the organizer, the source of hope and the final arbiter of all the life on Sanctum. The Tree controls the psychosphere.

Just now the Tree is suffused with an inner light. It throbs like an active muscle and sends pulses of light from its base right up to the outer reaches of its canopy. The Tree is transmitting and all the tunnels of Sanctum are alive with its thought. It is inviting the minds of the creatures that live on Sanctum to join with it.

A humble Gerbes, clamped firmly to its rock and enjoying the buffet of a cold salt wind, hears the call and rears and stretches its shiny trunk. A wave slaps the rock and sluices over it while the Gerbes (hereafter called Odin) begins to edge towards the land. He eases himself down and flops on to the wet shingle and toils up the shallow beach. The single basal sucker which anchors Odin to the land thrusts its lip forwards and then drags the domed body along. With a steady peristalsis Odin works his way over the wet rocks and up into a narrow tunnel which leads to one of the main passages. Before entering the bright blue passage, Odin pauses and worms his upper trunk into a black, bell-shaped robe which settles round him. This robe will preserve Odin's vital moisture. It seems that within the robe Odin has short stunted arms. Fine red tendrils emerge from the sides and take up a pale mask, like a travesty of a human face, and fit it up under the hood of the robe. Thus equipped, Odin glides out into the main thoroughfare and joins the other creatures who are hurrying to obey the Tree's call.

Far away, many strata above Odin, a Giant Hammer, belly deep in sand and dozing, rears suddenly. Its scaled legs lift it like pistons. It arches its sting over its hammer head and then begins to run, throwing up a cloud of dust and torn clods of earth. As it runs it drums, beating out a tattoo to all its fellows.

In a chamber filled with moss, where long ropes of dripping fibres reach from floor to ceiling, Spiderets tumble and crawl over one another. The senior Spiderets hear the call and stretch their legs and hump their bodies and shinny down to the cave floor. They scurry on hairy legs, jostling for a place.

Strangest of all, a Lyre Beast extracts its tendrils from the fissures of a rock wall and begins to descend. It is like a walking spider's web, like torn lace at a window. It spreads and dilates as it picks its way through lofty chambers and crawls down into one of the passageways. It is careful not to touch other creatures as its touch is lethal. As it moves it is accompanied by its own thrilling music, like the calling of many flutes.

And there are more. Many many more.

The focus of all movement is the beehive chamber where the Tree lives. This chamber has been designed and adapted for the specific needs of the aliens. There are cells of clear silica in which a private atmosphere can be maintained, and tier upon tier of seats and platforms.

The creatures that are gathering are the leaders of their species. And all the species gathered on Sanctum have one thing in common: they all have achieved self-awareness, the first requisite of civilization.

The tree emanates an aura of confidence and trust, and most important, of hope.

It is towards this hope that Odin toils. He does not want to be late, yet he cannot move quickly. He is scarcely three feet tall, and the Gerbes are slow in everything except their intelligence. The tiles are too smooth for him and offer no easy purchase for the delicate flukes which surround his sucker. He slips and then rears and works patiently on.

Other creatures pass him. A group of humans, head down and wearing a similar black gown, hurry past. These are servants of the Inner Circle.

Odin envies them their speed. A Giant Hammer jumps over him

and is gone like an express train. A Hooded Parasol with its petals extended flaps gently by.

Odin knows he will be late. But so be it.

Suddenly there is a shift in the intensity of the Tree's thought. The meeting is beginning. To Odin, who cannot see but who is sensitive to every slight fluctuation of thought, it is as though a furnace door has been edged open. He protects himself. There is no pain, just an awareness of raw power as the Tree takes charge of the psychosphere and brings all minds to singularity.

An image forms in Odin's mind. It is the face of a human, yellow eyed and imperious. Odin has seen it before. With the image come words. The Tree is speaking.

WE WILL CONSIDER PAWL PAXWAX WHO WILL, WE BELIEVE, BE THE SAVIOUR OF US ALL.

2

ON LOTUS-AND-ARCADIA:
THE PLEASURE WORLDS

All unaware of the interest being taken in him at that very moment on the distant world of Sanctum, Pawl Paxwax stood humped and angry in the palace of his mistress, Laurel Beltane. They were on Lotus-and-Arcadia, the pleasure worlds. She faced him squarely.

They had been arguing for hours in the friendly, serious way of lovers who know that they are broaching new territory and are therefore cautious. But the argument was real nevertheless. Finally Pawl threw his hands in the air.

"For the last time. Will you come with me?"

"No. The Families. . . ."

"To hell with the Families."

"Ha." She stood facing him with her hands on her hips and her bright cheerful face staring up at him. Behind her the lights of Lotus-and-Arcadia were coming alive as the day faded into evening.

"The Families would close on us before we could even reach Bennet Homeworld. Don't be a fool, Pawl. For my sake, for yours, for many sakes we must remain secret until you have talked to your father and won him over." Pawl laughed at that. "You don't win my father over to anything. You get the biggest hammer you can and hit him."

"Well, whatever. You must speak to him first. Wear him down like water on a rock. We have plenty of time. Why rush? Let him grow to the idea. Let him believe he thought of it."

"No chance."

"Your family and mine will be the happier for it."

Pawl knew that in this, as in most things concerning their relationship, Laurel was right. Still he cast about for arguments. "I'm sick of the pretence. I'm sick of creeping round here like a thief. . . ."

"So am I."

"I love you. I want the worlds to know it . . . and anyway, what if I can't win my father over? Suppose he says 'NO' flatly and forever? What then?"

"We will face that difficulty when we come to it. Just remember, I am of the Beltane Fifty-Sixth. You are of the Fifth Family. My family can be squeezed and pressured in any number of ways. We are very vulnerable. The safety of myself, my father and my brother depends on you. Don't treat that lightly. Be a realist, Pawl. What do you think the Xerxes sisters would do if they thought you intended to break the Code? Eh? What would they do?"

Pawl spread his hands.

"Well, I'll tell you. They'd call a special council meeting of the Eleven. They'd try to get sanctions against us." She paused and drew breath. "And the Wong, Old Man Wong, can you see him saying, 'Good, good. Go ahead, break the Code. You're only young once. You're in love, tra la la.' Hell no. He'd spit blood. He'd close the trade routes through his Way Gates just like that." She snapped her fingers. "Do you remember what he did when that fourteenth daughter of the twenty-seventh brother or whatever she was, tried to run away?"

"No, I don't re – "

"He sent out one of his pretty little death squads and they cut off her hands and feet."

"Rubbish."

"True, True, Pawl. Those are the people we are dealing with. They don't love you. They don't like you. They fear the Paxwax. Expect no kindness from them. Don't even give them an inch. *And* there's the Proctors. . . ."

"Enough."

"No, hear me out. The Proctors are silly, we all know that, but they are the First Family and they control more territory than your family and mine put together. They like nothing more than to wave the rule book. You haven't a chance against them, Pawl. Alone you are nothing. But with your family behind you, you have a chance. Thank God you are not the first son. Thank God you are not Lapis." Lapis was Pawl's eldest brother and next in line in the Paxwax family. "If you were the direct heir . . . whoosh, we'd have no chance."

"I'd still love you just as. . . ."

"I know. I know. Can't you see what I'm saying?"

"Are you trying to tell me you don't love me?"

"Away, silly man. I love you more than I can say." She spread her dark webbed hands and smiled. "It is because I love you that I am so careful. Our only chance lies in remaining secret. And then . . . well, if your father won't understand . . . we'll see what can be done. My family has friends. We know the Shell-Bogdanovich Conspiracy. We could probably arrange something. But I think you would have to renounce the Paxwax."

"I'll do it. I'll do it now."

"Pawl!" She pushed him. Though she was only small Laurel had a strong athletic body, the result of years spent swimming, and Pawl stumbled back, caught his clumsy heels in the carpet and fell down on to a low cushioned couch. Laurel Beltane rocked back on her heels and laughed. "You wait until we are married, Pawl my boy, you'll get worse than that."

Pawl scrambled to his feet. His hair had come unpinned and tumbled down over his shoulders. He was red-faced, but his eyes were not angry.

"By all the false gods that live on this god-forsaken shithouse of a planet, I've never met anyone as stupidly stubborn as you."

"Thank you, kind sir," said Laurel Beltane, lifting her skirts in a provocative mock curtsy.

"Do you realize that if I went outside this minute and hiccoughed, I could have any woman I wanted?"

"Go ahead. See how you like the kind of woman who'll lie down when a great man hiccoughs. I won't be there."

"Huh." Pawl sat down and as an afterthought blew her a raspberry. "So, where shall we eat?"

"We've already eaten. An hour ago."

"I'd forgotten. Where shall we go? What shall we do on my last night. Shall we stay at home like a happily married couple?"

"What would you like to do?"

Pawl thought. "What I would like to do," he said, "is kick a few heads in. I saw one of the Sith brood a while ago. You remember, at that party where we pretended we were only distant friends. Yes, well, he was looking at you and rubbing his hands up and down his horns and then he said something to one of his friends and they both started laughing. I almost picked a fight then."

"I'm glad you didn't."

"No, it would have been silly, wouldn't it?" He stood up and crossed to one of the windows and looked out at the kaleidoscopic night sky. From the distance came the sounds of laughter and loud music. Small lights danced in the air as private chairs, lifted by anti-gravity cells, darted about. The night was frantic with activity. "If I never see this place again it will be too soon. I only stay here because of you."

"Of course. It gives us cover . . . and freedom."

"So what shall we do?"

"Let's go to bed."

And being sensible and very much in love, that was just what they did. They tried to forget their troubles in passion and for a while succeeded.

But then in the early hours Pawl found himself awake. He listened to Laurel snoring softly and eased his arm out from under her without waking her. He brought the lights up to dimness so that he could look at her.

She slept like a child, with her lips moving, as in her dreams she mended the day. Magnificent sleeping woman. She was so beautiful that it made him hurt inside.

He was about to wake her, but didn't. Instead he reached across to the table near the bed and took hold of a scuffed old notebook and a stub of pencil that was attached to it by a string. With his knees up in bed he began to write.

*

This had become a habit with him.

Pawl Paxwax was different from the other children of the Great Families in many ways, but his writing was the strangest deviation of all. Literacy was not greatly admired and there were some among the Great Families who could do little more than scrawl their names: scribes were always available for more complex recording. But Pawl wrote for pleasure.

He did not understand it. He had discovered, almost by accident, that he could write bitter little satires which he directed against his real or imagined enemies. He gained more enemies than friends. But then he met Laurel and his bitterness drained away. Now, if he wrote at all, it was to try and find ways of expressing his love. It was all very simple to him, but he never managed to say what he meant.

Dissatisfied, he pushed the book aside and stretched out. His mind wandered over the day and into the future. Tomorrow he would visit Mako, some dreary little planet at the arse end of the Paxwax Empire, and thence back to Homeworld to visit his father. Whichever way he looked at it, the future was not attractive. What was wrong with life? Why did good things never get anywhere?

He became aware that Laurel was quiet and lying very still. He reached out a hand and touched her and she responded immediately. "Can't you sleep either?" she said.

"No."

"Worrying?"

"I suppose so." He lay quiet feeling her breathe beside him. "I mean . . . why is everything so hard? I keep asking myself . . . I keep wondering what has happened to us . . . I mean us of the Great Families. Why do we have a Code . . . ?"

"To keep your power together."

"Yes, but isn't it silly now?"

"It is what is. It is what will be for long after you and I are dust in the bottom of the sea."

"I doubt that. I have a sick feeling inside me. I think that we who are the children of the Families are as strange in spirit as we are in body."

Laurel had heard Pawl talk this way before in the quiet hours of the morning. "Hush," she said and reached up and placed one of her fingers on his lips. But Pawl was not to be stopped.

"No, let me talk. Don't you wonder sometimes when you see the Proctors . . . I mean, I saw one the other day. He'd set his mane in curlers and I swear that if his lower teeth grow any more they'll pierce his skull." Laurel giggled. "And the Shell-Bogdanovich can't leave the water for more than a few minutes at a stretch. And look at me. . . ."

"And me."

"We weren't always like this you know. There was a time when we were sturdy as beggars."

"Beggars aren't sturdy."

"But you know what I mean. I think we are rotting inside. Reverting. But still we live and breathe and breed."

Laurel *did* understand, for though she had a fine animal energy, outwardly she was piebald with delicate webbing between her fingers and toes. She tried not to think about it.

She wanted to quiet Pawl for she could see where this line of thought was leading him. Pawl had violence trapped inside him. He possessed a brooding anger with few outlets for it. When once set on a mood. . . .

"Well, some things we can't change," she said. "We must accept the reality that's given to us and hope for happiness."

"Yes," he sighed. "Yes." She felt him relax under her hands. "Even so. . . ."

A bell rang softly in their chamber, reminding them that there were only a few hours before Pawl was due to depart.

"I hope you'll write something for me when you are gone."

"Try and stop me. Hey, I scribbled this for you." Pawl reached down and sat up again, holding the battered notebook. He peeled through the pages and then found the page he wanted and tore it out.

"Here."

Laurel was used to this. She had often woken up in the night to find him hunched over his book, chewing his pencil and grimacing as he tried out words. It gave him release, she knew. Sometimes he never even made it to bed and she found him in the morning, snoring at the table. Sometimes he wrote with desperation, and once he had told her that the only thing with substance was words. She had not understood that. But in her mind she likened Pawl to a man who runs along a deserted beach until he drops, exhausted, on his knees in the waves, purged. She loved him for that.

Here are the words she read as the daylight brightened outside the windows.

I do not fear the darkness,
Or the shadow of a bat's wing
Across a full moon.

I do not fear the stranger,
Or the creature that dogs me and will
Beckon me soon.

I do not fear the journey,
Or the sad time that stretches from noon
To flickering noon.

But that veil behind the eyes,
The pause before the smile,
The emptiness that once was

Drum full,
When just to be near
Was enough.
That I fear.

She read. And when she had finished reading she kissed him. "Is the journey the visit to see your father?"

"Yes."

"Well, don't worry about the rest of it, Pawl. You'll never lose me. To get rid of me you'll have to kick me out."

"That. Never."

She smiled. More than Pawl she had sounded the depth of their love. She knew her own feelings, but she also knew that the heart of man is unfaithful. Laurel was above all a realist.

Over breakfast they discussed their plans. For at least the fifth time Laurel made Pawl check that the vivante cube they had made was safe. This was the cube which they hoped would help persuade Pawl's father that marriage with the Beltane family was not such a foolish idea.

"It is safe. Now don't worry. I'll talk to him straight. I won't lose my temper and I'll show him the cube. And when he has listened to me I'll get him to contact Lapis. I'm sure Lapis will help us."

"Mmmm."

"You don't think so."

"I don't know. I wish we'd heard from him."

"Ha. Don't worry about Lapis. The day he starts to act like anyone else is the day the worlds end."

"All right."

"Lapis won't let us down."

"What about Pental?"

Pental was Pawl's second eldest brother.

"I've told you before. Pental is with the Inner Circle. We haven't heard from him in years."

"Even so. Blood is thicker. . . ."

"Not where the Inner Circle is concerned. Forget Pental. We'll manage without him. We'll probably find that the Inner Circle are our greatest enemies. The less they know the better. They uphold the Code even more than the Proctors."

They faced one another silently over their breakfast. Neither had eaten much.

"I don't know what to say," said Laurel finally.

"Say nothing. Keep calm. Hold fast."

The bell which had rung in the night and which had rung at regular intervals since then, now began to sound loudly and urgently. Pawl was already late.

If he wanted to reach Mako in time for the festivities he would have to leave now.

"Away Pawl. Good luck. Take care. Contact me as soon as you have any news."

One kiss and he was gone.

Lotus-and-Arcadia, tawdry and drab in the morning light and as friendly as a drunk with a hangover, was just waking up as Pawl flew out to the shuttle port.

He checked in and the Way Guardian took his prints and enquired in its polite formal way, "Going away, Pawl Paxwax?"

"Family business on Mako."

"Will you be returning to Lotus-and-Arcadia?"

"Soon, I hope," said Pawl.

"Bon voyage."

3

ON SANCTUM

On Sanctum the creatures that led the Inner Circle studied the proud features of Pawl Paxwax. They did not know him and could scarcely understand the passions that drove him, though love is a universal engine.

What they did understand was that he was a rebel.

They encouraged rebellion wherever they found it, but in subtle and indirect ways.

There was more than that, however. From the moment of his birth, sensitives on Sanctum, groping their way to understand the future, had predicted that when the man with yellow eyes woke up then all the Families would fall. Like many predictions, this one sounded grand and apocalyptic. The seasoned minds of Sanctum treated it with caution. They had had their hopes raised before. They kept their eyes on the ground.

But the Tree seemed to take a special interest in Pawl and that gave some room for hope.

The Inner Circle watched Pawl. They knew about Laurel. They knew about his verses and his fights. He was certainly an interesting man, a different man. Whether he would be their saviour was a different matter.

4

ON MAKO

Pawl leaned back against the deep blue cushions of his palanquin and tried to ignore the throbbing in his head. Journey through the Way Gate system invariably left him feeling as though there was a creature inside his head, kicking at his temples, trying to get out.

There had been speeches at the Way Platform, then beefy handshakes, a lurching descent in the shuttle to more speeches, cheering crowds and a band. He had tried to listen to the Paxwax agent whose job it was to brief him on this agricultural world, but the man spoke with a thick accent and Pawl could not make sense of him. Finally he found himself hoisted in the air and dumped, not unceremoniously, in the palanquin.

So here he was on Mako, lurching along, carried by four bearers. It was not an easy mode of travel. They were not professional bearers but farmers, and they kept losing pace and rhythm.

As he swayed along he listened to the discordant voices of children. They were singing the Anthem of the Families and Pawl nodded and waved with as much grace as he could muster. Teams of scrub-faced children bordered his route. He saw their tiny mouths open and close in near unison.

For their part, the children stared at him with uncomprehending candour. They had been told he was a great man. For months their teachers had drilled them in songs and dances warning them that if they didn't behave properly the great man would be angry. They hoped to see something wonderful, like a god bringing bounty from the skies. But all they could see was a young man dressed in bright clothes and carried on the shoulders of their fathers. He passed them in a matter of minutes and they fell into line, singing as fervently as if the sunrise depended on it.

Here is the song they were singing. It is a song which all the children of human kind, scattered across the wide bowl of the galaxy, learn at school.

First are the Proctors, the greatest and best
They keep the great wheel spinning from the centre where
                                                    they rest.

Second are the Wong the warriors, saviours of our race,
They chased away the Hammer and put them in their place.

Third is the Conspiracy of the Bogdanovich and Shell
They fight for truth and justice and liberty as well.

The Xerxes de la Tour Souvent are fourth on our list
Where love is found and tenderness, they are never missed.

The Paxwax Fifth are generous to the meek and mild,
They give the food that keeps alive every little child.

The Lamprey Sixth love the light, their father was the sun,
Their children are the stars that shine upon us everyone.

The Freilander and Porterhouse hold the seventh place,
They stopped the alien in his tracks and kicked him in the face.

The Longstock and the Paragon,
The Sith and Felice too,
Help keep the goblins on their knees
And so I hope do you.

It is a silly anthem, and like most propaganda songs it is substantially untrue.

It was composed (no one knows by whom) shortly after the Great Push, when the Eleven Great Families were establishing their empire. Once it may have had meaning, but now it is merely a mnemonic, ensuring that the children never forget their leaders.

The palanquin halted and was lowered to the ground with a bump. Beside it was a high stage supported on wooden trestles. A flight of red painted steps led to the top of the stage, where the ornate carved throne of the Paxwax stood, looking ridiculous.

Pawl stepped carefully down and on to a carpet of freshly scattered petals. On cue, the children who had just sung to him came running round and surrounded him, offering flowers. It was a pleasing sight, for all its stiff staging, and Pawl smiled. *Laurel would have liked this*, he thought. He glanced round and his golden owl eyes blinked as though taking a picture. Then, when all was silent, he climbed slowly, and seemingly painfully, up the steps to the Paxwax throne.

It is in climbing that Pawl's deformity is most evident. A slight hump lifts one shoulder higher than the other and gives him a wrestler's stance. The crooked legs, set in wedge-shaped boots with high heels, look frail, as though they should be supported with steel rods. But the appearance is deceptive. Pawl can run and kick. Abnormality in the legs is a genetic hallmark of the Paxwax and Pawl is far less deformed than most of the members of the Great Families.

The true nature of the man shows in his hair and face. His hair is glossy with oil and he wears it braided after the manner of his boyhood. The tight plaits form a cone. The nose is aquiline and the nostrils large. But the eyes . . . it is the eyes that reveal his true strength and vigour. They are golden as flint and when Pawl stares at something he seems to devour it.

Pawl sat down on the uncomfortable carved throne and the children again burst into song. This time it was a jaunty song telling the story of how Mako had gained its prosperity.

Pawl sat straight in his chair. Even seated he was taller than most of the farmers who gathered close to him. He drummed along with the rhythm of the song on the arm of his chair and nodded to the singing children who waved flowers above their heads.

This is their day, he thought. *Let them have their day*.

Mako was celebrating three hundred years of Paxwax dominance.

While they sang the children divided into three groups. The first group held up a banner with the words "The Pioneers" emblazoned on it. They danced a dance showing how the first Paxwax settlers cut and burned the native forest to make clearings for their houses and fields.

When they had finished a second group took their place. They were called "The Planters". They mimed people digging the soil and wiping the sweat from their brows and pressing seeds into the ground.

The third group carried forwards a giant blue flower, the blossom of the Rand Melon. It was oils derived from the seeds of this melon which gave Mako its prosperity. Refined, these oils were

one of the main ingredients in a type of polish used to make
stonework shine. The flesh of the Rand Melon was inedible.

Pawl clapped when the song ended. He wondered just how
much these people knew about the true history of the planet they
called home. Pawl did not know much history. But this much he
had learned before departing for Mako.

The Paxwax gained the planet as part of a job lot when they
were re-organizing their economic frontiers. They bartered with
the Sith Tenth who had, for generations, mined the southern
continents.

Before the Sith, Mako belonged to the Freilander-Porterhouse,
who captured it during the Great Push. They had extracted salt
from its seas and released livestock and spread an epidemic among
the population of the only viable civilization that Mako had ever
known.

Before the Freilander-Porterhouse, Mako was un-named except
in the tongues of its native inhabitants, of which there were many.
Now, only remnants of that first population survived. The advanced
creatures which once had their cities here never managed the long
trek to Sanctum, and so became extinct. The present city of Mako,
Flower of Paxwax, was built on the site of one of the early alien
cities.

As the notes of the Mako song died, Pawl prepared to rise to his
feet, but was stopped in his tracks when the children began to sing
again. It was the wretched Anthem of the Families once more. The
damned song with its trite melody got on Pawl's nerves and he was
tempted to bring it to a halt by simply standing. But he didn't.

> "First are the Proctors, the greatest and the best.
> They keep the great wheel spinning. . . ."

Far away on a hillside, movement caught Pawl's eye. A small
colony of long-legged, green creatures was gathering. Their heads
were bobbing with the rhythm.

> "Third is the Conspiracy of the Bogdanovich and Shell
> They fight for truth and justice and liberty. . . ."

The creatures began to bang their small claws together and sway
and pace. One of them raised its head with a cluster of berry-like
eyes, and gave voice to a high whinnying.

Pawl watched as a farmer who had been patrolling the outer

fields waded through the thigh-deep fallow grass towards them and cracked his whip above their heads. They cantered back, graceful as giraffes, and fell silent.

Satisfied, the farmer turned his back on them and looked down towards the celebrations.

"The Paxwax Fifth are generous to the meek and mild.
They give the food that keeps alive every little child."

The singing surged with the breeze. The season for the gala had been well chosen. Springtime. A clean pale sunlight. The blue trumpet-shaped flowers of the Rand Melon were in full bloom in the fields, filling the air with their sharp sweet perfume.

Pawl rested his eyes on the blue hills and let his mind wander. The sight of so many children singing in unison and dancing with the same movements saddened him.

Life is diverse, not uniform.

Perhaps some of the philosophy of Laurel Beltane had rubbed off on him. Perhaps variety was, as she had told him many times, the essence of life. Pawl knew that to think of Laurel's delight in clashing colours and sharp rhythms as a philosophy was stretching the meaning of the word. But still. . . .

"The Lamprey Sixth love the light, their father was the sun.
Their children are the stars that. . . ."

The dark blue hills vibrated against the pale blue sky. The simple beauty of the scene sank hooks into him and held him. Why did nature always seem so right? What hand had placed that hill there, and that valley and that peak? So sure. So certain.

The hills gave Pawl comfort. There was a rightness to things, even if the reason for that rightness eluded him.

It was like his life. He was rolling down the path of his fate and there was nothing he could do, so why worry, why bother?

No! That was wrong. His life was not like a river following the line of least resistance and making its way to some ultimate sea.

He rode his fate . . . *he* could decide whether to dally in backwaters or race over rapids. The end might be the same; the means was all.

Pawl came out of his reverie with a start. The song was ending and now the speeches would begin.

"Help keep the goblins on their knees,
And so I hope do you."

The children finished on a triumphant note in which there was
also a hint of relief. They had played their part, and now it was
over to the grown-ups.

They sat down on the ground and Pawl quickly rose to his feet.
His short speech was prepared and memorized. He was first to
compliment the leaders of the Mako community on their hard
work and then present awards of merit to those farmers who had
achieved spectacular results.

The Senior Citizen who was in charge of the festivities came up
beside Pawl and opened a large sun umbrella which he held high
above Pawl's head. The farmers who were to receive awards
shuffled into a line at the foot of the steps.

Pawl was about to speak when a jabber of voices erupted behind
him. A tussle was taking place. A woman wearing a bright blue,
flower-patterned uniform forced her way on to the stage. She came
forward and whispered something in the ear of the official holding
the umbrella. He listened, looked surprised, and then glanced
uneasily at Pawl.

"Er. It seems there is a message received. An urgency. From
your father, Master Toby of the Fifth, in person. We shall delay.
We will continue singing."

The woman led Pawl to the back of the stage, down some
narrow steps and towards a low white building above which spread
the distinctive aerial of a vivante transmitter.

Behind him a dark, hooded figure moved quickly and stopped
him with a black-gloved hand. "Some misadventure, Essent Pawl?
Can I help?" The voice was whispery and sibilant, the way a cat
might talk.

"No problem, representative from the Inner Circle," said Pawl.
"No doubt a domestic call. I will take care of it immediately." The
dark figure bowed briefly and withdrew.

The less the Inner Circle knew about things the better. They
were everywhere, administering, advising. Fleetingly Pawl thought
of his brother Pental.

As he walked towards the vivante chamber he heard the concert-
master strike up the opening chords of the Anthem again.

A message from his father! This worried Pawl. In all the ten years
of his travel away from Homeworld, Pawl had only spoken to his

father a few times. Once when he graduated from the Military
Academy on Terpsichore. Once when an alien rebellion broke out
on one of the Paxwax concessions and Pawl had been instructed to
take charge of suppressing it. Once when he heard strange rumours
that all was not well on the Paxwax Homeworld.

Perhaps there had been a few other conversations – curt greetings, orders, instructions. Nothing of warmth or real interest. There
was no love between Pawl and Toby Paxwax.

And now his father had called. It could only be bad news. Pawl
wondered if somehow his father had discovered about Laurel
Beltane.

The vivante room was cool and dark. The machine was already
aglow and above the small black vivante plaque the air was
luminous. Pawl tapped out the linking co-ordinates and the shape
of a figure began to build up. It was half a figure. Pawl saw the
massive shoulders of his father and the forked beard and long,
braided yellow hair. The reception was poor and the figure wavered
and occasionally part of it dissolved into red and blue sparks.

"Pawl here, father."

The face of his father turned and his eyes squinted.

"Can't hardly see you."

"Reception's bad." Despite that, Pawl could see that his father's
face was haggard and that he had aged greatly since the last time
they had spoken. "Is there a problem?"

"Lapis is dead."

"What?"

"Lapis is dead. I want you home immediately." This was spoken
in a growl as though his father was just managing to hold his fury
in check. "Immediately."

"Lapis is. . . ."

"Are you witless? Are your brains addled? I've told you. He's
dead. Gone. Finished." There was a momentary break in his
father's voice and then he recovered. "So you get back here
immediately. Come alone. None of your fancy friends. And no
talking to anyone. The news is held. Not even Songteller knows."
His father turned as though to break contact.

"Wait Toby," shouted Pawl. "Sorry, it's just that . . . How did
he die?" The realization of what his father's words meant was
slowly becoming real to Pawl.

"On some god-forsaken moon. He was coming home. D'ye

hear? Coming home. It was going to be a surprise and then some tractor ploughed right over him." His father paused and breathed deeply. When he spoke again his voice was low and cold. "So now you move. Put away your pen and paper, boy, you're joining the real world now. You're all that is left. Now."

"Why haven't you told Songteller? He needs to know."

"We settle things in the family first. The administrators do what we tell them. No more talking."

The bulky figure collapsed in a shower of sparks and the chamber became dark again.

Pawl blinked in the bright sunlight outside. A close observer, one who knew him well, would have detected the change in his manner . . . perhaps a deepening of his yellow eyes and a stiffness in his walk.

"Can I help? I trust there is no . . . ?" The member of the Inner Circle was waiting for him. Pawl stopped and stared at him. With his finger he raised the front flap of the figure's hood.

The representative from the Inner Circle darted back, but not before Pawl had stared straight into the pale mask with the blank eye sockets and the smiling carmine lips. "You ask many questions. Let me ask you one. Do you know where my brother Pental is? He joined your order."

"We do not deal in names," whispered the voice.

"Liar." Pawl walked stiffly away, and then he could have bitten his tongue out. Why had he said that? Of all the stupid . . . Why had he been rude . . . Like a child. . . . Vainly he hoped that the member of the Inner Circle had not heard.

Behind him the dark figure stood in the sunlight. The alien, the almost-human, who occupied the black gown and hood smiled a cat smile behind its mask and thought to itself, *We have the right man*. Then it hurried away.

Pawl mounted the stage and waved for the singing to stop. In a daze he delivered his speech and handed out the Orders of Merit to smiling farmers. Suddenly magnanimous, he donated a new vivante console to Mako and then told the assembled citizens that he had to depart immediately.

"But the hunting and the concert. We had everything. . . ."

"Needs must when . . . I have to leave immediately. Your

friendship and hospitality will stay with me. My father wished me
to convey his thanks to you personally."

The whole of the city turned to wave goodbye.

Within an hour he was aboard the magnetic shuttle and rising
above the mottled blue face of Mako.

He had twenty minutes alone before he reached the Way
Platform, and he needed every second of them. The death of Lapis
changed everything. He was no longer the playboy younger son, fit
for diplomatic duties, responsible but second. He was now the
heir.

Pawl thought quickly. First he needed to contact Laurel and get
her safe.

Then. Then what? His mind was a blank. Panic began to build
up inside him. Unbidden, the words from the mantra for Calm,
hypnotically implanted during his time on Terpsichore, spoke in
his mind.

> The thundering hooves of the buffalo
> Stir not the leaves of the mountain tree.
> Only the mists
> Move in its branches.

Then? Then he would have to prepare a strategy to meet his
father. The old man would be wild and dangerous. He doted on
Lapis. Pawl would have to defeat his father on his own terms. One
thing was certain: he would not change his will to marry Laurel
Beltane, even if he had to fight the whole of the Eleven. There
would be a way. In this, the death of Lapis gave him leverage.

Unexpectedly Pawl felt a surge of excitement. His father did not
know him, did not know what was coming home. He would be
expecting an older version of the pudgy, dreamy youth who had
departed ten years earlier to serve his time on Terpsichore. He
would not be expecting the iron which Pawl had discovered inside
himself.

But Lapis gone . . . Pawl felt a hollowness open inside him. Of
all his brothers Lapis was the only one he had ever got to know.
Pawl had admired his strength and the wildness that made him
climb out of his bedroom at night and ride out to the servants'
building and get drunk and make love to the servant daughters.
Lapis, with the build of a giant and a deadly temper which once
made him try to kill their father with a hook torn from a side of

meat. Lapis, who fought a rogue stallion and strangled it with his bare hands. Lapis, who stole away one night from the great house, took the shuttle and escaped from Homeworld.

They had not heard from him for years. Then gradually news had begun to filter back of his exploits. How he lived like a despot on distant Zipra. How he detonated an asteroid in Xerxes territory. Finally, with some of the wildness burned out of him, he had contacted their father, and told him he was ready to become a Paxwax again. And now, perhaps on the eve of departure, he had died under the treads of a tractor.

The shuttle docked at the Way platform and Pawl quickly found the local vivante transmitter.

Within minutes he had located Laurel at her villa on Lotus-and-Arcadia. It was night there and she smiled at him sleepily, and then her face became anxious as she registered his expression.

"Listen love, I only have a few moments. I'm returning to Bennet Homeworld straight away."

"What's happened?"

"I don't know for certain. Something to do with Lapis. But you must leave Lotus-and-Arcadia immediately. Don't cause any ripples. Don't tell anyone you are leaving. Leave quietly and return to Thalatta. You'll be safe with your father. Wait there until you hear from me. I have the vivante cube safe. I'll contact you from my Homeworld as soon as I can."

"But. . . ."

"No buts. No questions. I'm taking a risk even speaking to you. Do what I say. Trust me."

She nodded. "I'm packing already. I'll be away before dawn. Take care." She blew him a kiss, and then in a swirl of covers was out of the bed and gone.

Pawl broke the contact.

Now for the long jump. He ran over to the entrance to the Way Gate proper. Once through this he would be effectively off the planet. An attendant held the door to the Gate open. She saluted, and closed and secured the locks when Pawl was inside.

He was in the small Guardian vestibule where the computer controller was located. He identified himself and tapped out the co-ordinates for the Paxwax Homeworld and waited while the computer verified that all stations were clear for transit. It would take three jumps. Pawl was far from home and each stage needed to be locked into alignment. While he was waiting he selected the clothes he wanted to have waiting for him on Bennet Homeworld. Each Way Gate had a wide range of disposable clothes. The Gate registered all clear and a second door slid open. A wave of cold antiseptic air engulfed him.

Sealed in the second chamber Pawl stripped and then popped a small purple pill into his mouth. He squatted down in the lavatory chamber while the pill did its work. Within minutes he had cleared his bowels and bladder. Sweat poured from him and was evaporated by a warm, sweet-smelling breeze. When his body had stopped its churning he showered and, still wet, pressed a red button to enter the Mirror room.

The light was cold and brilliant. The room was circular but with a flat floor. The walls were made of thousands of planes of crystal through which the light shone white. In the centre was a low platform large enough for six people to lie down. Pawl made himself comfortable on the flat surface. Almost imperceptibly the light changed from glaring white to violet and then began to flicker as though the whole chamber was revolving. Pawl felt a twinge of nausea and his head began to thump as the light began to tease open the interstices between the cells of his body. And then blackness closed over him like a bag.

As a pattern of coded references he was on his way.

5

ON LOTUS-AND-ARCADIA

Laurel did not leave Lotus-and-Arcadia immediately. During the morning she packed a small bag for herself. She casually told her attendants that she was thinking of returning to Thalatta for a short time. This was not unusual. Travel by Way Gate meant that any member of the larger families could come and go at will, without fuss or long preparations.

Then, as was her custom, she went to the lake and spent an hour diving and hunting among the roots of one of the giant dewfall trees.

Relaxed outwardly, she stretched out on the shore and let the warm rays of health lamps dry her and refresh her. She rolled over on to her back and stared up at the rainbow dome which covered the entire lake and protected it from the cold of space. She thought about Pawl and went over his message time and again, trying to squeeze more meaning out of it.

It was while she was thus occupied that a pebble landed squarely on her bare stomach. She glanced round but there was no one to be seen, only a couple of robot attendants, their eyes glowing redly as they watched for her signal, and a lone Pullah which patiently cleaned the white sand beach. She lay back and moments later another pebble landed close to her ear, sending sand into her hair.

She stood up quickly and ran up the shallow beach to where a bright green band of synthetic grass marked the end of the lake. Beyond were pavilions and the first of the palaces maintained by the Families.

Suspended in an anti-gravity hammock beneath a sun umbrella, and with a mound of pebbles on the table beside him, was Toro Sith. He wore a garland of flowers in his thick black curly hair and other flowers were wound up and round his black burnished horns.

"You are a remarkable woman," he called and pushed the chair opposite him out with his foot in invitation.

"Why did you throw pebbles at me?" asked Laurel.

"Join me and I'll tell you."

Thoughts raced through Laurel's mind. This was the young Sith who Pawl had wanted to pick a fight with. What better way to deflect attention away from her and Pawl than to be seen sitting with one of the eligible Sith.

"I'll just collect my things," she called and ran back down the beach.

When she returned, modestly clothed, one of the robot attendants was uncorking a bottle of Seppel wine. It produced two sparkling frosty glasses from its trolley and poured the wine expertly to within a finger's width of the brim. Then it withdrew discreetly murmuring, "Bon appetit."

"Now tell me why you threw those pebbles," said Laurel sitting down.

"Wouldn't you rather know why I think you are a remarkable

woman?" said Toro Sith, lifting his glass and touching it gently against hers.

"All right, why am I a remarkable woman?"

"Because you can move without your shadow."

Laurel absorbed this with a slight smile which she hoped would be enigmatic, and then took up her glass and sipped.

"Well? Where is the yellow-eyed one? You haven't drowned him, have you? Tied him up in a sack with stones in the bottom and left him lodged under the roots of the dewfall trees? No, fate would never be that kind."

"I don't know where Pawl Paxwax is. Business probably. We're not inseparable you know. Just. . . ."

"Good friends." He said it in a patronizing way.

"Something like that."

"Well, I'm glad to hear it. Does that mean that some of the rest of us can have a look in?" The accent he gave to the last two words left no doubt as to his exact meaning.

"I am the only daughter of the Beltane Fifty-sixth and I choose what companions I wish."

"Bravo. And I am a son of the Sith Tenth. That means something too." He stared at her and drank deeply. "Forgive me for speaking so bluntly. But we Sith are noted for our bluntness. I have watched you for weeks. I would like to be free to call on you." Still Laurel said nothing and the young Sith took this for encouragement. "The yellow-eyed one is well known for his faithlessness. He has had many lovers."

This, as Laurel knew, was true. Pawl, for all that he was ungainly and moody, held a fascination for women . . . possibly even because of these qualities.

"I would be a true companion," said Toro. "Perhaps, who knows, our association could lead to advancement."

Laurel did well to hide her laughter. The idea of the Sith dangling his family in front of her like bait was preposterous. But his words had a certain logic, for Lotus-and-Arcadia, apart from being worlds of abundant pleasure, were also a vast marriage market. All the important marriages were arranged but marriages among the lesser children were more relaxed.

"The Code forbids any such 'advancement' and you know it. I am of a low family."

"The Code is a heap of crap."

How often had Laurel heard Pawl express the same idea. "I'd

like to hear you say that to your father's face. I think Master
Singular Sith would have other ideas."

Toro shrugged and grinned and nodded his horns so that the
flowers shook. "Yes, he's old fashioned. Anyway, I'm glad I found
you alone. I wanted to invite you to a party. If your good friend
had been here I would have invited him too. So don't worry."

"What's the occasion?"

"A Terpsichore reunion. Everyone will be there. Even the Inner
Circle. There'll be games and hunting and a lot of loving. Will you
come?"

"I don't know."

"Go on. It'll do you good. Time you got out a bit more. You've
been living like one of the Inner Circle. And you're not getting any
younger."

"Thank you."

"That's not meant to be rude."

"I understand."

"So. I'll send a chair round for you. All right?"

Laurel thought. She reasoned, *I'll stay for a short time. Just a
few dances. Just long enough to be noticed and then I'll slip away to
the Way Port.*

And that was what she sincerely meant to do. Except the party
turned out to be great fun. There were lots of her friends there and
though she was worried about Pawl, she was glad of the distraction.

She fended off many questions about Pawl. Some of her friends
were especially kind to her, for they believed that just as they had
predicted, Pawl had finally abandoned her. That was to be
expected. Lotus-and-Arcadia was littered with daughters and sons
of lesser families who had become lovers of the Great and were
now abandoned and seeking matches on their own level. It was
part of the rhythm of things . . . and the Paxwax were the Fifth
Family. Pawl, it was commonly understood, when he married
would mate with one of the senior daughters of the Eleven.

One of those daughters was there: Dama Longstock, radiantly
beautiful in a gown of iridescent ice stones. Laurel avoided her for
it was well known that Dama and Pawl had enjoyed a passionate
relationship. In some people's minds they were still linked. With
her woman's instincts, Laurel knew that Dama was still fishing for
Pawl. It was best that they didn't meet.

*

Laurel watched the party. She danced with Toro Sith and danced with other men too. She observed that as Toro Sith drank more and more, so he became belligerent. The party reached a critical phase at which the good humour seemed to drain away and Laurel decided to leave.

She wanted to be unobserved and so slipped through one of the side doors which faced on to the dancing area and led out into the garden.

Seasons were unknown on this glass-domed world and the air was warm and perfumed. As she walked under the trees Laurel heard someone behind her. She turned and found her way blocked by the stumbling figure of Toro Sith. He towered over her with his horns catching in the lower branches of the trees. He reached out and his hand closed over her face, stopping her mouth. But Laurel was too surprised to scream.

She couldn't believe it was happening. She felt herself pushed back roughly and then dragged. She scrambled and tripped and managed to free her mouth and bit. Then Sith pulled his hand away and raised it to strike her. "Piebald bitch with your high and mighty ways. . . ."

Then before the hand could come crushing down, the Sith stiffened and tottered back on his heels away from her. His head was wrenched round as though his body was a bottle and his head was the cap that was being unscrewed. He fell on to his knees and smashed his face savagely into the gravel path. Not once or twice, but repeatedly, until his bull face was a running wound. Finally he lay still, face down in his own blood, with the crescents of his horns reflecting the artificial moonlight.

"Are you all right Laurel Beltane? I thought I heard a scuffling so I came to investigate." A figure in a dark robe emerged from under the trees. It was tall and Laurel recognized a member of the Inner Circle that she had seen that evening at the party. "Oh dear. One of the Sith is it?" The figure in the gown stooped over the prone body of Toro Sith and reached out a hand and took one of his horns and worked the head back and forth. "It looks as though he's had a seizure. Epilepsy is known in their family. I will take care of him. Don't worry. If I may suggest a few days on your delightful Homeworld might be in order. You look very pale."

Laurel was confused. "Did you. . . ."

"I did nothing except arrive at the right moment. We pride ourselves on that. Here, I will accompany you back to your

quarters. One of my colleagues will attend to the Sith." A second
figure gowned in the black habit of the Inner Circle glided into the
moonlight. Laurel felt that she was in a dream. So much . . . So
sudden. She felt the arm of the representative of the Inner Circle
slip round her and support her. "We try to be there when we are
needed." Vaguely Laurel realized that the voice of the member of
the Inner Circle was a woman's voice.

"You are very kind," murmured Laurel.

"We try to be."

Later, in her rooms, Laurel stood in the abrasive massage of a
particle shower and tried to cleanse her skin of the memory of
Toro Sith's hands.

Then she dressed quickly, collected her bag and within minutes
was riding high above Lotus-and-Arcadia towards the Way Port.
There was much she did not understand and much she didn't want
to remember. She was grateful for the way the member of the
Inner Circle had helped her but she was disturbed too. Of one
thing she was certain: whatever had felled Toro Sith, it was not an
epileptic seizure.

6

OF THE INNER CIRCLE

What is this strange order called the Inner Circle?

If you were to ask the Masters who controlled the Families you
would get many different answers.

"Doctors."

"Diplomats."

"Busybodies."

"Engineers."

"Grease."

"Advisers."

And all the answers are both right and wrong.

To understand the Inner Circle we must go back to the time when the mercantile fleets of Earth first captured the secret of Way Gate travel and began to spread out into the galaxy.

The Way Gate was an invention of the species called the Craint. They used the gates to transport their dead back to their Home-world and such was their casualness (for they were then reaching the end of their physical evolution) that they left active Way Gates in different parts of the Galaxy. One was close to Earth.

It was discovered and activated, and wholesale war broke out when its possibilities were realized. The Way Gate gave access to the wider galaxy. Fortune favoured the quick and the brave.

The early fathers and mothers of all the Families were traders and adventurers. They controlled their own private armies and they were ruthless. One such trader was called John Death Elliott, whose name is now remembered in that part of space called Elliott's Pocket. He need not concern us much at present though we shall hear a great deal about him later. Another was called Merry Proctor because he never smiled. And there was Li-Feng Wong and Claudia Bogdanovich and Long Reach Paxwax. And more.

Gradually these clans reached out, fighting among themselves and destroying or enslaving other populations, alien populations, when they encountered them.

This was the time known as the Great Push.

Most alien species encountered human kind and were vexed by them. Some species disappeared altogether. Others forsook their civilization and dwindled into savagery. To all the species it seemed as though the humans came from nowhere.

Thanks to the Way technology, the armies of the Great Families were able to appear in many remote solar systems.

Quick of intellect, able to breed faster than some species could blink, and brilliantly adaptable, the human colonists scourged opposition wherever they encountered it. Gradually they imposed their own economic lore and systems.

This time of turmoil and anarchy lasted over centuries, and it was during this period that Sanctum was established. It was the Craint again, clever bird beasts that they were. They saw the danger, and one of their last creative acts was to find this dying planet and prepare it as a haven for alien waifs and strays. Had they wanted to the Craint could no doubt have annihilated the bandit armies, but they were moving out of our space-time and conflicts among species mattered little more to them than clouds crossing the sun. They were concerned more with saving life than destroying it.

Non-human species flocked to Sanctum in their millions. They brought with them their cultures, their languages and their habits.

At first Sanctum was little more than a refugee camp and a museum. Gradually though, over the centuries, as the Great Families established themselves and pegged out their empires, a spirit of rebellion grew.

The question which exercised the best minds of Sanctum was how rebellion could be mounted. Safety lay in secrecy, in not being seen. For the aliens were under no misapprehension. They knew that if Sanctum were ever discovered, the human fleets of all the Families would quickly gather like wolves round a dying stag, and destroy it.

Then one day a new voice appeared among them. It was not heard as a voice but rather felt as a presence. It was a thinking, an attitude, an insistence. Attention focused on a sapling which had a trunk of silver and which grew, so legend had it, in the place where one of the last of the Craint had died. Year by year the tree grew and always it had one message: caution.

What manner of creature was this? The Hammer and the Spideret did not know, yet they heeded it. They could feel the pressure of an intelligence so vast that it made their darting sting and spat venom seem trivial. The alien creatures were wise enough to know that intelligence can be the greatest weapon of all.

One day the Tree did speak, clearly and incontrovertibly in their minds. It summoned them to its presence. At that same moment creatures that were eating paused and lay down, charging hunters cantered to a standstill, those that were sleeping awoke.

The aliens that lived close to the Tree's chamber made their way there and settled under its growing canopy.

"I feed on your feelings," said the Tree. "Give me your emotion."

The aliens gave vent to their wonder and their anger. The Tree listened and absorbed, and after three days it asked its first question.

"Can you bring one of the human aliens to me?"

"One? Several," said one of the old Great Hammers that had done battle against the Wong.

"Take no risks."

That day the old Hammer reactivated its ship, and taking two of its comrades set out. They travelled slowly, taking many years, until they were just within the boundaries of one of the small Families. They baited the trap by launching a small satellite beacon which bleated a call for help. Eventually the satellite was investigated and they pounced and captured the entire crew. Then they silenced the beacon and silently withdrew. They hid in a cloud of meteorites and joined the tail of a comet and finally made their way back to Sanctum.

The crew of the ship, now considerably aged, were paraded before the Tree and it stripped their minds like cotton wound from a bobbin: it emptied them, like wine poured from a bottle. They became the first members of the Inner Circle.

They were sent out and brought back more recruits. They brought children. A colony was established on Sanctum for the training of the Inner Circle and a special uniform was adopted. This consisted of a black overgarment with a hood and a pale neutral face mask.

They were trained as healers and word was put about that they were the harmless remnants of an ancient holy order that had once existed on Earth.

They concentrated their efforts on the Proctor Family, which was the most powerful and therefore had the most to lose and was noted for being very superstitious. They proved their worth by effecting cures, and so their influence spread.

Everyone trusts a successful doctor, and it was not long before they became accepted not only as healers but as diplomats. Over the generations they wound their order into the power structure of the Great Families.

They developed one planet as their official home, on the outskirts of the Proctor, and this was connected by a secret Way Gate to the true seat of power, Sanctum. In this way Sanctum gained influence.

The Inner Circle never presumed too much; they never threatened, and concentrated on serving the interests of the Families. They were a catalyst which eased relations among the Families.

They became masters of ceremony, carriers of discreet news,

and were generally regarded as valuable healers, upholders of tradition and fundamentally impotent.

Early on in the history of their activities, a strange truth was discovered; that so long as members of the Inner Circle were not blatantly alien they were accepted. The gown and the mask were the protection. They became synonymous with a careful, discreet, conscientious servitude. Of course, the Hammer and the Hooded Parasol and the Spideret could never sally forth . . . there was no way their alienness could have been ignored.

But the Tree was not omniscient. No entity is omniscient. Like most telepathic creatures it could scan the future by understanding the present. It could sense events while they were still shaping. Like a skilled climber who slides his hand up a rock face and knows which crevices will hold and which will crumble, the Tree felt its way into the future slowly, carefully and without making a mistake. The restoration of the aliens was not a matter of months or years or decades . . . it required millennia. For the fatal blow, when it was to come, could not be fudged, could not be partial. It had to be absolute.

Nor did the Tree serve only the aliens. Its actions were not altruistic. It served its own kind as well. In its growing it had devoured the Craint. Far away, deep in that region of space known as Elliott's Pocket, its fellows were becoming hungry. Their planet, called in the language of the first Earthmen that discovered it Ultima Thule, swung round its own sun and fought an unending battle with the darkness of a world called Erix.

Little did the aliens or the creatures of Earth realize that everything that they considered meaningful in life depended on the strength of Ultima Thule.

However, that need not concern us now. For the moment the attention of the Tree is directed towards Pawl Paxwax. It senses in him something different: a vibrant awareness of life, a creative drive, a capacity for hatred and love and a deep and unresolved anger. The Tree knows Pawl Paxwax better than he knows himself. It is preparing to use him.

As for the other Families, the Tree watches their hatreds and their machinations. Take Clarissa of the Family called the Xerxes de la Tour Souvent.

She is plotting the downfall of the Paxwax at this very moment. . . .

7

ON MORROW

Far away on Morrow, the Homeworld of the Xerxes de la Tour Souvent, Clarissa was sauntering among her ancestors.

She walked down a long, wide stone-floored corridor. On either side were tall glass cases within which glimmered the pale faces of long dead Xerxes. Eighty generations were preserved here, and Clarissa knew just where her niche would be.

The ancestors sat or stood, each in her preferred attitude, as natural as in life, each a tribute to the taxidermist's art. They wore their finery and stared impassively out into the corridor.

Dame Clarissa often came here when she was worried. The silence and stillness were an anaesthetic. Here in the dark passages in the deepest roots of the tree, Clarissa found a permanence which escaped her when she was conducting the day-to-day affairs of the family.

She had a favourite ancestor, Dame Rex, to whom she came to talk most often. She stopped now in front of her. Dame Rex, fifteen generations dead, and with a face like an old apple, stared at Clarissa with glittering queenly eyes.

It had been during Dame Rex's tutelage that the Xerxes Empire had expanded almost to its present limits. It had come to rub against the Paxwax, and the friction had never ceased. Dame Clarissa, who studied history, saw this conflict as inevitable as fate. The Paxwax and the Xerxes could not share the same sunlight. There was something in the life principle of the two families which meant that they were antagonists. All the treaties and the demands of the Code were so much chaff in the wind when set against this irresistible feud. Yet if you had asked Dame Clarissa exactly what it was about the Paxwax she detested she would have shrugged and replied, "Their manners."

The crude vigour which was the pride of Master Toby and which had been epitomized in his eldest son, Lapis, made the Xerxes shiver with disgust.

"We're gambling this time," murmured Clarissa, scratching the glass softly in front of Dame Rex's eyes. "You would be proud of us. If we win we will carve the Paxwax to the bone. If we lose, well, we won't lose too much. Either way we will have stunned Toby." Clarissa's feathers ruffled at the thought.

Her reflection in the glass matched the face of Dame Rex. Their similarity, despite their differences in age, was startling. A genetic bridge joined them, though in Clarissa tendencies which were just visible in Dame Rex had come to full prominence. Most distinct among these were the feathers. The neck and bare shoulders of Dame Rex were downy like the breast of a bird but her hair was natural and silky. Dame Clarissa's neck, head and shoulders were totally plumose. The scarlet and black feathers completely framed her pale beautiful face. When she was in a passion the feathers would rise into a crest and stiffen to spikes.

"Soon," she whispered, "soon."

A distant bell chimed, sending echoes down the long corridor. It was the summoning call for the daily ceremony of Gelding. Today it was Clarissa's turn of duty. She touched the glass case for a final time and turned away and began to hurry down the long corridor.

Out of the shadows behind her emerged three little men with bald heads, wearing white smocks. They hurried after her, trying to keep up.

The corridor became narrower and more distinctly rounded and began to twist. Steps hewn from rock replaced the gradual slope. They came to the last of the glass windows. Inside a stone figure stared out with glass eyes. It was clothed in silver mesh. This was the oldest of the Xerxes matrons. She was wearing the ancient space suit she had worn when she first stepped on to Morrow. About her were relics of that time beyond memory. An old radio loud hailer. A broken thermos flask. The worn tip of a three flanged drill once used to bore into the base of the giant silica tree which had been their earliest refuge and which had since become their constant home.

The name of this first ancestor was stencilled on the front of her space suit: Maria de la Tour Souvent. *Xerxes* was the name of her ship.

Clarissa paused before the window and bowed to the image. Behind her the three little men bumped into one another and then got down on to their knees and touched their noses to the stone.

The corridor ended in a massive wooden door which slid open as Clarissa approached. Beyond it were brilliant lights and the roar of giant fans. The air was thick and smoky. Clarissa stepped on to a small balcony set in the wall of a vast amphitheatre. They were now deep underground, in the very roots of the tree.

A shout went up when she appeared. It rolled round the stone walls. She raised her hand in recognition and shaded her eyes from the searchlight that was trained on the balcony.

Below her were caverns and a long line of naked little boys who stood, each with his hands on the shoulders of the boy in front. They stood proudly, to attention.

Dame Clarissa snapped her fingers and one of the little men ran forward and handed her a small scarlet package tied up with gold cord. She undid the cord and a long red ribbon tumbled loose and began to fall down to the floor of the cavern. When it was fully extended she shook it sending long snake waves down its length. A drum began to beat and fires flared.

The primitive ceremony of castration began. Each day the ceremony was performed. As each boy born on the Xerxes Home-world reached the age of ten he was ritually robbed of his manhood. There were no fertile men on Morrow. Impregnation of worker women on Morrow was artificially accomplished, using sperm collected centuries earlier, long before the time even of Dame Rex's rule.

Clarissa stayed long enough to watch the long pale procession begin to shuffle forward and then she turned and left the balcony.

Jettatura should have contacted her by now. Not hearing a word was vexing. Jettatura knew how important it was.

Clarissa entered a small communication alcove and called her sister. Jettatura's disembodied head appeared half-size in the dark-ness. Though they were sisters they were completely unalike. Where Clarissa was richly coloured and loved bright clothes and jewellery, Jettatura was a pure white albino with bright clear pink eyes. She wore simple tight-fitting athletic clothes. Her composure as ever was glacial.

"I said I would contact you if there was news. There isn't. If you can't keep your anxiety under control I suggest you come up here and join me. We can wait together."

"Yes, I will," said Clarissa and broke the communication.

Beyond the communication alcove was a transit niche. Clarissa sat down on a golden couch and one of the little men arranged her dress round her feet. When he had withdrawn, another of the attendants lowered a domed screen in front of Clarissa. The screen glowed briefly and then faded.

The three little men looked at one another, and shrugged. Clarissa had neglected to give them any orders. "Bed now," said one.

"Food, food," said another.

"Better wait," said the third, and sat down.

Dame Clarissa ascended the tree. The path she traced followed the natural twists and contours of the trunk and branches. Only once, briefly, did she emerge into a transparent tunnel which connected two branches. But she could see nothing, as a violent sand storm was blocking the ports.

Soon she was high and approaching a central nodule which contained the main Xerxes living quarters and the administrative centre. Unlike most of the Great Families, the Xerxes did not use a separate planet exclusively for administration. The nerve centre of their empire was here, in the silica tree. Their only contact with wider space was via a heavily armoured shuttle which lifted from the top of the tree to the Way platform.

Over the generations they had occupied the whole of the lumpy, dust-shrouded planet of Morrow. The trees were a natural home. They lifted their branches in all the main valleys from the frigid poles to the cool equator. Their roots twisted together to feed on the rich rivers which flowed beneath the planet's surface and which had been adapted to form a network of communication tunnels.

Why the first pirate women of the Xerxes had chosen to inhabit such an inhospitable planet was anyone's guess. Perhaps simply because it was so inaccessible and forbidding. In the early days that had been important. Morrow, snug in its orbit within a torus of asteroids, had provided an impregnable fortress for all except the skilled pilots of the Xerxes. With the coming of the Way Gate System its isolation was lost, but by then there were other defences.

*

The transit couch slid silently into a bare oval room walled with grey panels. The door clicked open and retracted and Clarissa stepped out. She shivered briefly in the chill air, for this was a room that was rarely used on Morrow. It was the main docking bay for the shuttle and there were few visitors to that planet.

Jettatura was waiting, seated incongruously at an ornate lacquered table which she had had shifted there from her apartments. She was playing cards. She sat straight-backed and radiant in a silver tunic. Her long white hair, which reached almost to the ground, was brushed into neat smooth waves.

Standing apart from her and at an easy watchful attendance was Latani Rama. She was a beautiful broad-shouldered woman in her late twenties. She was highly trained in all the arts of attack and defence and was Clarissa's personal bodyguard.

Clarissa was surprised to see her there. "Is it coming?" she asked. "Is everything all right?"

"I believe that everything is all right," said Latani Rama. "But the Way Gate has reported that an alien of the type called Spideret is accompanying the cargo. I thought it best if I was with you."

"Yes. Thank you. Disgusting things. I er . . . didn't know that the . . . er cargo was to be accompanied. Should we have other guards?"

"I can cope with any problems and I understand that secrecy is required for this cargo."

"Yes," Clarissa said.

"Calm down. The shuttle is descending now," Jettatura said. She did not pause in her game or glance up as she spoke.

Dame Clarissa looked at her. "You are as ever an island of elegance. I did not think to dress for the occasion."

"Obviously. How was the ceremony?"

"As normal. Look. . . ."

"I brought this for you. I hope you don't mind. I thought it appropriate." She motioned to Latani Rama, who stepped forward and held open an ancient polished wood box. Inside, on a bed of crushed velvet, lay a diamond pendant wrought in the design of four interlocking comets. It was the official emblem of the Xerxes de la Tour Souvent and was normally only worn on the occasions when Clarissa had to face in full conference the other members of the Eleven Great Families. "As senior sister you should show your rank at an important moment in our family's history."

Dame Clarissa placed the heavy pendant over her shoulders and

6 PHILLIP MANN

made it comfortable among her feathers. She glanced round the room. Apart from the table where Jettatura was playing, the only other piece of furniture was a low wheeled trolley.

"Is everything ready?"

"It is."

"Where is Rose? She should be here."

"Mooning about probably. I sent for her."

"Is she not well?"

"She seemed spirited the last time I saw her. Now let me concentrate. I want to finish."

"Cards! How can you play cards at a time like this? I'm almost climbing the walls . . . but in you tension is manifest as calm."

"Don't be obscure."

Dame Clarissa's feathers ruffled briefly and then subsided. She began to pace round the walls. She halted and touched one of the panels and it immediately cleared to reveal a view of Morrow.

They were above the sandstorm. It poured past below like the back of a giant swollen snake. In the distance, the tips of other trees could be seen poking up like stiff fingered hands.

Clarissa clasped her hands behind her and stared out. "Oh for summer, when the wind drops and we can see for miles across the crystal plain."

Jettatura did not answer but played on, slapping her cards down on to the table.

Abruptly a section of the wall slid open and a second transit couch glided into the room. A heavily built, squat woman swung her legs out and heaved herself up. This was Rose. "Sorry I'm late," she whispered, glancing at the two sisters as though she expected to be scolded. "I dozed off again. I hope I haven't missed anything."

Rose was considerably shorter than her sisters, a fact accentuated by her heavy pregnancy. She had mouse-brown hair and it was pinned back into a bun except where lank threads had escaped. Her eyes were large, too large, and gave her face the appearance of a Pekinese dog. "I seem to be tired all the time now." She looked round for a chair and finding none sat down on the trolley and joined her hands over her belly.

"We are still waiting," said Clarissa. "You have missed nothing. But when we know where we stand we must get the Lamprey Sixth on vivante."

Silence, except for the slapping of the cards, and then Jettatura finished her game with a flourish and after carefully shuffling them packed her cards away in an ivory box. Then she sat back, quite still, with her hands folded in her lap and her eyes closed.

A bell began to ring and immediately Latani Rama came to attention and swung a blunt-nosed rifle from her shoulder. Jettatura stood up and stepped to one side and slid her chair neatly into place. Clarissa spun round and then smoothed her feathers, which were attempting to rise. Rose licked her lips and worked her way forwards off the trolley.

Above them the ceiling darkened. A crack appeared in the roof and widened as the two halves slipped back. The blunt end of the shuttle nosed down into the room and halted a few feet from the floor. Facing the sisters were twin iron doors and a bright red release handle.

Silence.

"Will you open it or shall I?" asked Jettatura.

Dame Clarissa fingered the Xerxes emblem as though it was a talisman and then stepped up to the doors.

"No. Let me," said Latani Rama. "There could be some trickery."

Clarissa stepped to one side and Latani Rama took firm hold of the release handle. She swung it and then shuffled back and dropped to her knees with her rifle held stiffly in front of her.

The door opened and Rose screamed. Immediately inside the door was the squat shape of a Spideret. Its dull grape eyes stirred and its mandibles worked as it chewed slowly. Latani Rama released a low charge which singed the creature's hairy legs and it scuttled back into the shuttle and then shinnied up a white web rope and hung, looking down at them.

Directly beneath it, spreadeagled on a couch, was the body of a man.

Holding the Spideret covered with her rifle, Latani Rama activated a mechanism which brought the body forward and to the edge of the shuttle.

The Spideret exuded a sticky gum and lowered itself to the floor. There it carefully turned on its back and worked its eight legs in the air.

"A sign of submission," said Latani Rama. "These creatures have intelligence. It was probably his servant."

"Keep it covered."

"I will."

The Spideret rolled over on to its legs and then stood up as high as it could. It advanced, placing its legs carefully until it was crouched over the body. Then it gathered it up and walked stiff-legged from the shuttle. Under the surprised eyes of the three sisters it placed the body, loose-limbed, on the trolley and then it scampered back into the shuttle and climbed to the roof.

Latani Rama kept it covered while the sisters gathered round the body.

"Behold the enemy," said Clarissa grandly.

Naked on the trolley lay the bruised and torn but still breathing body of Lapis Paxwax.

8

ON SANCTUM

Odin glided down the wide tiled thoroughfare which led into the chamber where the Tree lived. He was a late arrival and could feel the Tree's thoughts gather like smoke about him. The Tree was inviting the assembled creatures to share their thoughts. It had revealed that Lapis Paxwax had been captured by the Xerxes and this was a new move in the complicated slow game which needed to be comprehended.

Carefully Odin worked his way past bright reptilian eyes which blinked slowly. He squeezed between scaly and shaggy flanks. Once he had to pass beneath the stiff and hairy-jointed limbs of a Giant Hammer. Here, in the presence of the Tree, he was in no danger and knew it, though his nerve fibres screamed caution as he moved close to creatures who in other circumstances would have flashed at him with their gummy tongues and sharp teeth.

Despite the common purpose of the aliens, Sanctum was not a peaceful planet. The species which made up its population all remained true to their natures, be they hunter or herbivore. Here, traditional enmities stretching back to the dawn of time itself lived on.

Odin worked his way through the ranks of aliens until he reached the rich loam at the base of the shining silver tree. The damp soil gave him ease. The presence of the Tree was a balm which dulled his chafing sense of worry. For a long time Odin had felt dull premonitions in his fibres. At times the stone which he carried deep inside his body felt hot, as though it was burning. Ever since the time of his hatching he had been aware that there was a strangeness in his future. He both feared the strangeness and was thrilled by it, and at the same time did not understand it. Odin felt the future in the same way that a mouse feels the beating wings of the diving owl.

He settled close to the Tree and let himself be swept up by the gentle assured systalsis of its thought.

Other Gerbes were already there, each in its black gown and hunkered down. They were sifting the rich thought patterns in the cavern. Gerbes were very important to the workings of the Inner Circle for they belonged to that minority of species which are mobile, intelligent and magnificently telepathic.

Settled, Odin cast about with his mind to discover a creature with eyes. Though blind in himself, Odin loved the spectrum of visible light. He encountered a Hooded Parasol which floated tall and graceful on the upper tiers of the chamber. He slipped gently into the Parasol's mind, being careful not to disturb the creature's repose. He adjusted to its eyes and was amused to discover that at the moment of possession, the Hooded Parasol was staring down over the backs of the aliens to where Odin himself sat.

So many species. So many different ways of looking at reality. How could they all pull together? Yet Odin knew that gathered here was only a small percentage of the population of Sanctum. These were the policy makers of the Inner Circle.

Odin noticed that a human was standing close to him and was surprised that he had not detected the human's presence earlier. There were many others too. More than he had expected. That must mean something.

Suddenly in Odin's mind there grew the image of a waterfall. The water fell in long ragged strips of lather and there was a roaring. It seemed that the water pelted him. He recognized the distinctive thought-call of a Diphilus. He located the Diphilus

which was transmitting, lapping in a fissure high on the wall. It had the nature of its own slow-moving planet. It swirled in its clear sack body like coloured oil. The complex mosaic of its thought built hues on colours and elaborated strange images. On its own dark world the Diphilus, like all of its kind, lived in shallow depressions among cold rocks. Unimpeded by any atmosphere, it mirrored the stars from which it gained its strength and wisdom.

With a convulsion it clarified its thought.

SO THE XERXES FEMININE HAVE CAPTURED THE PAXWAX MASCULINE. WELL. WELL. WELL. WELL. WELL.

I DON'T THINK THIS ALTERS OUR POSITION. THEY WILL FIGHT. THE HATREDS WE HAVE NURTURED WILL FLOW LIKE MANY STREAMS CUTTING THE DRY LAND. AND ONE WILL WIN, AND THE SAME ORDER WILL PERSIST, PERHAPS EVEN STRONGER, AND OUR POSITION WILL REMAIN THE SAME. SQUABBLES WILL NOT SAVE US, THOUGH THERE WILL HAVE BEEN MANY DEATHS.

The Diphilus paused and into Odin's mind floated the image of a burning planet, of oceans vaporized, of columns of ash, of lava twisting in coils like worms on a sheet of glass. The image faded slowly but left a residue of fear.

WE MUST BEWARE OF LONGING FOR DEATH. IT IS A VILE LONGING AND THE ONLY DEATH WE MAY FINALLY ACCOMPLISH MAY BE OUR OWN.

Odin saw himself caught up in a spinning wheel of fire and carried away like a scrap of burned paper. Of all deaths, Odin feared death by fire most. He was aware of a restlessness among the aliens in the chamber. Each was facing its own dread. In their minds they saw themselves splayed and helpless, the bright lamps of their life dimming.

THIS NEED NOT HAPPEN. IN OUR REVENGE WE MUST BE LIKE STONE GODS WHO NEITHER LOVE NOR HATE.

AND LIKE STONE GODS WE MUST BE PATIENT. OUR TIME IS NOT YET BUT IT IS COMING.

The Diphilus settled and its colours sparkled and subsided.

YES, IT IS COMING.

The thought touched Odin like a burn and he felt the stone inside him begin to throb. It was as though the Diphilus had spoken directly to him. For the first time he felt an urge to address the assembly but he withdrew the wish when he saw a Giant Hammer stiffen its legs and rise up, its sting advanced. It lifted on to its four rear legs with its front legs crooked in front of its head.

In this fighting position it began to speak. Tentacles rippled and
beat against its sides, drumming out its message.

I AM NOT SO NICE AS YOU KNOW. I DO NOT FEAR DEATH, ANY DEATH.
I HAVE SMELLED IT LIKE PERFUME FROM THE EARLIEST DAYS OF MY
FEEDING. I HAVE LIVED WITH IT, AND I WILL NOT CHANGE. I SAY,
WHEN THE DAY COMES THAT THEIR HOUSES ARE DIVIDED, WE MOVE.
TERROR WILL WALK IN MY SHADOW AND I WILL MAKE A GREAT
SLAUGHTER IN THE WOODS OF AN.

The Hammer reached forward over its head with its sting and
jabbed it down into the ground. Its venom leaked. In this way it
signified that it had finished speaking.

The Diphilus swirled briefly.

DO YOU HATE? HATRED CORRODES.

The Giant Hammer beat out its reply.

HATRED? WHAT DO I KNOW OF HATRED? I LOVE THE PREY THAT
MOVES IN RANGE AND GIVES THE STING TO BITE. THAT IS ALL I KNOW.
BUT WE HAMMER WERE WRONGED MORE THAN MOST . . . AND THERE
WILL BE A RECKONING. BUT DO NOT FEAR FOR ME. WE HAMMER
UNDERSTAND BALANCE. HOW ELSE COULD WE WALK? I WILL AWAIT
THE DUE TIME BUT WHEN I MOVE I WILL BE LIKE THE SETTING SUN AND
DARKNESS WILL FOLLOW ME.

The Hammer settled again until its long body rested on the
ground and its sting was retracted into its sheath.

Silence in the chamber. The fierceness of the Hammer took a
long time to evaporate. Finally a Spideret, crowned with a hard
froth of pearly eggs, scampered up its rope and hung above the
assembled aliens. Its legs worked in complicated semaphore.

TO THE POINT. THE HUMAN IS A WITTY ANIMAL AS WE ALL KNOW TO
OUR PAIN. ONE OF MY BROTHERS IS WITH LAPIS EVEN NOW. IT LOVES
HIM EVEN THOUGH HE IS OF THE ELEVEN. IT SPINS CEREMONY ROUND
HIM. GIVEN THE CALL IT WILL END THIS XERXES FOLLY IN AN INSTANT.
AND WHERE ARE WE THEN? CAN ANY OF YOU WHO CAN SCAN THE
FUTURE TELL WHEN WE CAN ACT? I DO NOT BRING WARRIORS INTO THE
WORLD FOR THEM MERELY TO CLUSTER AND SWING IN THE CRADLE.
NONE OF US DO.

The call to Odin was as palpable as a slap on the back. Without
thinking he began to glide forward until he stood alone, the focus
of all eyes. His domed cowl, where a head might have been, raised
and revealed the glimmering pale mask of the Inner Circle. The
mask seemed to smile and then red tendrils writhed in the vacant

eye sockets and sprouted from the parted carmine lips of the mouth. The feelers undulated as though tasting the air.

I AM A DEFENCELESS CREATURE. NO WEAPONS, ONLY MY MIND. I CAME FROM A DEFENCELESS PLANET AND MANY OF YOU KNOW THE FATE THAT ALMOST OVERCAME MY RACE. THIS I SAY.

OUR ENEMIES ARE NOT MEN OR WOMEN. OUR ENEMY IS ABSTRACT. IT IS HUMAN ORDER. IT IS BASED IN THEIR TRADITIONS . . . IN THEIR TRADITIONS OF MASTER AND SERVANT. I DO NOT HAVE A WORD FOR IT. BUT THIS I KNOW. WE CAN NOT DESTROY AN ABSTRACT FOE. ONLY THE GREAT FAMILIES WHO GUARD THAT ORDER AND GAIN THEIR STRENGTH FROM IT CAN DESTROY IT. DESTRUCTION MUST COME FROM WITHIN. AND ONCE IT STARTS IT WILL NOT STOP. THERE MAY BE NO NEED FOR VENGEANCE AND THE *DEATH* YOU FEAR (here the Diphilus glittered in recognition) WILL NOT BE THE DARKNESS OF ANTI-LIFE BUT A PROPER WITHERING, AS HEALTHY AS AGE.

Odin paused, amazed at the thoughts which raced through his mind. It was as though it was not him speaking, but another . . . Again the tumble of thoughts.

I SPEAK TO YOU, FOR ALTHOUGH I CANNOT SEE THE FUTURE I KNOW IT FEELINGLY. I AM THERE IN THE FUTURE. THE CAPTURE OF LAPIS IS NOT ALL. IT IS ONLY A BEGINNING. SOMETHING BIGGER IS WAITING. TO UNDERSTAND OUR FUTURE WE NEED TO LEARN THE HUMAN MIND.

The flow of thought dried up suddenly and left Odin standing confused. He bowed down and retreated. For a second he had glimpsed the future and the vision had appalled him. *We who serve*, he thought privately, *but know not what we serve. We who are responsible but lack authority. What is our reward?*

The tall human who had been standing close to Odin stretched and raised his arms.

I WAS HUMAN. I AM NOW A TWO-IN-ONE. I WAS PENTAL, SECOND SON OF THE PAXWAX. LOOK INTO ME AND BEHOLD THE HUMAN ONLY.

Deep inside Pental, the creature that inhabited his veins and coiled in his blood stretched for a second and then contracted. The movement brought Pental ease and pleasure and he slipped quietly into trance.

Pental became simple as all humans become simple when in seizure. He became vulnerable as sleeping prey, as shellfish at ebb-tide.

The aliens wandered in the alien human garden of Pental's mind.

They saw and recognized his beauty and darkness.

They discovered something of what it means to be human.

9

ON BENNET:
THE PAXWAX HOMEWORLD

Pawl Paxwax materialized as a wheeling pattern of darkness. Black motes coalesced and gradually tightened to the solid reality of a man. The bright silver lights in the mirror chamber slowed in their spinning and finally stopped, bathing Pawl in a steady hard light.

He lay still and stiff. After a few moments the rigour of transformation eased and he was able to draw in a deep, life-giving breath.

His body knitted. There was movement in his face, a twitching about the eyes.

Pawl became aware of himself and of the nausea which always accompanied travel by the Way Gate. It burned briefly in his stomach and then subsided, leaving him in complete possession of himself.

He sat up, placed his deformed feet firmly on the floor and eased his body forward. Reflected in the mirrors about him, an infinity of clones moved with him.

Moving as quickly as his stiff muscles allowed, he found the door and released himself from the mirror room.

In the vestibule the air was cold and he shivered. It was all part of the waking-up process. He studied himself in a tall mirror. *What changes have we this time?* he wondered.

The tuning of the Way System was almost perfect. The entity which was re-assembled was in most respects a replica of that which was disseminated, but slight changes did frequently occur.

There was a new greyness in Pawl's hair and a rash of freckles had appeared on his throat and chest. His face looked patchy and dirty. But the eyes were the same, and the strong long-fingered hands, and the feet. He felt like Pawl and that was finally what was important.

He remembered a commoner he had once met who had maintained, not knowing who Pawl was, that passage through the Way System prolonged life. This was not true. The small deaths endured by the body all left their mark. Those who by circumstance were forced to use the Way System regularly ended their days looking like wizened babies.

The particle shower buffed and stung him and brought a healthy redness to his skin. The clothes he had selected, neatly pressed and still warm, were waiting for him. When he was dressed and groomed he felt fighting fit, and stepped out to identify himself.

The door leading to the Way Platform was already open. Pawl had expected a welcoming party. He had expected the Way Attendants to greet him with their customary salute. But there was no one. The Way Platform was grey and deserted. Pawl looked out and the empty room stared back at him. He noticed that the air was stale and that a patina of dust covered the chairs and table. Even some of the lights were out.

In the centre of the chamber a spiral staircase clanked jerkily into life and began to revolve like a giant steel gimlet. It would carry him down to the Shuttle.

Before advancing further Pawl placed his hand flat on a black square just inside the door and identified himself to the Way Computer.

"Welcome home, Pawl," boomed the computer, its voice unnaturally loud in the still chamber. "Your father says you are to descend immediately. The shuttle is waiting. Your trunk and other luggage have already been loaded."

"Thank you," said Pawl. "Anything else?"

"Nothing else."

"Where are all the people?"

"No information."

"What about the guards and attendants? Is the Gate protected?"

"We are on full automatic alert."

"Since when?"

"Two months."

Pawl digested this information and looked again at the drab reception room. "What has happened?" he asked.

"No information."

"Is my father well?"

"No information."

"Was I expected?"

"You were expected. Your father says you are to descend immediately. The shuttle is. . . ."

"Thank you," said Pawl. "I already heard you. I am on my way."

Pawl sat on his trunk in the shuttle and waited while the ceiling closed and secured. With a slight lurch the shuttle detached from the Way Platform and began its controlled descent down to the surface of the Paxwax Homeworld.

A thick muddy red light filled the chamber as the windows cleared.

Pawl moved to one of the bubble windows and looked down. Below him stretched the vast redness of Homeworld. Dawn was advancing across the smooth face of the planet, pushing back the luminant purple of the night sea. Where day was established, the sea glowed a brilliant, almost fiery red. Flecks of brown marked the numerous low muddy islands which lifted above the sea. On those islands, life would be active. The Maw would be waking up.

The Maw were the closest to an indigenous population that the Paxwax Homeworld still possessed. Their sentience was limited, and it was probably that fact which had saved their skins. Pawl knew that at that very moment, the skins of the Maw would be turning from grey to a dark brown as they soaked up the sunlight. They would be gathering the strength of the sun into their bodies and flopping about as they prepared for a day's grazing among the red algae.

Pawl remembered how, when they were boys – him barely eight and Lapis a sturdy nineteen-year-old – Lapis had taken him out hunting in his flyer. They had set out at dawn and swooped over the red ocean, no more than a few feet above the sluggish waves. Whenever they saw the inflated bellies of the Maw, they fired. Hit, the creature would roll over and evacuate the contents of its stomach in a vain attempt to jet itself to freedom.

How long ago that seemed.

Pawl stared down. Clouds were forming above the islands as they warmed up. On the surface of the sea, giant purple stranded whorls curled and twisted all the way to the horizon. These marked the currents that stirred the sea of Bennet Homeworld.

Pawl thrust his head completely into the bubble window and stared directly down to where the distinctive heart shape of Bennet Island was already visible. It stood out green and hard against the mottled red sea and its high sculptured cliffs cast a long shadow. Clouds hid most of the central peaks of the island, but one dark fumarole, higher than all the rest, poked through the mist like a small round mouth. This was Frautus, a picturesque volcano.

Pawl had wondered what his reaction would be to seeing the island of his birth after so many years. Now that he was actually here, dropping down like a stone, he felt detached . . . empty . . . an observer. Everything looked unreal.

Somewhere down there, no doubt monitoring the descent of the shuttle, was his father. That thought obliterated all other feelings.

The shuttle was dropping quickly. The clouds shifted. The sea sparkled, and details on the island became clear. Pawl could see the circular fields, though they did not seem as sharply defined as he remembered. He saw the ornamental woods where he had played and rode as a boy inventing hideaways. There were the valleys, too, each carefully constructed to give a feeling of space and distance. Frautus now stood clear and firm, a perfect volcanic cone.

He could see the roofs of the larger buildings. From this height they looked like tumbled bricks. Most of Bennet Island, as Pawl knew it, had been constructed during the reign of Sceptre Paxwax. This man had been a dreamer with the means to realize his dreams. He had fancied himself as an architect and had planned game parks and boulevards and vast domes which housed exotic creatures from the far reaches of the Paxwax empire. He had grafted spires and towers on to the old stone buildings which were the first home of the Paxwax. It was Sceptre Paxwax who had moulded the island into its heart shape. He had hoped that the Paxwax Homeworld would become a centre of culture.

But its flowering only outlived him by a few years. The Paxwax family contracted and its interests changed. The city which he had built fell into disrepair. The works over which painters and sculptors had laboured were packed up or left to moulder behind locked doors. Whole thoroughfares which once had echoed to the songs of vendors were left unrepaired. Nature invaded the city. Trees and shrubs broke up the mosaic pathways, blocked gateways and climbed and tangled in the high balconies.

When Pawl was a boy only a small part, the oldest part, of the once-bustling city was still occupied.

Looking down, Pawl could still see the outlines of Sceptre Paxwax's city. Here and there a tarnished spire jabbed up through the trees. There was a tower too, made of bright cherry-red tiles, which Pawl had admired when he was a boy. This still stood out clearly.

And even while Pawl was watching, something strange happened. It was as though the island was beneath clear water and the surface had been suddenly disturbed. The whole island wavered. A ripple travelled outwards from the occupied part of the city. It sped over the hills and trees. When it touched the sea the water churned and the red algae was pushed back. Within seconds the whole of Bennet Island was surrounded by a dark circle, as though a wine glass had been placed over it.

"So Toby is awake," murmured Pawl and nodded to himself. "Playing with his weather machine. Planning a welcome, no doubt."

Pawl eased himself from the observation bubble and crossed to the shuttle controls. He altered the speed of descent, slowing it to its lowest speed. He was now less than a mile above the buildings. He threw open the shuttle windows and allowed the cold morning air to blow through and chill him.

Birds.

As the shadows of the shuttle slipped and jumped over the hills and trees, Pawl noticed that there were thousands of birds circling. They looked like carrion crows and flew with a lazy flapping motion.

Then, suddenly it seemed, the ground was rushing up to meet him and he felt his weight increase as the auto brakes took effect. The windows darkened as he left the morning sunshine and entered the shadow of the buildings and trees.

With a bump, harder than he had expected, he was down. Seconds later a section of the wall cracked open and lowered to become a ramp. Pawl looked out. Nothing moved. Still no people. Then he heard a loud harsh barking coming from the direction of the nearest buildings and a giant slab-shouldered and box-headed dog appeared. It ran jerkily on the grass in front of the building and stopped and looked at him with one paw raised and its ears pointed. Then its ears flattened and its lips drew back and it darted straight towards him.

Pawl recognized Punic, the giant mechanical dog, which had been in his family for generations and was one of the few surviving relics of the time when such creatures were the delight of the Families. Like all of its kind, it was designed for single-minded devotion – a fearless, tireless watchdog. When Pawl was a small boy the dog had often terrified him.

Punic reached the ramp of the shuttle and sat down with its steel and plastic paws stretched out in front of it. Clenched incongruously in its oily jaws was a folded sheet of paper.

Pawl advanced, extracted the paper, and ordered the dog back. It growled and hunkered down and then retreated with its head low as though it was about to try and slink round behind him. Its glowing eyes never left him.

The paper bore a curt message from his father. "See me this evening. My rooms."

How silly, thought Pawl. He looked at the dog with its obvious hostility and realized that he was facing a complicated charade. No doubt his father had instructed the dog to try and frighten Pawl. "Silly old man," he muttered, and the dog snapped at the air and growled. "Listen Punic, you may have frightened me once, when I was a boy. But not now. Not any more. Those days are long past." Deliberately Pawl turned the paper over and rested it on the side of the shuttle and wrote his quick reply. "I'll be there." Then he screwed the paper into a ball and threw it to the dog. It caught the message in its damp jaws and scampered away scattering the birds which had settled on the lawn.

When it was gone Pawl stared out at the deserted buildings and empty windows. "Halllooo. Is anyone there. This is Pawl Paxwax. Is there anyone there?" The only answer was a fading echo.

No one came to help him with his bags. No smiling face said welcome home.

Pawl found a pneumatic trolley and shifted his gear himself. Uncertain where he should go, he decided to move back into the small suite of rooms that had been his since the days he took his first uncertain steps. He was sweating when he finally dragged his trunk up a short flight of steps and deposited it in the centre of his former bedroom.

The room had been completely stripped. The only furniture was a plain bed, a small domestic vivante machine and an old speaking grandfather clock. This had been given to him on his eighth birthday. It looked incongruous and lonely, but it still worked and greeted him with the news that the time was now "Eight th . . . th . . . thirty."

The air in the room smelled oppressive and musty and Pawl opened the casement window to let the morning air stir the dust. Below him he could see a large courtyard fringed with trees. This was his main playground when he was a boy. At the far end of the courtyard were low buildings which had once been stables. Many times in the past, Pawl had awakened to the sounds of hoofs clattering on the courtyard cobbles. Beyond the stables the woods began, and beyond them there was the open countryside. A tunnel of branches led under the trees. In Sceptre Paxwax's time, this had been the main thoroughfare leading out of the city.

Pawl glanced round hoping to see movement. But there was nothing. His eyes came to rest on a high ferro-plastic building which looked like a giant brick rammed, end on, into the earth. Slit windows stared down into the courtyard. It was here that his father had his rooms. The entire roof and half the courtyard was shaded by the silver spokes of the vivante aerial.

The silence was uncanny.

Grim faced, Pawl turned from the window and opened his trunk. He selected a particle pistol and strapped it to his side. He pulled out a satchel and his notebook and a small vivante cube enclosed in a transit box. He handled it with care. This was the vivante cube which he and Laurel had made on distant Lotus-and-Arcadia.

Thus equipped, Pawl set out to explore the house.

Pawl quickly discovered that the house was uninhabited. Many rooms were locked. Some had boards nailed roughly across them. Cobwebs showed passageways that had not been walked in for a long time. He found windows through which branches poked and stair carpets that were sodden and glazed with mould. The only life he encountered in the whole of his wanderings was a sheep with a dirty, heavy fleece which stopped in one of the corridors and stared at him stupidly. He shooed it away and the sheep barged into a once-elegant room and out into the garden through a broken French window. Pawl tore the grass free from around the base of the door and dragged it shut and forced its rusting clasp to close.

None of the flow-ways worked, or the mobile staircases or the vacuum lifts. The power cells which activated the lights were for the most part dead. Once when he tried a switch, lights blazed on and then died in a fizz of sparks. But at least there was power flowing somewhere.

Several times in his wanderings he came back to the base of a wide flight of stairs which led up to his father's rooms. But he did not ascend. He avoided the stairs and finally, beginning to feel oppressed by the silence and the decay, he made his way outside.

He pushed through a narrow walkway choked with shrubs and eventually came to the large courtyard. The sun was bright, dazzling after the dark house.

Pawl noticed then that the trees in the courtyard were just coming into leaf. Springtime. He smelled the air and it was wholesome and clean. He looked up into the sky. High fleecy clouds, a bite in the air. It was a perfect spring day . . . too perfect.

Pawl recognized one of the basic weather plans which his father could control at will.

Avoiding the temptation to look up at his father's windows Pawl set out down the long courtyard. The sound of his boots echoed loudly in his ears. He expected Punic to come scrambling round one of the corners at any moment but nothing happened and finally he found himself at the door of the old stables. The main door which faced into the courtyard stood half open and hung at a crazy angle with its upper hinges broken.

The horse doors, half doors where the horses had stood looking out, were all closed with bolts of wood.

Pawl tiptoed inside. By the smell he could tell that it was a long time since anything other than sheep had lived there. He walked down the empty stalls and heard the scuffle of rats.

At the end, in a corner, in a place where the hay had been stored, the sunlight blazed white and sharp through a broken window. It fell on the scattered skeleton of a horse. A collar was still round its neck and the lead chain was shackled to a stall pillar.

Now who could let a horse die like that? wondered Pawl, thinking of its whinnying and kicking and thrashing. The horses had once been the pride of the Paxwax Homeworld.

Tightlipped he left the stable, for there was nothing he could do there.

He wanted to get away from the house, as far as possible. None of it made any sense to him. What had happened to the horses?

What had happened to the rooms? What had happened to the people?

He walked into the tunnel under the trees. He pushed through stiff-branched shrubs and his boots squelched in the mud and ooze of decaying leaves. He came to the domed houses where the servants had once lived. One had a ragged hole in its roof. He threw a stone through the roof and startled some nesting birds. But no one came angry and red-faced to the door.

After about a mile Pawl came to the end of the outbuildings and the wood. This was a place he recognized. He broke through a tangled hedge and made his way to a grove of trees beside a small stream. Grazing sheep had kept the grass cut short and the place was almost as he remembered. The water still gurgled over the pebbles, flies still danced and buzzed in the air.

Pawl threw himself down on the grass and rested his chin on his hands and stared at the flowing water.

On an impulse he elbowed himself to the edge of the bank and then plunged his face down into the stream. Its cold stung him and felt good and he kept his face under until he could hold his breath no longer. He emerged puffing and blowing and with the water running down his neck and into his jerkin. He wiped his face with his hands and shook his head.

"Laurel."

He whispered the word. God, he felt lonely. Laurel would have known what to do. If he had known what was waiting for him on his Homeworld he would have insisted she come with him, dragged her along if need be. He felt angry that she was not with him, angry with the Families, angry with the Code, angry with himself, and that feeling was close to love.

He reached for his satchel and opened it and pulled out his notebook. This was typical of the man. For when his thoughts became too complex, he found that sometimes they gave themselves shape in words. He wanted to talk to Laurel in his mind and so he dug out a pencil, turned to a clear page and began to write.

Pawl wrote what he called songs.

Sometimes they were shouts. Sometimes gentle soundings. Feeling was immediate and complex . . . blessed words took time and space . . . Oh Laurel. . . .

>Why do I see your face in the water?
>Why hear your voice in the bubbling stream?

I am not satisfied with shadows
Though shadows of you are all that I see.

Oh I am a foolish man.
Being thirsty I throw open my mouth
And gulp and gulp, drinking you down,
So much that breathing comes hard.

Oh I am a foolish man
For when I have drunk, I lie on my back,
And wish and wish, thinking of you,
That I were thirsty again.

"Why now? Why a love song now?" Pawl smiled. At least he felt better. Something was off his chest and out in the open. He lay back and listened to the gurgle of the stream.

Like the ringing of bells . . . the singing of eels . . . the. . . .

Pawl awoke with an insect crawling up his nose. He sneezed and noticed that the sun had moved in the sky. It was hotter now and the buzzing of flies was louder, like a machine.

There were more birds too, and they were circling just beyond the hill on the opposite bank.

Pawl roused himself and pushed his notebook and pencil aside. He jumped up and in growing excitement scrambled down the bank. Something was happening over there . . . perhaps a man ploughing judging by the birds . . . something normal.

The water was chill as he waded across the stream.

The buzzing grew louder as he hoisted himself up the bank and climbed the hill. He pulled himself up gripping the stems of the small bushes and reached the top panting.

Pawl stared.

He stared, and his yellow eyes were unblinking as he looked down on the dark confusion of bodies. Birds which had been pecking and pulling at the remnants of clothing to gain the maggots flapped into the air as his head appeared. They soon settled. The buzzing of black flies was like the beating of hammers.

The mass grave was in a natural hollow beyond the river bank. It had always been a seepy place of weeds. Now it was a small oily pond.

The bodies lay tangled and confused as thrown. The eyes

were gone, and the exposed hands and bellies were ravaged. Occasionally, the clean whiteness of bone showed.

Pawl sat down slowly, cross-legged at the edge of the pond. He was oblivious of the ants which quickly found a path across his hand.

10

ON MORROW

Clarissa viewed Humility Lamprey with disgust and hoped that her feelings did not show in her voice.

"Your Lowliness, I hope I have not called at an inconvenient time."

The old man, his face streaked with dirt, his eyes like sewn-up button holes, shook his head at her. "Devotions completed." He was sweating. Dame Clarissa could see the dark stains on the grey tunic round his scrawny neck and under his arms. *And God alone knows what else he's been doing*, she thought.

He sniffed the air like a rodent following a scent. Being blind he had no notion of how ugly the movement was. "Have you news or do you just want to talk to me?"

"News," replied Clarissa. "Important news we felt we should share with you."

"Tell it, child. Take the weight from your mind. A troubled mind becomes a troubled spirit."

Clarissa hoped he was not warming up for a sermon. Once she had had to sit for two hours while he lectured her on the text that reason was the enemy of faith. That was long ago, when the association between the two families was just beginning. In those days Humility Lamprey had often tried to get Clarissa and her sisters to join him in worship of his blind ancestor.

"The fox is in the net."

He stared past her blankly. "You speak in riddles. The fox is. . . ."

Clarissa threw her eyes to the sky and her quills fluffed briefly and settled. She cursed the workings of fate which had made it necessary for the Xerxes to ally themselves with the dirty bigoted stupid Lamprey. She forced the words out of her mind and concentrated.

"I mean that we hold Lapis Paxwax."

That elicited a positive reaction. The Lamprey face screwed up like a baby's. "Good. Good. When can we have him?"

"You can't. He is ours. It was agreed. Don't you remember? Your turn comes later. Later."

The old man chewed on this. "We hold rights to vengeance too," he muttered.

Vengeance. Who did not want vengeance on the Paxwax? It was Seppein Paxwax who generations earlier had ordered a strafe party to invade the Lamprey wine worlds. What should have remained a small economic war had escalated into a bloody conflict in which the honeycomb of cells occupied by the Lamprey slave workers had been flooded. The Paxwax, having defied the Code which absolutely prohibited violence between Families, were punished. But still the offence lingered, nursed like a religious flame, and the armies of the Lamprey were ready.

"And vengeance you shall have. Are you in readiness? The time is close, perhaps only a few days."

"Our Saints stand ready for the call."

Clarissa had seen the Saints once. A pale army of drugged creatures; a spawning of alien and human who, from the cradle, had been taught that their sole purpose was to obey and that their own lives were dispensable. A chilling force, amoral as a knife. On order they would emerge from the Lamprey worker worlds and invade the Paxwax.

Their purpose was a carefully-guarded secret.

"Do not move without a word from me. Toby must be on his knees and begging before we invade. He must see his empire torn open like a leaf."

"We will wait. Patience is strength."

Clarissa sensed a text emerging and hurried to end the contact.

"So you will hear from me. We will keep you well informed. Peace to your ancestor."

"Honour to the dead."

The vivante space on the two Homeworlds became milky and then cleared.

Behind Humility, well out of range of the vivante, stood a man clothed in a similar tunic, but with a wispy beard and eyes like catkins.

"Can we trust the Xerxes?" asked Humility when the vivante glow had faded. He groped around with his hands, feeling expertly until he encountered the fabric of the other's tunic. "She sounded strained."

"She was just excited. You know how women are. She wants to eat Paxwax flesh and drink their blood just as we do. We can trust Clarissa. She knows she cannot manage without us. Her self-interest is involved."

"Ah. You give me comfort. Shall we bring the Saints to readiness?"

"Without delay. They await but the word."

Hand in hand the two walked away from the vivante, feeling their way along the walls of the catacombs in which they lived.

Behind them, with a sound like leaves in the wind, moved a detachment of their grey mindless army.

Lapis Paxwax of the Paxwax Fifth was kept in the dog-hutch, a deep pit quarried from the living rock in the roots of the tree. Generations earlier it had been a settling tank for water and its sides were steep and smooth.

The Spideret was with him. Latani Rama had wanted to kill it but Clarissa had intervened, saying that there had been enough killing so far and that they, the Xerxes, were not simple butchers. "If it is his servant, let it stay with him. It cannot be a danger to us here, I think. Not on Morrow itself. It is in small things that the truly magnanimous spirit shows itself."

Jettatura had sniffed. "Just so long as I don't have to see it. Keep it penned in the dog-hutch."

The Spideret showed every symptom of fear and submission, scuttling behind the trolley as it was rolled down into the deepest part of the Xerxes tree.

"But if it shows any sign of aggression, cut its legs off," said Clarissa as an afterthought.

So there it was with Lapis in the dog-hutch. It fashioned a web across the top of the tank and hung there at its centre, its eyes glittering.

Lapis groaned and shifted on the cane and canvas bed which supported him. He lifted a hand and explored his hair and face. The other arm was a stump. One eye was closed under clean bandages. His chest was numb with anaesthetic and he could not tell whether he still had legs. But he was alive. His one good eye opened and he looked straight up at the Spideret.

Immediately it detached and spun down into the pit until it was beside him.

Lapis took one of its feelers in his hand and squeezed. "You here Tirit. Thank God. How'd you manage to save me? No forget it. Too complicated."

The Spideret detached its feeler and began to stroke Lapis gently. It moved small feelers in front of Lapis's eyes.

Lapis watched and then stretched flat. "Okay, I'll rest. But where are we? Was there a cave-in? Last I remember was the tractor coming round and then starting to topple. Thought it was on me." The Spideret made no reply but continued to stroke.

Abruptly, bright arc lights blazed above them, throwing black shadows into the pit. The Spideret scampered back to its rope and climbed a few feet.

Over the lip of the pit appeared the face of Jettatura. Her long white hair gleamed and tumbled.

"Awake, are you?" she called. "Get away from him, you thing, and come up here. I want to see him." Obediently the Spideret shinnied up to its web. "Can you hear me, Lapis Paxwax? You have made a good recovery. We have treated you well. I am now going to make a vivante recording of you. This is for your father. He believes you are dead. You may say anything you like."

Lapis stood up painfully from the bed. "Where am I?" he called.

"You are on Morrow and I am Jettatura of the Xerxes de la Tour Souvent Fourth." Lapis sat down heavily.

"Is this truth? Why are you holding me? When my father knows he will. . . ."

"He will what, small man? Come raging to find you? He may, but he will not go far. I think your father will come to us. But on his knees. And we will kill you. And him. The Paxwax are ended. They finish with you."

Jettatura fixed Lapis in the viewfinder of the vivante camera and began to make a silent recording. "Come on, speak, man. Where's the Paxwax spirit we've heard so much about? Why don't you rage? Call me names. Insult me. You've said enough in the past."

Lapis did not move. He sat and stared at the floor.

"I'd like to see you in action. Banging your fist on the walls."

Still Lapis did not move. Jettatura became impatient.

"You know, I've talked to my sisters about you. I want you as my pet. A pet pig. I want to remove your arms and legs so you can only wallow and squirm. And I'll put a bracelet round your neck and parade you in a cart before all the Eleven."

Lapis spoke but his voice was so soft that Jettatura had to lean to hear. "Have pity," he murmured. "Have pity. If ever I rule the Paxwax, we can live in harmony. We'll settle disputes. . . ."

"You haven't been listening, pig-man."

The faces of Dames Clarissa and Rose joined Jettatura.

"Is the recording finished?" asked Clarissa.

"Yes, but he wouldn't perform," replied Jettatura and turned away. She handed the vivante camera to Clarissa. "Here, see if you have more luck."

"All we need is a simple recording to show that he is alive. No exotic touches." She paused, "Have you been trying to goad him?"

"I talked to him."

Clarissa studied her sister. There were times when she feared her. There were movements in Jettatura that she did not understand. She turned back to Lapis.

"Listen to me, Lapis Paxwax. We shall speak with your father. Perhaps tomorrow. If he agrees to our terms we may even let him speak to you. We shall exact concessions, naturally. Both you and he must accept the hopelessness of your position. If you wish to live – if you wish the Paxwax to have a future – you must accept the reality of your position. We believe your father is a realist. Live in hope that he is. When your father has agreed to our conditions we will move you to a more comfortable place of keeping. You will lack for nothing to keep you alive. Do you have anything to say?"

Lapis sat unmoving.

"Very well, we shall speak to you later."

Clarissa and Jettatura left the rim above the pit. Lapis heard their voices fade as they moved away.

Silence. Lapis looked up and saw the bright eyes of Rose staring down at him. She was sitting at the edge of the pit with the hem of her skirt trailing down into the hole.

"What are you doing here?" he asked. "Gloating?"

"I wanted to see the face of the enemy."

"Well, look your fill."

"I shall." She stared in silence.

"Are you Rose?"

"I am."

"Why do you and your sisters hate us? It was all a game to me. We could have got on. Rubbed along."

"It was never a game to us."

"The Families are a game. Look at my father."

"What will he do?"

"He will never agree. He will fight. You could lower me in acid before his eyes and he would not change."

"I think you are wrong. Blood is thicker than water."

"Well, what about Pawl?"

"The boy is lost in his dreams."

Lapis studied his bandages. "How did *your* father die?"

"We have no father."

"Mother, then?"

"In childbirth bearing me."

"Doesn't that make you think?"

Rose stood up awkwardly, heavily. She moved back from the rail, away from the staring Lapis.

"Well, doesn't it make you think? Make you think?" Lapis shouted.

But Rose was gone.

"So, tomorrow then. We are agreed." Clarissa spoke with finality. "I will speak to Toby Paxwax and then show him the vivante. I will give him five minutes to comply. I will outline the conditions but will not mention the Lamprey. We will hold them in reserve in case of trickery."

"I still think you should let *me* speak to him," said Jettatura.

"No. I am senior sister and I have conducted affairs so far. I will not be robbed of my triumph."

"And if he says war . . . ?" asked Rose.

"He will not. Toby is mad but he is not stupid. Our advantage is absolute. We have him. We should be rejoicing."

"I shall rejoice alone," said Jettatura.

"I shall retire," said Dame Rose. "I am tired again."

"I shall sit with Dame Rex," said Clarissa, and the meeting came to an end. "Till tomorrow, then."

Clarissa did not spend long with Dame Rex. She was too jumpy and found it uncomfortable to remain on her high stool in front of the glass case. She called the little men to her and ordered them to begin cleaning all the glass. Then she bade Rex goodbye and set off to her private quarters.

Comfortable in her own rooms she called Latani Rama to her.

"I want to review the attack schedules," said Clarissa. "Bring all the details in here."

The two women settled down to comb through, for perhaps the hundredth time, all the details of their carefully-laid attack plan. The plan was simple and elegant. Assassination teams and Way technicians were waiting at key points round and within the Paxwax empire. Their exact positions were known only to the Xerxes sisters and Latani Rama. The establishment of these positions had taken years, and only the help of a traitor in the Paxwax hierarchy had made them possible. On cue, the teams would attack the Way Gates, thereby paralysing the Paxwax empire while Latani Rama herself led the final thrust to Bennet Homeworld.

Everything depended on surprise.

"It will work, won't it?" said Clarissa.

"It will," replied Latani Rama with confidence, "given surprise."

11

ON SANCTUM

That Pental was a human animal made him interesting. Odin had often drifted through the minds of humans and taken delight in their swift passions. They were capable of love and hate at the same time, of despising and desiring an object simultaneously. They were endlessly inventive but profoundly ignorant of their own natures. Odin was not surprised that they were great conquerors but he could not understand the contradictions which were at the heart of their natures. This made them almost unique and interesting objects of study.

That Pental was a child of the Paxwax made him very important at this moment in the aliens' history. But Pental could tell them almost nothing about the Paxwax. He had left that family at the age of thirteen, scarcely more than a boy.

As Pental stood open before the aliens on Sanctum, Odin could read a deep self-loathing within the man. He was like a child that should never have been born: a loveless entity that wanted to escape from itself. This made Pental an almost perfect host for the eggs which lived in his body and blood and which would one day hatch and devour him . . . but it made him almost useless as a source for understanding the Paxwax.

Certain memories stood out: hiding in the bushes while his father raged about, dangling from his life-support mechanism, looking for him; finding a bird's nest in which the birds were just hatching; scooping up the red algae of the sea and boiling it to a pulp; watching his mother cry; standing wondering by a grave while a young Paxwax child was buried and wishing it was him; riding on one of the big horses with Lapis; observing a couple make love under a tree and thinking he was witnessing murder; crying himself to sleep while a giant dog padded and growled outside his door.

But what did these memories add up to? Very little.

Pawl Paxwax figured in Pental's mind as a fat little child who was always crying. That was all. The memory had no individuality or colour.

By the age of ten Pental had decided he wanted to join the Inner Circle though he had no idea what the Inner Circle was. He wanted a solitary obedient life. He even took to wearing black clothes which he made himself and stopped speaking to anyone. He hobbled about the house, watching but never commenting, and his family were glad when finally the Inner Circle accepted him.

Odin touched the memories gently. There was a darkness here that repelled him.

It made him wonder what forces were at work in Pawl Paxwax.

It made him wonder in what strange way the survival of the alien community was linked to Pawl Paxwax.

12

ON BENNET

Pawl sat and stared at the tangled heap of corpses. They had lain for several months, Pawl could not tell how many, and individuality had been gradually lost.

The heap had settled. Leaves, water, insects and birds had done the rest.

Pawl had seen death before. The carcases of the land whales on distant Phonir made mountains of flesh after a month's hunting. But there was a difference between the animal you had stalked and felled and the bodies of people you had grown up with. He stared and tried to give the mound a meaning . . . and failed.

As the day crept through, and Pawl sat, clouds gathered round the dark peak of Frautus and in the Mendel Hills. They became grey and then dark with rain as the spring day disappeared and the temperature dropped. The sky became leaden and heavy with snow.

Pawl's first awareness of a change in the weather came when the sun faded and then finally became a milky glow behind the haze. With the loss of the sun came the breeze. A sudden wind, surprisingly harsh, bent the trees and sent cat's paws curling across the broken surface of the pond.

When Pawl looked up there was thunder.

He stood up and faced the storm. He could not make sense of the killing, but one thing he had come to understand. Someone was responsible and that someone could only be his father. That evening Pawl had to face him. He wondered what he would say.

The first large flakes of snow wheeled down as he slowly began to make his way back. The broken collection of buildings was before him, strangely luminous in the storm light, but grim and deserted. No friendly lights shone at the windows.

Inside his bare rooms Pawl made himself as comfortable as possible. He activated the power cells and was relieved to discover they still worked. He gained heat and light. He went down to one of the disused rooms, pulled down some curtains, dragged them back to his room and tacked them up over his window. Outside, the courtyard was already grey with driven snow. No lights were showing in his father's quarters. Pawl was not surprised. He knew the windows would be heavily curtained. His father hated the outdoors.

Pawl unpacked slowly, arranging his possessions neatly. He unwrapped a rare picture of his mother; he set the picture on a ledge and looked at her smiling face. It had been taken shortly after her wedding. Burn marks blackened the edges. Pawl had rescued it from the fire when his father burned all his mother's belongings. Pawl remembered that sad savage day and his mother's face as she walked past the bonfire on her way to banishment. She had not cried. Her chin was high and defiant. She had not made a sound even when confronted by the tortured body of Jon, her lover, being dragged round the shuttle port by Punic. Pawl heard shortly afterwards that she had died in a distant part of the Paxwax domain.

Pawl's last memory of her was as she mounted the ramp. She had not turned, but her fingers had crinkled behind her in what Pawl had taken to be a wave of farewell.

He had cried, and Lapis had cuffed him. Pental, his other
brother, had stood stiff as a statue and watched like a man looking
at the sea.

Pawl could remember little else except that that night he heard
words in his head as though someone was speaking to him and he
wrote them down and that became his first song. Years later his
father found that first writing and destroyed it, but by then it didn't
matter.

Behind Pawl, gears meshed and a voice spoke.

"Th-thirty m-minutes to your m-meeting."

Pawl whirled round and then smiled at his own nervousness.

It was the old grandfather clock.

"Thank you. I haven't forgotten," he said. The deep bell tones
faded into the silence leaving only the slow stuttering *t-tick, t-tock*.
Every second sounded as though it were its last. It had sounded
this way ever since Pawl could remember.

Outside the wind howled. Pawl drew aside the curtain and stared
out into the courtyard. Darkness had fallen. Bright quartz lights
blazed down in the courtyard and in their glare the snow swept
past like wraiths.

Pawl knew that the storm was for his benefit.

Pawl spent the last few minutes before seven o'clock sitting on his
trunk in front of the simulated wood fire that blazed in his hearth.
Then, at five minutes to seven, just as the grandfather clock was
winding itself up to speak, he opened his trunk and selected a
heavy mantle and threw it over his shoulders. He made sure that
the vivante cube of Laurel Beltane was safe and set off down the
stairs to the small door that led outside.

The wind was steadily working up to gale force. Fine snow had
blown in under the door and covered the porch like the skin of an
arctic fox. Pawl unlocked the door and held it firmly against the
buffeting wind. Then he slipped through quickly and dragged the
door shut.

Outside the wind caught at Pawl's cloak and blew it up round his
shoulders. The snow swirled down and plastered him. Grim-faced
and hunched he trudged straight into the teeth of the wind. He
crossed the courtyard under the harsh glare of the overhead lights
and came to a door made from a single segment of a silica tree.

This had been a gift from the Xerxes many years ago during the time of Sceptre Paxwax's reign. Low on the door was a small portal and it was through this that Pawl entered.

Inside the house was dark and creaking. Dim roof lights led him down corridors until he reached the main central staircase. He climbed, taking the stairs two at a time, at any moment expecting the mad dog Punic to come snapping at him. But the only sound was his own footsteps.

Finally he reached the passage which led directly to his father's rooms. Like the rest of the house it was filled with shadows. Busts of the long dead masters of the Paxwax family stared down on him. But at its end there was a glimmer of light.

Pawl tapped at the door and it yielded smoothly, opening to his touch. Staring straight at him was his father. Pawl entered and the door hissed shut behind him.

The room stank. It was a smell of staleness and decay.

Long dark cables ran in festoons across the walls and terminated in a giant console which occupied, wedge-like, a third of the room. This was the weather machine. It was active now and fine green graph lines curled in space, monitoring the storm. It had other powers too. With it Toby could create images in the sky and on the land.

One entire wall was taken up by a clear glass screen behind which billowed a frothy orange liquid. In the liquid large snails moved. Pandora Boxes. Liberated, these creatures exuded a dark semen which crept and fed on any life it encountered. Inside the host, new Pandora Boxes developed and so the cycle continued.

Beside the screen was a cage full of rats which were the food for the giant snails.

Most of the rest of the room was as Pawl remembered, though he had only been allowed in there a few times. At one end was a curtained alcove behind which was Toby's bed, and beyond that a specially appointed lavatory. Opposite the weather machine was a shallow alcove in which stood an old-fashioned vivante machine. This was Toby's only contact with the outside world.

The room was sparsely furnished but seemed cluttered. In the centre sat Toby, immersed to his hips in soft warm plastic which churned in a steady massage. His chair was as expansive as a bed and was the only hint of luxury. Above him, hanging like a giant jelly-fish, was his life support system which kept his blood clean and which, by means of its anti-gravity cells, allowed Toby to move about. He had been fitted to this machine when he was a child and it had grown with him. Bio-crystalline cords stretched from the "chandelier", down to points on his body. A control band, strapped to his wrist, allowed Toby to lift and glide and swoop.

In his massive hands Toby held a half-empty carafe of wine and he motioned with this for Pawl to sit down opposite him.

"So, Lapis is dead. Did I tell you?" Toby Paxwax waved his hand in front of his face as though wafting the thought away. "Yes, course I did. Just can't get used to it. You and I have a lot to talk about, but I'll tell you this. If I'd had any choice I'd have strangled you with my bare hands rather than let him go. So that's how we start discussion."

Pawl looked at his father without speaking. He saw the long hair plaited into ropes. It was the colour of pale straw. The hard face and the sharp blue eyes. The tight bodice which strained across his shoulders and which was partly hidden by a ginger beard. From the waist up his father was a giant: below the waist a dwarf.

"No tongue? No lip? No fancy words? What's wrong with you?"

"Where are all the people? What happened?"

"Didn't you find them? You were out today."

"I found them."

"Well?"

"What happened?" His father didn't reply but merely chewed on a corner of his moustache. "I have a right to know."

"You have no rights, boy. Not till I'm dead."

"Does it hurt you to tell me?"

"They rebelled. I taught them a lesson. It's history. And who needs them? We Paxwax are independent. We need no one. No one!"

Toby was suddenly angry. His face darkened. But whether his anger was directed at the memory of the Paxwax people or some other cause, Pawl could not tell.

They faced one another in silence again.

"Tell me how Lapis died."

"He was coming home."

"I know."

"Out on Auster. Digging for ore. A tractor fell and he was under it. It dragged him under its tracks. They found the top half of his cover-suit. He'd been sucked clean out of it. Just a hand left. They sent it."

"Do you want to see it? I've got it here." His father pointed to a standard Way box which stood on the table.

Pawl shook his head. "Who sent it?"

"The creatures he'd been working with."

"What creatures?"

"Those big spider things . . . I don't know what they're called." Toby looked away and drank quickly.

"I'm sorry," said Pawl.

"Sorry. You're sorry. Spare your tears – or are you going to write some pretty words. . . ."

"If you like," said Pawl. It was a goad and his father reacted.

"Well, don't. He was my son. My real son. He should be sitting where you are. I don't want you messing up . . . I don't want you to be a part of anything. Lapis was mine. You belong to your mother."

Pawl looked for a long time at his father and then stood up and crossed to the wall near the weather machine. Thick curtains hung there. He pulled the curtains open and looked out into the night. The weather had changed. The snow had settled and the clouds were gone. Beyond the Mendel Hills the twin moons of Homeworld were rising silver and gold.

"Close them," ordered his father. Pawl ignored him.

A faint purple tinged the night sky at the horizon.

"You know, this place could be beautiful if only you'd let it. I could enjoy life here. I could marry and. . . ."

"Close them."

Pawl still ignored his father but turned and faced him. Then he walked round the room touching the weather machine and the case containing the Pandora Boxes. Finally he sat down again and faced his father.

"You are a silly old man," he said.

With a bellow his father tapped his wrist and immediately the chandelier contracted and lifted, hoisting him from the plastic bath. His dwarf legs with their nodules of flesh, lacking sinew or bone, were revealed. He spun over to the window and wrenched the curtain shut.

"Get out," he shouted.

Pawl smiled and shook his head. "Not now, father. Not after all these years. Sit down and look at me. I'm all you have. You didn't drag me back here just to trade insults. One day I shall be Master of Paxwax. God knows I didn't want that, but there we are." He shrugged. "Let us begin talking seriously. Sit down."

The effect of these words on Toby was strange. He breathed deeply, angrily, and balled his fists as though he would smash the window. Then he relaxed and just hung there.

"Lapis wouldn't have used those words. He would have tried to fight me."

"I am not Lapis."

"He wouldn't have used that thin clever voice."

"I am not Lapis."

"He'd have bawled and I'd have bawled and then we'd've had a drink."

"I'll drink with you."

The carafe Toby had been holding when he lifted had fallen to the floor and poured out its contents into the carpet. Pawl rose and fetched a new one and broke its seal. "Come and drink with me, father. We'll drink to Lapis."

Toby swung away from the wall and hovered over his plastic bath. Then he descended and the soft plastic received him gently.

"He was coming home, you know. He'd forgiven me. Forgotten everything. He said he wanted to be a Paxwax son. He was going to ask you to take charge of Elliott's Pocket. Did you know that?" Pawl shook his head. "Well he was. Said he knew you had friends there and it's an important region. Perhaps you should go out there . . . get the feel of running a whole sector. That's how I learned things." He reached out for the carafe. "And we've got the Xerxes on the run. I've been mounting an offensive. What do you say, Pawl?"

Pawl shrugged his shoulders non-committally.

"I think that before we begin talking about sectors we should settle another question first . . . my marriage."

Toby looked at him with surprise and then bellowed with laughter. "You're quick off the mark, son. No sooner do you hear that you're heir to the Paxwax . . . than you want to get married. Want to get your line established, eh? Well, take my advice, boy: women are trouble. Love them. Leave them. Use them to get yourself an heir, but don't give them your. . . ." Toby clenched his huge fist like a boxer. "Don't give them your . . . spirit. They'll only destroy you, turn on you. I know."

"I want. . . ."

"Who cares what you want? You're going to be Master of
Paxwax one day. Forget about what you want. Paxwax rules. The
family rules. Kiss goodbye to your freedom. You do what is
necessary. Clear?"

"I'll do what I want."

Toby cleared his mouth and spat on the floor. "You're just a
boy." He drank deeply, until the wine spilled into his moustache
and down into his beard. "And you'll do what *I* want. Now. You're
right about one thing. A Master needs a wife. Lapis and I had
been communicating. We had things worked out. Stupid boy. Why
didn't he wear a harness? Why didn't he clear out sooner? He
could have been back here. Lapis would have kicked the shit out
of the Xerxes and laughed while he was doing it."

Toby's eyes focused on Pawl. "But he's gone, isn't he? And that
leaves you and me. God help us. God help the Paxwax. God
knows how we ever became so thin." Toby was beginning to rave
. . . wandering in his mind. "You know, I had five sons, and only
one of them was any good. And now all I've got is you."

He drank again and took a deep breath. "Well, anyway. Like
my father used to say. Take what you're . . . I mean, there's
nothing any of us can do about it anyway. So come on. Let's mix
it. I've been thinking about what sort of alliance would suit us best.
You're right about one thing Pawl. Marriage is the next step.
Come on, I've got things to show you."

Toby placed his wine glass carefully on the table in front of him
and then tapped the panel on his wrist. Immediately the chandelier
glowed and its strings tightened and it lifted him and swung him
over to the vivante. He selected a cube and popped it into the
machine and then swung back. "Want you to see this. See what
you think."

Pawl watched. *So that's it,* he thought. *The old bastard's got it all
planned out.* He wondered whether now was the moment to stop
his father, but he was already too late.

The room darkened and a fine point of silver light appeared
above the vivante machine. It grew larger, became a vortex, and
suddenly blossomed into the image of Wong Xiou-lung. The
wavering notes of the Mei-lan flute filled the air.

She looked ghastly. She looked like a shrivelled child. She was
gowned like a doll, but the thick brocade could not hide the
deformity in her arms and shoulders; nor could make-up conceal

the symptoms of Ivory sickness. She had been invaded at about the age of ten and the parasite had arrested her development from that hour.

Stranger matches had been made. Pawl knew.

Physical deformity among the higher Families was more the norm than the exception and was frequently a cause of pride. In his time on Lotus-and-Arcadia, Pawl had made love to women with tusks, to androgynous creatures, to the scaly, silken and webbed. It was the way.

"She's of age, you know," said his father. "I know she looks small but that's no disadvantage. And she is of the Wong Third. I've already spoken to Old Man Wong and he seems keen enough. Think, an alliance of the Wong Third with the Paxwax Fifth. We'll carve up the Xerxes in no time. There's a contract almost ready. What do you say?"

"I say I laugh at you," said Pawl carefully. "There's about as much human blood left in her as there is in this wine. She's hosting a parasite. She'll be dead within the year. I've seen that lost look before. Listen, Toby, stop playing games. We are wasting time. I've already. . . ."

"I knew it was a long shot but it is serious. All right, so she's dead in a year; we still gain and you can marry again."

"I've already made my choice."

His father dismissed this with a wave.

"Have you? Well, good. We can talk about that later. For the moment we're just surveying the field. What about this lady?"

He stopped the vivante machine and popped a new cube into it. The anthem of the Longstock Eighth rang out and Dama Longstock appeared. Pawl had known her well on Lotus-and-Arcadia and their names had been linked more than once. His father had a crafty look on his face.

Dama Longstock was a respected beauty. Her hair was so blond it was almost white. She was tall and well-formed with a strong profile and full lips. A small frill of bone encircled her neck and this was her only strangeness. The frill was sensitive as Pawl well knew, for he had often kissed it in the time before he met Laurel Beltane.

"Is that your choice? Is it, lad? Your names have been linked. I've been keeping my ears open. I thought she might fit Lapis but. . . ."

Pawl decided he could delay no longer.

"Dama is a rare beauty and there is no denying that in other circumstances I could be happy with her, but she is not my choice. I have already decided. The lady has agreed, so there is an end to the matter. It is not Dama Longstock, much as I like her; it is Laurel Beltane."

This speech was greeted in silence. Toby's face was expressionless. Then he wrinkled his eyes. He leaned forward. "Did I hear you right, boy? Will you repeat?"

"I said I'd already made a choice of my own. I was on my way back here to tell you when you contacted me. It is cut and dried, so there's no need to go flashing any more vivantes at me."

Again silence. Pawl's father's face darkened and a pulse began to beat in his temple. When he began to speak his voice was soft.

"Dama Longstock was adopted by the Longstock Eighth and you know what that means. Higher blood. She is protected and looked after by one of the greater Families. I have reason to believe that her protector is from the First Family. Get that?" His voice became suddenly shrill. "The First! And you want to throw yourself away on the first status-seeking little bitch that takes your fancy. Well, I won't stand for it." He began to beat the sides of his chair, driving himself to fury. "Sort yourself out, boy. I am still Toby Paxwax. Master of the Fifth. You will marry Dama Longstock whether you like it or not. Do you understand? I have spoken. You may go."

Pawl sat still. He calmed himself, and when he spoke his voice had a cold edge.

"I will not go. And you will hear me out. You do not know Laurel Beltane. You have not studied her. She is not on your lists."

"Beltane." Toby turned the name over contemptuously in his mouth. "I have heard of that name. She is not of the Eleven."

"Correct. She is not of the Eleven."

"Then the Code forbids it."

"To hell with the Code."

"Brave words, cock spaniel. But the Eleven will forbid it."

"To hell with the Eleven."

Toby studied his son. He was not used to disobedience and was at a loss for a moment. "She does have rank, I presume, or are you planning to turn the entire family over to carrion?"

"Her family is the Fifty-Sixth."

"I'll kill you first."

"You'll have to."

"I'll. . . ." Toby moved quickly, but Pawl was ready. He had anticipated just such a move. He leaned forward and swept his hand over the controls to the chandelier. Toby, who had been reaching out to grapple with his son, was completely off balance when the chandelier lifted and spun him round. The movements were random. He banged against the wall and struck a corner of the weather machine with his head. The support system, linked to his nervous system, sensed that something was wrong and immediately cut to neutral support. Toby Paxwax hung in its wires and shook his head groggily. Pawl took his advantage. He crossed to his father, seized him by the shoulders and propelled him to the liquid chair. He pressed him down into it until the liquid plastic reached his waist. Then he kicked the power pack from the base of the chair. Immediately the plastic began to harden. By the time Toby regained consciousness, he found that he was set in the chair as firmly as a wick in a candle.

Pawl stood behind him. He took hold of his father's long braided hair and forced his head back. Toby strained and then relaxed. "One move. One false move and I'll cut all the strings on this contraption and then lug you out into the snow. Clear?"

His father muttered something and Pawl slowly released his hair. "Now I am going to talk to you and you are going to listen. I'm no longer the little boy you sent off to Terpsichore. I'm my own man now and I'm very much your son. That alone should give you warning."

He came round to the front of the chair and faced his father. "I'm also my mother's son and I will marry the Beltane."

His father's eyes glittered with anger.

"And don't go thinking up clever ideas about trying to kill her. She's on her Homeworld and that happens to be close to the domain of the Xerxes and there's nothing they would like more than to catch one of your assassination squads trying to slip through. I shall warn them if I have to."

The fight seemed to go out of his father. He slumped forward over his chair. "Not the Xerxes, son. Never the Xerxes. Those ladies are closed as fists. I know."

"Well, the Paxwax don't have much honour, come to that."

To Pawl's surprise Toby nodded. "I know. I know. We're all the same fish. But understand one thing. Everything I've done has been for the good of the family. I think Lapis began to understand that. You can't rule and be nice. Try to be nice and everyone thinks you're either weak or a liar. When I heard that Lapis had died I felt that the sea had washed over my grave. It's true. And I thought of you. An unknown son. I hated you because you'd lived, but I thought, *Ah well, perhaps he'll come true,* and I thought it out. I got it all arranged. You could build on my foundations. The family, Pawl. We've never done like the others, had litters of children, with bastards all over and honorary children. We are us. That's all. The family. . . ."

"There's nothing going to happen to the family. We'll pull through. We'll build. Now I want you to meet Laurel. She'll bring no shame on the Paxwax. Look."

Pawl removed the vivante cube of Dama Longstock. He felt in his satchel and produced the cube which he and Laurel Beltane had made on Lotus-and-Arcadia. "Now watch. She's no great beauty, but you'll like her."

Toby Paxwax watched with his craggy face cupped in his hands and his fingers knotted in his beard.

Laurel appeared. First her dark face with the piebald markings. Then the camera drew back revealing her motley arms and pointed breasts. Her webbed hands entered the picture and she fanned them so that there could be no mistake. Her hips were broad and her legs short. Her feet were long and webbed. About her waist was a purple and yellow scarf.

She grinned, winked and waved. "Well, Toby, you've seen the worst." She tapped her stomach. "But I'm all there where it counts. Pawl is running the camera and he's told me what to say but I'm going to improvise. I've never seen you, Toby, but Pawl has told me all about you and I think I know what you want. Grandchildren. Am I half-right? I can give you those. What is more, I am not an adventurer. I don't know what kind of a talk you and Pawl have had but knowing him it won't have been easy. You have a rough son, Toby. But know this: we Beltanes are proud, even if we are not part of the Eleven. I love Pawl. He loves me. I don't want to fly in the face of the Code but for a second son it shouldn't be so bad. Besides, the Beltanes are not without some wealth and I am an only daughter. What else can I tell you? Good health to you, Toby. Smile at me. Give us your blessing." She waved and the vivante faded.

Toby's face held no expression.

"I'm leaving this vivante with you," said Pawl. "Study it as long as you want. But get used to the idea that she is my wife."

Toby sat back. "Aquatic, is it?" he asked. "And you'd give up Dama for that?"

"Yes."

"Does it smell of sea-weed."

Pawl hit him before the words were fully out. "The last time," he said through his anger. "The last time you speak that way. You think, Toby. I marry her with your blessing or without. I don't care. The choice is yours. I'm leaving you now. I'll speak to you again in the morning."

"She's. . . ." Something stirred in Toby. "She looks fun."

"Right, she is. If you've any wit, Toby, you'll wish us well in the morning. Where's your fighting spirit? We'll spit in the eye of the other Families. You'll like that."

Pawl crossed to the door. "Are you going to leave me like this?" called Toby, throwing his arms wide.

"Yes," said Pawl. "It'll give you something to do. Take your anger out on the chair. Rip it to bits. I'll see you in the morning." And he left.

Toby watched him go and felt an emotion he could not name. His son had bearded him in his own den, and what father could ask for more?

Then he set about the chair. He tore the sides open with his bare hands. He seized a paperweight and began to beat at the plastic. It chipped and then cracked wide, revealing a smooth mould of Toby's lower body.

Once released Toby brought the chandelier out of its trance and lifted.

He hung for a long time staring into the tank which contained the Pandora Boxes. He fed them rats and watched the snails scurry. He drifted round the room and found a small, delicate hand bell. He rang it. Somewhere in the depths of the lonely house a dog growled and barked. After a few minutes there was a scrabbling at the door and Punic entered.

"We're going to have a party, just you and me. Bring me something of all the best wines and liqueurs. And don't drop them."

The dog barked and departed.

Toby settled himself at his weather machine.

*

Walking back to his rooms, Pawl thought about his father's madness. Power and madness: an unholy union, but one which was not uncommon among the Eleven Great Families.

Pawl saw the pattern. Solitude, fear, the ambition to master the Xerxes, the destruction of love, distrust: all had combined to unbalance his father's precarious sanity. The man still had something magnificent about him, but he was diseased. He was like a giant oak tree that has been struck by lightning and burned right down to the roots.

Pawl knew that he would have to be on his guard that night. Madness followed unpredictable paths. In his anger his father was imaginative.

As quick as he could run, Pawl crossed the courtyard – crisp now as the snow was frozen – and slammed the door leading to his rooms.

13

ON THALATTA

About a hundred yards from shore Laurel accelerated, driving her arms through the clear water and feeling it run deliciously down her sides. She pulled strongly through the surf, lifted on a wave's crest and let herself be carried up on to the shingle. She lay there while the water hissed round her and the retreating wave scoured hollows under her knees and arms.

Home. It was a wonderful feeling. The sound of the waves, the smell of the sea, the gulls tumbling and diving in the air and skimming inches above the waves . . . everything conspired to make her feel whole and herself.

She rolled over on her back and felt a wave buffet her, lifting her webbed arms and legs and transporting her several yards down the beach. She loved the sea . . . strong as a masterful lover, gentle and warm as a great mother that lifted and engulfed her. In the tickle and caress of the waves she felt clean. Memories of Lotus-and-Arcadia, which hung about her like a sticky second skin, dissolved at the sea's touch.

Laurel jumped to her feet and splashed through the shallows and up on to the dry land. There she threw herself down on a patch of blue moss. It received her yieldingly. Fine tendrils reached out from the moss and began exploring her warmth and wetness, devouring the particles of salt. She stared out over the sea.

A mile from shore hovered her house. In shape it was like the skeleton of a pale-green sea urchin. It looked as delicate as blown glass but was woven from the ubiquitous bio-crystalline fibre and could withstand storm and waves and the chill of near space. Its colour mirrored her moods.

Green told of worry.

She had arrived in the night at the Way Gate above Thalatta. Rather than take the shuttle down to the main island of Saprosma, she called her house up to her, and spent her first hours drifting gently through the thin air above her Homeworld. She settled in a part of her world where there were no people, and where the seas were warm and thousands of islands dotted the seascape. From there she put a call out to her father and brother, telling them she was home. She heard them respond.

Already the great galleon of her father was gliding from the north to join her. Closer was her brother Paris in his giant tumbling silver coil. Despite her need to see these two close members of her family, she hoped they would not arrive too soon. She still needed time to herself.

She had hoped that a message from Pawl would be waiting for her, but there was nothing. And she dared not call Bennet Homeworld. All she could do was wait and worry.

Idly she looked out over the sea and wondered if it was all worthwhile. Why give up the beauty of her Homeworld, her peace and privacy, to be locked into the machinations of the Eleven Great Families? But the thought was passed in an instant. She really had no choice in the matter. Women like Laurel, when they love, give up everything.

She knew Pawl well. Knew that he had come to depend on her. Knew that without her beside him he would become moody and strange. And what was this trouble with Lapis? Even now, as she lay in the sun, Pawl might be locked in argument with his father.

The trouble as she analysed it was that Pawl and his father were not quite opposites. Opposites when they clash can neutralize one another. But they were oblique forces and oblique forces always devour the space about them when they clash, like waves running up the sand.

On a simpler level, Laurel was missing Pawl. She felt that part of herself had departed. It was worse than she had expected. Pawl was rough in his love-making . . . rougher probably than Toro Sith, and Laurel liked that. The thought of Toro Sith made her flesh creep and she hoped that his face would never mend, even that he was dead.

A lattice of shadows passed over her. Paris's house curved round the bay and settled towards the sea. He was standing at its apex. He waved and when he saw that she had seen him he dived, turning gracefully head over heels in the air. He entered the blue water like a black arrow. He broke surface in the foam close to the shore and blew out lustily.

He slapped the waves as he pulled himself on to the shingle and raced towards her. He splashed her with spray and threw himself down half on top of her. She received a wet kiss in the nape of her neck and rolled over trying to throw him off.

"Welcome home."

She did not respond and Paris released her. His dark face showed surprise and then concern. "You are sad? Not well?" He looked into her eyes, trying to read there signs of what had made his sister withdrawn.

"I am well. And I am very happy to see you." She slipped her arms round his neck and squeezed him close to her. "But I am sad too and cannot tell you why. Father will be here soon and I will talk to him."

"Ah. You have fallen in love." His young face looked so serious that Laurel Beltane burst out laughing.

"Love. Ha. What do you know about love?"

"I know that it makes people happy or sad and there are no middle paths."

"Well you have learned something. Come and swim with me. I brought you presents from Lotus-and-Arcadia. I will be happy again when I have spoken to father."

Side by side they swam out to the two floating houses.

Perhaps there will be a message waiting for me from Pawl, thought Laurel, and she began to swim more quickly.

14

ON BENNET

The barricades were up. Across the door which led to his room Pawl established a particle screen. Anything trying to pass through would be randomized. From his trunk he took a small dark block which resembled a vivante cube. He warmed it for a few moments in the palms of his hands and when the yeasts that powered it were active, he placed it close to the small domestic vivante. It would jam all incoming signals and stop his father spying on him.

Pawl studied the window. It was twenty feet from the ground and stoutly framed. There was no danger unless Toby, dangling from his chandelier, should try to break in, and that was most unlikely. But to be safe, Pawl left the curtain down.

Outside the twin moons, each half-full, sailed like majestic boats above the Mendel Hills.

Pawl made himself comfortable on the floor, facing the fire with his back to the trunk. He had his notebook and pencil and tried to concentrate. Something was burning up inside him, a memory.

> Once upon another time, on the cliffs,
> On a blustery day, I saw a tree burn.
> Being a boy, I looked for a bucket.
> Being a man, should I have prayed for rain.

He set down his pencil and rested his head back with his eyes closed. There was no relief. The words would not come and the problems remained.

*

He was startled awake by a sound which anyone who had undergone alien combat training on Terpsichore learned to fear – the
soft, fluting call of the Sennet bat. The trill of its warning notes
faded and Pawl heard the snicker, like the wind rustling dry seed
pods, as the creature unfolded its wings.

Pawl felt sweat start on his brow as he turned slowly and faced
the bat, hanging a mere six feet away above his bed. In response to
his fear the mantra for calm and courage in a time of peril began
whispering through his mind. It released his paralysis and allowed
him to think. Reason pinned fear.

Reason. The Sennet bat is a tropical creature and can only
survive in the moist warm jungles of Pandora. In a chill such as this
the bat would doze and then die.

Reason. Why had Pawl not smelled the creature's foul skin and
dribbling poison sacs the moment he entered? He could not smell
them even now.

Reason. The bat could not have entered through the particle
screen and thus . . . the bat did not exist. Somehow his father
had. . . .

The bat released one claw from the beam above it and flexed its
talons: a warning sign, as Pawl well knew. It trilled again and Pawl
saw the pulse in its lower belly begin to throb as it built up pressure
to squirt its venom. The poison orifices located in each bony
junction of its grey wings opened and then narrowed like a cat's
eye. The dark furry holes which were its ears pointed straight at
Pawl's face.

Reason.

Moving slowly Pawl stood up and inched forwards until his face
was a mere six inches from the bat. "You are a fake," he said
slowly and distinctly.

If a Sennet bat can look surprised then this bat was surprised.
The ridges of skin below its bright eyes flicked up and then down.
It lowered its grey wings until they shrouded Pawl. He stood his
ground. He remained firm even when the bat, with one flap of its
wings, loosed its poison. Nothing happened.

Pawl laughed and then, strangely, the bat laughed. It transformed
into a simulacrum of his father.

"I am not afraid of ghosts, Toby."

"You should be."

"What do you want?"

"Come and talk to me."

"No. We can talk in the morning. I want you to think about things. I'm glad you got out of the chair easily."

The simulacrum shrugged. "Why didn't you shoot at the bat? I thought that was what you were taught on Terpsichore."

"My gun was not near me."

"Lapis would not have been so careless."

"I am not Lapis."

"True."

The image shrank to a point of light and then vanished.

Pawl found his particle gun and climbed up on to his bed. He knew what he was looking for. Implanted in the ceiling and roughly covered with tape Pawl found two silver wires. He tore them loose and traced them to the wall. There he cut them and fused the ends. Then he searched the room and found two other implantations. He treated them in the same way. He felt a fool that he had not foreseen this trick. Probably the whole house was wired so that Toby could ghost about at will. *Well, no more visitations tonight*, thought Pawl, and settled again by his trunk. His pistol rested beside him.

Slumped across the weather machine, Toby scowled at his reflection in its smooth surface. "I fought without spirit," he said. "What is wrong with me? Catch my father behaving like that, eh? He would have skinned me alive."

Close to him Punic growled low and rested his long head on his paws.

"Let's see your teeth." Punic bared his gums, which were crusted with broken glass and splinters. "Set you on him, eh, and he'd see reason?" Punic snarled and snapped his jaws shut.

"Well Toby, you've seen the worst. But I'm all there where it counts. . . ." Laurel Beltane began her speech for the fifth time. Toby picked up a bottle and threw it at her. It passed through her image and smashed against the wall containing the Pandora Boxes.

"He'll not have you," he shouted. Punic trotted across the room, picked up another bottle of Carpetal Wine and brought it to Toby. "I'll see him bedded with the slugs of Opiate first. I'll infect you with the Ivory disease like that poor Wong girl. I'll . . . I'll. . . ." His anger became incoherent and guttural as he poured another drink. It poured thickly, without bubbles. Then he laughed to himself with his fingers matted in his beard, thinking, *The bat made him jump. I'll give him a show.* Toby checked the registration panel on his weather machine and saw that the power was building up. His fingers danced across the patterned keys. *I'll give him a night to remember.*

Toby hit one of the switches with his fist and immediately lightning crackled and seemed to stalk over the Mendel Hills. Toby tuned the static. Again his fingers danced. "Now me. Prince of Fire." He struck the machine again and outside the sky grew red.

Pawl saw the redness and stood up and looked out of his window. At first he thought that Frautus had come to life but then he saw the patterns in the sky.

Pawl watched as hazy lines of blue and red fire began to form shapes in the air. The pattern built slowly until finally it was recognizable. Pawl stared at the fiery face of his father. Colours and tones crept into the picture until it was a passable likeness. Suddenly the figure grew taller as though it had just stood up after kneeling. Pawl's father stood on the horizon. He looked as he never looked in life. He had legs like giant trees and these were heavily rooted.

The image of Toby raised its arms in a gigantic salute and lightning dribbled and fell from its fingers.

Another giant figure began to build up beside him. It was hazy and indistinct like a figure made of smoke. It came to sudden focus. Laurel Beltane.

Gradually more and more details were filled in. Flesh tones hardened and individual markings appeared. The eyes sparkled with fire.

The image of his father placed its hands round the neck of Laurel Beltane, and squeezed. Her mouth opened and the head popped up and detached and rose slowly into the air.

Spinning it fell to the earth, bounced once and then began rolling towards him. As it rolled it grew larger. It rolled through the outbuildings and over the deserted stables. It came to rest exactly outside Pawl's window. One giant eye stared miserably through at him.

Pawl stared back with cold yellow eyes. "Mad, Toby. You're completely mad," he whispered and on the far horizon the figure of his father danced.

Carefully Toby monitored the flow of charged particles which held the shape of the head intact and steered it to Pawl's window. When

it was in place he placed the machine on hold and groped round
for his glass.

He knocked it from its place and the contents spilled across the
floor. "More," he said and the mechanical dog obediently trotted
over with another bottle.

Toby surveyed his handiwork with tight concentration. He drank
quickly, absentmindedly, and hunched over the machine again.

On Terpsichore Pawl's training had been thorough. While learning
the mantras he had also learned to face fear. He stared at the eye
of Laurel Beltane until he had reduced it to lines and shading. He
saw it for what it was, a pattern of charged particles, robbed of any
emotional tones. The only disturbing element was the mind of its
creator.

It was going to be a long night. Pawl sought in his trunk for a
flask of his favourite Seppel juice. He sat with the bottle in his
hand and stared at the giant eye. For some reason he found himself
thinking about his family.

His mother, passionate and tragic, but who had somehow managed to communicate her sense of love. Fingle, five years younger
than Pawl, who had died in a fit three months after he was born.
"He was never meant to live," said his mother as she cried over
the little body. Fingle had never become real to Pawl.

Ramadal, Pawl's twin and elder by an hour; of all the brothers
he was the gentlest and the most deformed. He was piebald and
covered with short thick hair like a horse. His mouth and nose
were joined like a fish and there was some irregularity in his
stomach so that he could only take liquid food. Toby Paxwax had
hated him from the moment of his birth. Pawl could remember his
father shouting, "He should have died in the womb, and so should
that other weakling" (meaning Pawl). And then Ramadal did die.
He just curled up. It was Pawl who had found him, stiff and
clutching a towel, and with his eyes open. He was buried by the
coast and his father had not even bothered to attend the funeral.

Five years older than Pawl was Pental, the silent one. He had
always been apart, a brooding presence, always observing, never
commenting. Then had come the summons that Pental was to join
the Inner Circle. The black flyer with its red markings had arrived.
It stood on the lawn with its dark door open and Pental had
entered without a backward glance or a wave of farewell. When
Pental left, something in Toby died. They had never seemed to be

close and yet a bond was there. For days Toby hovered above the grass, turning a stone over and over in his fingers until it was worn smooth. Then he made drawings of Pental using a thick brush and black paint. Finally he ordered that all Pental's belongings be carried into the courtyard and there he burned them.

Last of all was Lapis and now he too was dead.

And that leaves me, thought Pawl, finishing the bottle. *Me and a madman and a mechanical dog. If I survive this night, I'll put this place to rights.*

Pawl's reverie was interrupted by a movement at the window. The eye had gradually become fuzzy. Now it came back to sharp focus and stared straight through him. Slowly it closed and then dissolved into a random cloud of sparks.

Round two beginning, thought Pawl, and crossed to the window.

In the courtyard a figure appeared. It was his father, complete with a ghostly chandelier. A brilliant light shone downwards from it, bathing him in a cold, harsh glare.

"Look at me," called the figure. It was the voice of his father and it had a sob in it. "Look at me. I'm all you have for family. For pity's sake, look at me."

This was new. This was different. Pawl had come to expect horrors. He had not expected to be pleaded with.

"Come to me. You're all I have. Call me. Let me talk to you. I can't help what I am, but I'll change. I promise. Everything I've ever done was for the family. I'm drunk and sad and alone. No tricks. Please. Let me come to you."

Pawl considered. He remembered the white face of his mother. He remembered the rolling head of Laurel Beltane. He remembered the bodies he had seen that afternoon. In the balance it was too much and he hung the curtain back in front of the window.

After calling for several more minutes, the figure of his father slowly faded.

Toby Paxwax was slumped over the weather machine. He was crying. His chest and back ached as they had ached so many times and he felt a stranger inside his own body.

Punic was licking his feet in an attempt to comfort him.

"He won't hear me. Won't see me. I didn't mean all those hard things . . . it was just me . . . chafing. I. . . ."

The dog brought another bottle and Toby slapped it from its rubber lips. "I've got to talk to someone."

Toby lifted above the weather machine and floated to the vivante console. He tapped the code for Veritas.

Veritas was the administrative planet of the Paxwax Fifth. It was part of the same solar system as Bennet Homeworld and on fine nights could be seen clearly as a bright point of silver light.

On Veritas it was late afternoon and Songteller, as ever, was on duty.

Like Punic, Songteller had been with the Paxwax family for generations. Unlike Punic he was not mechanical but mainly flesh and blood. He was an adapted man. Part of his brain had been preempted and modified to enable him to cope with the vast legal and economic lore that attended the running of the Paxwax Empire. He was a sifter, a finder of loopholes, a watchdog. Between the computers which handled the day-to-day business, and Toby who made the long-range decisions, stood Songteller.

He was not a tall man and had long thin hands which he rubbed together restlessly as though washing. Like Pawl Paxwax, he looked slightly humped, and his deformity was always covered by a shiny defensive shield. In the hump was his expanded brain. It was supported in a cradle of flesh and bone which grew out from his shoulders. The weight of the brain, especially when he was tired, pulled the skin of his face, making him look mongoloid.

One consequence of the adaptation which he had undergone when he was a boy was that he was emotionally stunted. He hardly knew what laughter was, smiled rarely, and conducted all the affairs of the Paxwax with a cold and bloodless logic.

Songteller turned and looked at Toby, showing neither surprise nor pleasure.

"You should be resting, Master Toby. I have told you before. It is now the middle of the night on Bennet Homeworld."

"I know. I know," growled Toby. "Can't sleep. Need to talk. Private."

"There is no one here with me. We are on shielded circuit. Talk away. How can I help?" Beyond Toby's vision Songteller placed his vivante on record. There might be information coming that was valuable to Dame Clarissa. Long ago, in the years shortly after Toby became Master, Songteller had succumbed to the temptation of being a traitor.

*

Toby hesitated. Now that he had companionship he didn't know
quite what to say. "Everything all right with the Paxwax?"

"Everything is fine. The concessions we have made to the
Longstock Eighth Family have been received with surprise and
pleasure. I think they expected harder bargaining. I could have
squeezed more, but your instructions were. . . ."

"Yes, yes. Go on. Anything else?"

"The Sith are still arguing about the skin allotment and trying to
get us to lower our tariffs."

"Ha. Screw them."

"I am. I have received information from The Shell-Bogdanovich
Conspiracy that they want to re-open negotiation for Way Rights
through Elliott's Pocket."

"Are they after the Wong again?"

"No. My interpretation is that they want to get closer to the
Xerxes' Industrial ring. The Conspiracy always tries to steal its
intelligence."

Toby nodded absently. "Grant them. Special rates. We shall
soon need all the friends we can get."

Songteller nodded. "Is there anything else, Master Toby? It is
my opinion that you have more on your mind than the affairs of
the domain."

Toby lifted his craggy face and stared at the administrator.
"Have there been any rumours?" he asked.

"Rumours? About what?"

"Anything about Auster?"

Songteller's eyes narrowed slightly. "Well now, there was something . . . let me see, Auster. Yes, a report came of a minor
accident, some Spiderets in a mine, none survived. Nothing of any
consequence. Production won't be held up."

"Lapis was on Auster."

"Was he? I thought. . . ." Songteller stopped in mid-sentence.
"Is Lapis in any way connected with the accident?" he asked
slowly.

"Lapis is dead."

There, it was out. Toby stared angrily at Songteller as though
challenging him, daring him to offer words of sympathy. No such
words came. The only change was that Songteller's pale face grew
even paler and he leaned forward.

"Dead? When did you hear? Why wasn't I. . . ."

"I was keeping it secret until I got Pawl back to Homeworld."

"Is he there now?"

"Yes."

"Then he is now the next in line?"

"Yes. Damn him."

"I don't follow. If Pawl is. . . ."

So the conversation continued. To Toby there was relief in the clear, cool questions of Songteller. To Songteller there was a growing excitement such as he had never experienced before in his life. Bit by bit, tacking back and forth in his questions, he built a mosaic.

Toby talked too freely. Perhaps he was drunk and tired. Perhaps he misinterpreted Songteller's keen questions for concern about the welfare of the Paxwax. He talked about Pawl and about Laurel Beltane and even showed Songteller the vivante of Laurel. Finally Songteller drew back. He knew every letter of the Code. "We must seek," he said, "to make Pawl see reason. He has always seemed to me to be persuadable."

"Not now. He's as pig-headed as his mother."

"Well, I suggest we talk more in the morning. You need to rest now. I am glad you have revealed the situation to me. I can make plans now in case the news breaks before we are ready. Leave matters in my hands."

Toby nodded and moved to break the communication. "Oh, one last thing," asked Songteller. "What was Lapis doing on Auster of all places?"

"Skylarking."

The communication ended.

The talk with Songteller and the grief he felt for Lapis both worked on Toby. He rocked round his room with his head in his hands. He thought about Pawl, hard and arrogant. So different. He wanted the boy near him. He tried the vivante and found it jammed.

Bracing himself in front of his window he drew the curtain back and let the moonlight and snowshine enter his room. He could just see Pawl's room across the pale courtyard. The curtain was still in place.

"One last try," he murmured.

Pawl was awakened by shadows. Someone was on his windowledge, waving. His drowsiness vanished as he found his pistol and crawled over against the wall. He pulled the fabric down from below.

Standing in the very window were his mother and his dead brother Ramadal, like a foal.

"Pawl. Pawl. Go to your father. He needs you. He's not well. Pawl, I know you can hear me. Don't be like him. Have mercy. He will let you have Laurel Beltane. If you ever loved me, go to him."

Pawl stared speechless into the white face of his mother.

"Go to him," came the thin whining voice of Ramadal and he raised his stumpy arms to his eyes and cried.

Two tragic faces stared at Pawl through the window.

Slowly they faded when Pawl made no reply. He stood panting and shocked. The attack was more insidious and subtle than he expected. He did not know what to think.

Commotion in the courtyard. Figures came to light. The whole family was there; they were playing in the snow. Toby was in the middle of the three elder brothers, swaying under his chandelier, and laughing as the kids pelted him with snowballs. Pawl's mother stood to one side, resplendent in rich furs. In her arms was Fingle, and little Ramadal stood at her side. She was laughing in a way that Pawl had never seen her laugh in life. Pawl saw himself as a boy of five scoop up a snowball and hurl it at Lapis.

But the snowball never arrived. It stopped in the air a few feet after leaving his hand. All the figures stopped moving at the same time. They froze in whatever attitude they were standing. And then, after several minutes, they began to fade.

Slowly they lost substance. They became translucent. Pawl could see arms through bodies and the untrodden virgin snow through backs. They faded away.

An awful silence filled the courtyard and then began a steady drip, drip, drip from the roofs. The snow was beginning to melt.

Beyond the Mendel Hills, the salmon pink of dawn began to stain the sky.

Pawl stood at his window, indecisive. He didn't know what to do or what to think. But he needed to do something. He picked up his particle pistol and strapped it to his thigh. Within minutes he was downstairs and out into the courtyard. The air had lost its chill edge. It smelled fresh and there was a hint of warmth.

The snow was melting quickly and a morning breeze stirred the tops of the trees, sending down a spatter of slush.

Opposite Pawl, in the building occupied by his father, the small portal door banged open and Punic tumbled out into the snow. He seemed not to see Pawl but ran to the centre of the courtyard and there stopped and lifted his head and howled. Then he loped away, head low, in the direction of the stables.

The howl broke Pawl's trance. *It's a trap. It's a trap. I know it's a trap, but so be it. I've got to know what has happened.*

Memories of combat training were in his mind as he ran across the courtyard and flattened himself against the wall near the door. Here he could not be seen from his father's window. Perhaps he was being foolish, perhaps there was no threat, but somehow the defensive attitude made action easier. He could not have walked calmly to his father's room.

Holding his gun at the ready, Pawl dived through the doorway, rolled and waited. Nothing. No Sennet bats or other monstrosities. Nothing. Silence.

He ran through the silent house.

The door to his father's room was open. "Toby. I'm coming. I hope you are not planning anything. I'm armed."

No reply. Nothing moved. He ran silently down the corridor and paused at the door. The smell of spilt liquor reached him.

His particle pistol at the ready, he stepped into the room. It was in ruins. The carpet was pulled across the floor. Broken glass was everywhere amid the scattered ruins of Toby's chair. A bottle had smashed against the wall holding the Pandora snails, and a crack had opened in its smooth surface. Two snails were working at the crack and already a creamy substance was seeping through. Pawl cauterized this carefully and the snails withdrew. That would need attention urgently.

Pawl moved fully into the room. "Toby, where are you? I've come to talk."

A trace of blue lines in the air above the weather machine showed that it was still active but in the holding mode. The machine had not been cleared. Toby's last co-ordinates were still in the circuits. The machine had simply switched itself to base plan. Whatever had happened to his father had happened quickly, before he could complete his programme.

Pawl's eyes were drawn to the alcove where his father slept. He noticed that a light was shining behind the heavy curtains and that the curtains were straining downwards, trapped by a weight.

He moved over to the curtains and reached forward and gripped them. He tried to lift. Something was holding them. They were caught at the bottom. They were trapped under a bulge.

Pawl heaved upwards and the curtains came free with a jerk. Toby's shoulder and arm flopped into view and his hand rested open-palmed on Pawl's boot.

Quickly Pawl opened the curtains wide and revealed Toby's body, half-collapsed off the bed. It was still partially supported by the straining cords of his support system. Toby's Viking face, purple and ghastly and wide-eyed, stared up at Pawl.

The impossible accident.

Of all eventualities connected with the life-support system, this was the one that was "guaranteed" not to happen.

Round Toby's neck and still pulling was one of the fine support cables. Another cord was tangled with the bed and looped round Toby's stunted legs. Between the two tensions, and no doubt flailing about, Toby had been strangled.

Pawl reached up and hit the breaker switch on the underside of the chandelier. Immediately the machine settled and the body slumped and fell on to the floor. Pawl sliced through the bio-crystalline cables and heaved the machine to one side. It was surprisingly heavy.

Then he gripped his father under the arms, lifted him bodily on to the bed and let him flop. He straightened the arms, arranged the silly legs and finished by pulling the covers up under his father's beard and smoothing his long hair on the pillow. That done, he sat by him at a loss. There were other things he should do, he knew, but he could not think of them. He sat and looked at the hardening face.

Unkempt and fierce, mottled with broken veins, the face still retained some vitality. He had not died easily, and there was dignity in that.

Behind Pawl there was a sudden movement. Punic was standing in the doorway. Pawl eased his pistol from its holster and watched without making any sudden move.

The great dog advanced slowly, its head bobbing, until it was close to Pawl. It stared into Pawl's eyes and then its tail began to wag jerkily, brushing the broken glass and fragments of chair. It went through all the motions of sniffing him, after which it unfurled

six inches of leathery tongue and began a thorough licking of his
hand. Its touch was like sandpaper.

At that moment it finally dawned on Pawl that he was now
Master of Paxwax, lord of the Fifth most powerful Family in the
Galaxy, answerable only to the Code and his own conscience.

An alarm bell jangled and the vivante came alive, clamouring for
attention. Punic jumped and barked. Pawl cuffed the dog and
ordered it outside. It left obediently, crushing broken glass under
its feet.

Who could be calling at this hour? Surely not Laurel.

Pawl checked the co-ordinates. Veritas. Songteller. Now what
the hell was Songteller doing calling at this hour? Pawl had hoped
for just a few hours of peace and quiet to settle his mind. Pawl
thought of shunting the call on to record, but didn't. Now or later,
the demands of the Paxwax Empire would not wait. *The long night
is over*, he thought, dramatically. *And now the long day begins.*

He punched open the transmission.

The hunched, small body of Songteller built before him. He
looked eager and nervous.

"Hello, Pawl. I need to speak to your father. Where is he?"

The suddenness of this question surprised Pawl. "I thought you
would have been surprised to see me. It is many years since we
have spoken. Did you know I was on Homeworld?"

"Your father asked me to call him."

"You haven't answered my question."

Songteller hesitated just that fraction of a second too long. "So
you did know. My father kept it a secret. How did you know?
Come on speak."

"Your father contacted me last night."

"I see."

"Can I speak with your father? The matter is urgent."

"Yes. That I can believe. And what did my father tell you? Did
he speak about Lapis?"

"He did."

"Then you know to whom you are now speaking?"

"Yes. Pawl, let me speak to your – "

"Songteller, why are you so unwilling to speak to me? Did my
father mention other matters?"

"We talked about many things."

"Such as?"

"Your prospects." Pawl was amazed to see Songteller squirm. He was retreating before Pawl's questions. He was holding back.

"Songteller, I advise you to speak clearly and openly. Just now I found my father dead. I am now Master of Paxwax. You must speak to me as directly as you did to my father."

Songteller gaped. For a creature who depended on logic, that information was too much. It overloaded his mental circuits.

"Dead? Then you are Master of Paxwax," said Songteller, stupidly.

"Correct."

"Forgive me. I am not as young as I was. It takes time to. . . ."

"I know. I have not grown accustomed to the idea yet. Apart from myself you are the only person who knows. Anyway, here are your orders. Suspend any negotiations which are going on at present. Say Toby is thinking. Do not initiate any new contracts. Buy me time. Apart from that, let business be as normal with the Paxwax. No disturbances. But keep your eyes and ears open. We live in dangerous times and the Paxwax must move with care." Songteller nodded. His eyes were completely enigmatic. "I want a freeze on everything, but I don't want people to know there is a freeze. Is that quite clear?"

"Yes, Master Pawl."

"Good."

Songteller was becoming his cool, business-like self. "I hope I can serve you, Master Pawl, as well as I have served your father."

"So do I."

"Do you know the demands of the Code?"

"Tell me."

"You must inform Proctor Central immediately. The circumstances of two deaths are most unusual. They will want to send out a Death Inspector. The protocol is very clear."

"I see. And then?"

"Then?"

"When the news breaks out, lives will become very interesting."

"Yes. Interesting," echoed Songteller. "I cannot read the future."

"Nor can I," said Pawl. "End contact."

He tapped the keys of the vivante and Songteller's face vanished.

The discussion with Songteller had not been satisfactory, but Pawl could not tell why. He supposed that he'd expected more. More

what? Friendship? Support? Encouragement? All of these. And
yet he knew it was not in Songteller's nature to be other than cool
and rational. Still there was something . . . an evasiveness, a
shiftiness. And that was not in Songteller's nature either. Perhaps,
thought Pawl, Songteller was so used to being loyal to one man
that he found it difficult to shift allegiance quickly. After all, Pawl
was the newcomer. A playboy son fresh from the boisterous nights
and sleepy days of Lotus-and-Arcadia. That was how Songteller
would regard him. And when all was said and done, Songteller
knew more about the workings of the Paxwax at this moment than
any other man alive. He could even resent Pawl's sudden elevation
. . . that is, if resentment were part of his nature.

There was no end to such speculation.

Meanwhile there were things to be done. With a sudden chill
Pawl realized that he was probably the only man alive on the
planet. The survival of his entire family depended on him alone.
Somehow he had never expected Toby to die. Death was abstract.
Now it was actual . . . as real as the grim-faced man that lay
unmoving on the bed.

The Code demanded that he contact the Proctors on Central
immediately. Death and succession were central to the Code.

Well, to hell with the Code, thought Pawl. *I need some private
time. I need to sort things out.*

He looked round the smelly derelict room.

"Your poor, poor, poor man," he said to the stiff body of his
father. "What have you been doing all these years?"

He began to leave the room and then paused. Methodically he
turned off all the controls on the weather machine and then he tore
it from its power supply.

"No more ghosts."

But Songteller, sitting in his rooms on Veritas, didn't move for
some time. He sat staring blankly at the space where the image of
Pawl had stood and rubbed his hands methodically.

The game was ending. He knew that. And in his subdued way
he felt regret. For Songteller, betraying the Paxwax had been a
purely intellectual matter. He was not tempted by money or
position or power. The Xerxes sisters could offer him nothing that
the Paxwax had not already given. To him, the pleasures of

betrayal had been those of finesse; of working plan upon counter-plan; of watching greed and ambition inter-react. He neither liked the Xerxes nor disliked Toby.

He surveyed the two Families. Given his present knowledge he was in no doubt about the outcome. He had watched over and assisted the Xerxes and although he did not know their plans in detail, he could make accurate guesses. The Xerxes would pounce on Pawl. They would be fools if they didn't and Pawl, isolated, immature in the ways of the Families, would be crushed.

It was time to move. He would join the Xerxes. The escape route had been planned long ago.

15

ON SANCTUM

It may be true that space is infinitely vast. But it is balanced by thought, which is infinitely fast.

So, even as Toby banged back and forth in his room, choking and tearing at the bio-crystalline threads, something of his spirit spread out wide beyond the confines of his planet.

To a creature as highly tuned to human emotion as the Tree of Sanctum, and concentrating moreover on Pawl Paxwax, the death of Toby was palpable as a slap.

In the great hall on Sanctum there was a sudden hush. Pental, still locked in his trance, stumbled and came to himself and withdrew.

At the very moment Toby died, crashing into his alcove, every creature on Sanctum was aware.

A great cry went up, for whether it is a fly caught in a web, or a sparrow caught in a storm, or a Giant Hammer threshing, or a man lying in peace surrounded by his friends, the experience is the same. Death is as universal as love.

The creatures sighed with the passing. Little Odin, crouching by the Tree, knew that this, more or less, was what he had foreseen.

So now where were they?

The Diphilus once again was the first to fill the chamber with the tumbling waterfall of its thought.

IT APPEARS WE HAVE A NEW EQUATION. I BELIEVE WE HAVE ONLY TWO CHOICES. EITHER WE SUPPORT AND TRY TO SAVE PAWL PAXWAX OR WE DON'T. THERE IS NO MIDDLE GROUND.

The Diphilus's message was uncharacteristically brief.

Silence. And then the ghostly mysterious music of the Lyre Beast filled the entire chamber. It was like the piping of an organ, like the wind blowing over reeds on a marsh. The Lyre Beast rarely spoke. Even the Tree, which modulated and translated all the thought in the chamber, found it difficult to explain the Lyre Beast. But this time its message was simple.

I WOULD LIKE TO HEAR THE OPINION OF THE TREE.

All eyes turned on the silver Tree. It began to pulse and pale lights, like the reflection of fire, raced up and down its trunk.

PAWL PAXWAX IS A LOVER (*it began*). WE MUST WIN HIM TO OUR CAUSE. HIS LOVE IS HIS STRENGTH AND HIS WEAKNESS. WE MUST NOT LOSE HIM. LATER WE WILL DISCOVER HOW TO USE HIM. BUT FIRST WE MUST SAVE HIM. YOU MUST SAVE HIM.

WHY WILL HE HELP US? HOW WILL HE HELP US? The questions came from many creatures.

HIS LOVE IS HIS GREATEST STRENGTH AND HIS GREATEST WEAKNESS. WE WILL USE THAT. WE WILL BEND HIM TO OUR NEEDS. BUT FIRST HE MUST TRUST US.

The creatures did not understand, but the Tree spoke with confidence and for the time being that was enough.

Only Odin, close under the Tree, felt his fibres stir when the Tree talked of the future. *What is my part?* he wondered, unaware that the thought would escape from him.

He was amazed when he felt the aura of the Tree expand and contain him.

"You have a special part to play, little one."

The Tree was talking to him, to *him* alone. It sounded like a friend from the same hatching.

"When the time comes, you will offer your kindness and gentleness to the Paxwax. He needs one as wise and sensitive as you. You will see him through his troubles and finally. . . ."

"Yes?"

"Finally you will destroy him."

Odin shrank from the contact, for in the word *destroy* he could feel his own dying. But the Tree held him firm. Monstrously, it thrust its will upon him, overwhelming him.

With a fragment of his untouched mind Odin screamed against the imposition. He saw with stark clarity that he was singled out for martyrdom. And he screamed and he screamed and he screamed: and the screaming lapped away to silence.

That last fragment of Odin's natural mind died slowly, like a drowning man who struggles on the surface of the sea and then is swamped by a wave and gradually sinks.

And when it was gone, Odin was whole and hopeful and ready.

Martyrdom seemed like honour.

The Tree released him gently. Its last lingering thought which stayed with Odin was: "We none of us choose the parts we play. Not even me. . . ."

In the chamber many creatures were contending for the right to speak.

A Spideret shinnied high and broadcast. WELL, SINCE THE PAXWAX MUST BE SAVED, I HAVE A SUGGESTION. MY BROTHER IS WITH LAPIS NOW, ON THE HOMEWORLD OF THE XERXES. HE CAN KILL LAPIS WITH CEREMONY; THAT WILL LESSEN THEIR HOLD ON THE PAXWAX.

At the back of the assembly, a tall grey-haired woman who had thrown back her black robe called, "I am Lorca. I am known to the Xerxes. I will travel there again at the bidding of the Inner Circle. I will find a way of speaking with the Spideret."

AND I, Odin heard his own thought crackle like a sheet in the wind, WILL TRAVEL TO THE HOMEWORLD OF PAWL PAXWAX AND ATTEND TO HIS WELL-BEING.

16

ON BENNET

Pawl walked from the house to the sea. He trod a narrow path; behind him trotted Punic. Finally, at the end of the path, he stared down the sheer rock face a thousand feet to where the red algae sea churned slowly and heavy waves beat the shore. It was still early in the morning and the Maw were just easing themselves into the water. A brisk wind blew from the sea and teased out his hair, which he had uncoiled.

Pawl wanted to make a quittance, and the redness of the dawn sea matched his mood.

On your way, Toby. You silly, great, silly man.
I can't hate you now you're dead.
I don't know if there is a life after death,
but I can't think that all that was in you,
your spirit, your anger, your pettiness and pride,
are gone like a stone in a river.
You are here in the air I breathe,
your marks are on this sad island,
you are in my hand and beneath my feet.

On your way, Toby. You were my father and we parted at odds.
That is no way for a life to end. Death
never comes at the right time does it?
I'd like to have spoken to your face, just once more,
But life's not like that, is it? After the farce
the tragedy. That's the way of things.
No matter. No regrets, eh? But you could have been a better
                                                                     man.

On your way, Toby. You great, silly, great man.
You are what you made yourself and I don't cry for you,
though I do cry. Unmanly by your book.
You could have made us happy but you didn't.

You could have made my mother smile,
you could have given your sons some feeling of purpose,
but you didn't. Why do you think we all escaped?
We escaped *you*.
Now Pental is gone and Lapis is dead and I'm . . . well I'm here.
What were you afraid of all those years? Laughter?
And what price do you place on gentleness, Toby?
Or kindness? What price do you place on love, Toby?
What price?

The best and the worst I can say of you is that I never
knew you, father.
I am now as though you had never been born.
On your way, Toby.

The words disappeared into the air without an echo. The gesture
was ended. Pawl did not see it, but as he limped back towards the
deserted towers and passages of Bennet, the spirit of his sad father
howled in the psychosphere.

Pawl waited as the vivante space in front of him darkened and
became spangled with beads of light. Clarity came suddenly and
Pawl found himself staring down at a naked man with a lion's
mane of red hair. He was lying on a bed and a large slug with
sucker feet was working its way slowly up his back, massaging the
tight skin. The man glanced up dreamily when the vivante came
alive and Pawl saw the distinctive fangs of the Proctor First Family.
They were lower teeth which curved outwards and then up, like
ram's horns.

"Sorry," said the man lazily, "just getting ready for bed. Had a
hell of an evening. Party, you know. Need to get myself uncreased.
Is this really a priority call? Can it wait a few hours?"

"I'm afraid not. Do you handle death reference?"

The man came awake. "Among other things." He sat up,
dislodging the slug, which fell heavily on to the floor. "Who's
calling?" He looked more closely. "Hey, you're Pawl Paxwax,
aren't you? Didn't we meet on Lotus-and-Arcadia once? I'm
Lobesang Proctor, seventh son of the eighteenth father."

Pawl nodded. "We may have." There were so many Proctor
sons, Pawl couldn't keep track of them. "I wish to announce a
death in my Family."

The man registered Pawl's lack of warmth and became brisk and business-like. "I see." He stepped off the bed and crossed to the vivante machine and sat down. "Have you contacted anyone else?"

"No," lied Pawl. "I am following the Code."

"Good. Now I am switching to record. Please give me the details slowly and carefully."

"First, I wish to report that my brother Lapis Paxwax is dead."

"Circumstances?"

"I don't know. I only have my father's word."

"And where is your father? Why isn't he making this report?"

"He can't," said Pawl. "He's dead also."

It was comical. Lobesang Proctor stared. Then he opened his mouth and his coiled fangs wagged but no words came. He quickly checked something to the side of his vivante and then he found his voice again.

"Would you repeat?"

"My father is dead. I can show you. I found him just a few minutes ago."

"And that means that you are . . . er, subject to confirmation, of course, er, Master of Paxwax."

"I am."

The Proctor looked at him differently. "Look, er, sorry, this is way out of my . . . I usually only deal with kids and squabbles. I'm handing you on to someone higher up, all right?"

The screen blanked out whether it was all right or not.

Pawl was handed on three times until he found himself facing Lar Proctor, the Fourth Senior Proctor of the Proctor First. Pawl knew him only from pictures.

He was an old man and his teeth stood out in spirals. He was dressed in a green bathrobe, and when Pawl first saw him he was spitting into a silver basin after gargling. He removed his teeth with a twist and worked his jaw and smiled at Pawl.

"More comfortable this way. Damned things get in the way when you want to talk. Well, Pawl. Sad news, eh? Well, perhaps not. Hard to say in these matters. But I've received the report and I'm not going to delve into details. We believe you're telling the truth and the Death Inspector can find out the rest. There'll be one with you shortly. You can expect her in a few hours and I've also contacted the Inner Circle. They get tetchy if they don't get told about things like this pretty soon. They will want to send someone to take care of the ceremony. Have you had much dealing with the Inner Circle?"

Pawl shook his head.

"Well, good fellows basically. Discreet. Get things done without too much folderol, if you take my meaning. But you don't tell them too much. It's going to be a hard time for you, my boy, the next few months, so if you want someone to talk to you can regard me as an uncle. All right?"

"Thank you, sir."

Lar Proctor waved his hand. "No formality. I just wanted a chat with you. Well, my commiserations and congratulations in that order. In truth I was worried about Toby. I was going to give him a call. Thought he was taking a few too many risks . . . and Lapis. Well Lapis was Lapis, wasn't he? We all loved him, but I could never see him buckling down to running the Paxwax, could you? Many's the time I've said to Toby, 'You're lucky to have Songteller. A man of judgment. You can trust him.'"

Pawl nodded. "So Toby is gone. I shall miss him. One of the colourful ones. We were on Terpsichore together, you know. A fine shot. Shame about the legs . . . still, he never complained. Did he get a chance to talk to you much before he died?"

"Not much. I only gated home yesterday."

"Yes, quite. Well, is everything calm on your Homeworld? No troubles or worries?"

"Everything is peaceful."

"Good. I probably don't need to tell you but there are some tensions in the alliance of the Eleven at present. Nothing too serious, but this civil war in the Freilander-Porterhouse doesn't help. I like to think of the Eleven as one big family. Yes, we have our squabbles and misunderstandings, but we all pull together when it counts. We all understand the same things, share the same human values, don't we?"

"I believe so."

"Do you have aliens on your Homeworld?"

"Not intelligent ones. I think our planet was cleared at the time of the Great Push."

"Good, good. But there is unrest and I would be doing less than my duty if I didn't warn you to keep your eyes open. Toby ran a tight ship and that is good. Remember the price of our freedom remains constant vigilance."

Pawl's knowledge of aliens was limited. He had hunted somewhat

and had helped put down a small rebellion when one of the Paxwax
mining stations was overrun. He had once seen a team of Spiderets
assembling a derrick and he had admired their speed and skill. But
that was about all.

"Well, one last thing, and perhaps the most important," continued Lar Proctor. "I have taken steps to convene a Council of
Eleven as soon as possible and we shall welcome you formally.
You are an important man now. You should look to establish
yourself firmly. Do you have many relatives?"

"Some. Father kept them at a distance."

"Yes, I heard. So. Good luck to you Pawl, and as I said, if I can
be of any assistance don't hesitate to contact me. As soon as the
Death Inspector has seen you, the formal death announcement will
be made. Something brief and dignified, eh?"

He smiled and his image faded.

How little he knows, thought Pawl. He wondered what Lar Proctor's
reaction would have been if he had seen how dismal was the state
of the Paxwax Empire.

Pawl let the vivante cool. He was at a loss as to what to do next.
He was about to leave his father's room when, on an impulse, he
turned back to the vivante and summoned up the Way Gate
Guardian high above his island.

"Essent Pawl?" enquired the computer in its cool polite voice.
"Can I help you in any way?"

"Are you still at full alert?"

"Yes. I have received no order to – "

"Good. I want to extend that alert to all our Way Gates."

"All?"

"Yes."

"I see. Does your father – "

"My father has asked me to do this."

"I see." There was a brief pause. "It is done, Essent Pawl.
Please inform your father. I have logged this order."

"You are very efficient." Pawl was not sure how he should speak
to the Way Guardian. It possessed one of the most advanced
brains on the planet and its loyalty circuits were finely tuned. He
did not want to do anything which might upset it until it had been
re-registered to respond to him as Master. That would be the work
of the Inner Circle.

PHILLIP MANN

"Can I help in any other way?"

"Yes. There will be a contingent of the Inner Circle gating through. I don't know how many. Make them welcome."

"I shall, Essent Pawl."

Pawl closed the circuit and sighed to himself. The computer could have demanded that Toby Paxwax give the order in person. But it hadn't. Now all the Way Gates were at alert. This meant that if there were a disturbance at any Way Gate all the others would close automatically, thereby sealing off the Paxwax Empire. It was a common stratagem, one often used by the Wong Third, and it meant that Pawl was moderately safe for the time being.

What next? thought Pawl. *Laurel.* She would be worried sick. He tapped out the co-ordinates for Thalatta and then delayed. He dared not try to speak to her in person. He knew that the Proctor might already be monitoring signals from Bennet Homeworld, and so he dispatched a simple standard message. "THE PAXWAX ARE HAPPY TO GRANT CONCESSIONS AND LOOK FORWARD TO A CLOSE ALLIANCE WITH A MUCH RESPECTED MINOR FAMILY." Laurel would understand.

The empty house creaked and sighed. Pawl wandered through the rooms, throwing back curtains and opening windows wherever he could. Finally he made his way outside.

He came to a private place. Only the silence remained the same, the peculiar hush that envelops cemetery gardens. Pawl stood with a handful of the tough native wire-grass in his hand and breathed in the moist, perfumed air. He had torn the grass from around the small white door which led from the house into the cemetery garden. Now the door stood open. Soil was scattered over the stone steps. Pawl surveyed the ravaged graveyard. He remembered it as a place of stillness and beauty where shrubs, selected for their fragrance, bowed beside brilliant flame trees. Above the garden, a milk white dome regulated the temperature and humidity and spread a timeless, shadowless light.

As a boy, this had been his private garden, a place where a boy could romp and hide and disappear. Only the long dead of the Paxwax had shared it with Pawl.

Now the flowering shrubs were tangled and wild. Many had grown top-heavy from lack of pruning and had fallen from their supporting trellises. Grass grew hip-high. The Boniface Irises, with flowers as big as the head of a horse, were strangled and trapped

by native vines. Away to one side, the satin surface of the dome
was breached and loose fabric slapped in the breeze. A well-beaten
track showed where sheep had wandered, no doubt carrying native
seeds such as the wire-grass in their wool.

The white cylindrical pillars which marked shafts leading down
to the graves were all smashed. All the lamps were out. Some of
the shafts were exposed, revealing dark tunnels leading into the
ground.

But the single most obvious mark of devastation was the statue.
Once a giant statue of Long Reach Paxwax, the founding father of
the Paxwax Family, had stood at the centre of the garden. That
statue, with its blind pupilless eyes and hand raised in formal
greeting, had been deliberately toppled. The rope which had been
looped round the upraised arm was still there, trapped under the
massive shoulders. The exposed rectangular plinth showed grooves
where drills had prepared access for levers. When the statue came
crashing down, the head had broken free and rolled a few feet and
come to rest, nose down, in a small ornamental fish pond.

The rest of the statue was broken. Sledgehammers had smashed
the fingers and chipped the legs and fractured the ears.

Pawl clambered up on to the head and surveyed the ruin. He
wondered at the desperation of the people who had broken in here
and committed this symbolic outrage. Only people who know that
their fight is to the death go so far.

While he stood the dome above him darkened, as a shadow crept
over it. Following the shadow came a roaring which rattled the
windows in the old house and shook the catacombs. It was a
roaring that did not fade, and Pawl clapped his hands to his ears,
jumped down from the head and ran to the break in the dome.
Above him was the underbelly of a cruiser from the First Family.
It dwarfed the buildings, dwarfed the hills. He felt a prickling on
his arms and scalp and knew that he was in the anti-gravity field of
the giant ship. Slowly, like a boat in the tide, the great dumbbell
shape swung round until it was clear of the high translucent towers.
The roaring ceased, leaving only a muttering in the hills. In
awesome silence the cruiser settled towards the ground.

Pawl had seen giant ships such as this during his time on Lotus-
and-Arcadia, though he had never been in one. They were the
only true starships, and only the Proctor First possessed them. The
technology was a closely-guarded secret. The rear of the craft was

a black sphere. This contained the symbol transformation generator which allowed the ship to slip independently from point to point in space. It was a Gate within a Gate. When the ship was preparing to jump, the forward smaller sphere withdrew into the larger. The surface sealed and turned silver as its density grew. Then it flickered and vanished. Pawl had seen this once and it had bewildered him, as though reality itself were inconstant.

This ship was fully extended. In this configuration it could manoeuvre in the proximate space of any planet.

The giant ship settled. Pseudolegs stabbed down, probing the strength of the earth, digging into field and marsh, spreading the load. Gradually an equilibrium was established and the great ship rocked, as light as a leaf on water.

A round door opened high in the ship's forward section and a figure dressed in red looked down on Pawl. The platform detached and began to carry the figure down to the ground in a controlled flight. There was something familiar. . . .

"Hello, Pawl Paxwax, Master of the Fifth. Remember me?" It was a woman and she removed her helmet and shook her head, fanning out her mane of hair. "I am your Death Inspector."

Pawl recognized the voice and face of Neddelia Proctor.

She stepped to the ground as Pawl ran up. "Remain formal," she instructed, holding up a small black case. "Business first."

As she spoke she displayed her magnificent curved fangs. Pawl noted that they had been tipped with gold since the days he had known her on Lotus-and-Arcadia. "You are looking well," he offered.

"Well, at least I haven't grown any taller." At full stretch Neddelia would have been a good six inches taller than Pawl. But she could not stretch; at least, not when standing. A deformity in her upper back kept her head jutting forward. Many Proctors were afflicted in this way, just as Pawl's legs told that he was a Paxwax. Her deformity did not detract from Neddelia's personality. She was a jovial and sensual woman. Roused to anger, her bluntness and caustic wit left those who antagonized her bloody-witted and confused. In view of their former association Pawl wondered if it were pure chance that had assigned Neddelia to the Paxwax Homeworld, or whether she had made it her convenience.

"I'm glad to see you," he said.

"I know," she replied. "Let's have a look at the body."

*

Punic was guarding the door. It growled when it saw Neddelia and lowered its head and slunk to one side. Neddelia sniffed. "Dogs," she observed, "even mechanical ones – in fact, animals in general – seem not to like me. Perhaps it is the aura I carry with me these days. Something of my work rubs off. It is the price I pay, for I much prefer the living to the dead." She surveyed the room. "And this was where the late Toby lived? The meanness of the very rich never fails to amaze. What a mess. You must have had a hell of a fight."

"There wasn't a fight. We had an argument, yes, but then I went back to my rooms across the courtyard. At dawn I came here. The room was like this and Toby was pretty much as you see him. I tried to tidy him up a bit."

Neddelia looked at Pawl shrewdly. "What happened over there?" She pointed to where Pawl had cauterized the tank containing the Pandora Boxes.

"Yes, well, that *was* me," said Pawl. "This morning, when I came in. He'd cracked the case and the things inside were trying to get out. I burned them."

Neddelia shivered. "If I were you I'd shoot them all. I suppose keeping creatures like that adds spice to cloistered lives but to me they are wholly loathsome. My father has banned them on all our Homeworlds and there are moves underway to exterminate the entire species."

Pawl nodded. "As soon as this business is over I intend to clear them all out."

Neddelia looked round the room and then back at Pawl. "Well, I have seen some strange sights in the course of my work but this I didn't expect. Did Toby really live here? What happened to the house? Where are all the people? I feel as though I'm standing in a museum."

"It's a long story," said Pawl.

"Then you can tell me later."

Pawl smiled a sad smile.

"You look a mess," said Neddelia. "Why don't you go down, mix a couple of spicy drinks, and wait for me. This won't take long and it's very boring."

"I'd rather watch."

"Well, suit yourself, but sit down and don't get in my way. I'll be as quick as I can."

Neddelia became brisk and business-like. She opened her case and removed a small vivante camera. With the camera running she explored every part of the room, turning over the chairs and sifting through the rubbish. She made a thorough survey of Toby with the covers pulled back. "Been dead about twelve hours, I'd say. Strong looking man. Except for all this." She motioned to Toby's lower limbs. "Not much family resemblance, is there?"

She stowed the camera away neatly in her case and then removed a black container and a small pair of antique scissors. "Been in the family for centuries, these," she said, holding them up and snipping them. "Cute, aren't they? Now, snip snip and we're halfway there." She clipped a lock of Toby's hair, a fingernail, and a small segment of flesh from his ear. These she dropped into the container, which she then placed in its niche in the case. She pressed a switch. "Be about a minute while it does the analysis." She sat on the bed and smiled at Pawl. "Not like the old days, eh, philosopher? Did you know that I'm married now?"

"I heard. One of the Felice, wasn't it?"

Neddelia nodded. "Can you imagine that? Me and one of the Felice. He's so small. It's like sleeping with a teddy bear. And about as satisfying. Not that we sleep together often. God knows what political need my marriage served."

"Apart from that, are you happy?"

"I have my work. And I'm free to rove. What more could a girl ask for?"

"Doesn't your work bother you?"

She shrugged. "Not now. Used to once. Thought I'd never be able to sleep, but you get used to it . . . hardened I suppose. The trick is not to think you are dealing with human kind. Last week I had to exhume someone after a month in the crypt. They'd been infested by one of your pet snails. You should have seen the. . . ."

A soft chime sounded in the case and a green light flashed on. "What does that mean?" asked Pawl.

"It means," said Neddelia, removing the small receptacle, "that the samples I took from your father have been analysed and compared with his birth prints and that the man you *claimed* was your father was *indeed* your father and that he *is* dead."

"Glad to know it," said Pawl.

There was a whirring from the case and a sheet of paper unrolled. "Here you are," she said, tearing off the sheet. "Here is your receipt and a full analysis." She glanced at it and then looked more closely. "Cause of death, asphyxiation . . . cerebral haemorrhage

. . . insult to the brain . . . oh hell, he had a cancer in the stomach too. He was a very sick old man." She handed the paper to Pawl and he read it through quickly.

"Now for you." She handed him the scissors after sterilizing them. "Would you care to do the honours?" She cleared the receptacle by throwing the small pieces of Toby on the floor, and then sterilized it. "Don't bother clipping your ear. A drop of blood from your thumb will do. Primitive, isn't it? But efficient. This will confirm that you are who you say you are, and tell you what state you are in."

Pawl complied and a minute later the case flashed green. When the receipt snaked out, Neddelia handed it to Pawl without reading it.

There were no nasty surprises.

"And what happened to Lapis?"

"He died on Auster. Crushed under a mining tractor. Apparently they never found the body."

Neddelia raised her eyebrows.

"Yes, it does sound strange, doesn't it. They sent his hand. That's all they could find."

"Where is it?"

Pawl led her to the small Way box and opened it. She looked at the stiff, blackening hand. "Well, indisputably, this hand is dead," she said. "Sorry, Pawl. Don't mean to be flippant. I'd better carry out what tests I can."

She worked quickly and expertly and within a minute the analysis case blinked green.

"Well, I can confirm that this was part of Lapis. What happened to the rest of him will perhaps never be known. Thank God Auster isn't part of my diocese. No doubt the Death Inspector for that region is already on the job and will ferret out whatever evidence remains. Come on. I've done everything I can here. I'll report that all is in order. Shall we go down and sip a Seppel juice? I trust you do have Seppel juice on this forlorn little planet."

Pawl hesitated. "Can I ask you one last thing?" he asked. "You're experienced in such things. How come he was strangled by that machine? I thought they were supposed to be infallible."

"Do you want me to take a look?"

Pawl nodded.

"All right." Neddelia got down on her knees by the side of the bed and probed gently round one of the places where the fibres

from the anti-gravity unit entered Toby's body. The skin was
discoloured. Using her scissors she removed a tiny segment of skin,
and then scraped some particles from the bio-crystalline fibre.
These she placed in the analysis box.

The machine was silent for a long time. Finally its green light
flashed on and a long sheet of paper purred from the case. The
report was full of technicalities and Neddelia translated it for Pawl.

Over the years the support system had developed a symbiotic
relationship with his father. This was not uncommon. What was
strange was that the machine had contracted Toby's ailments. It
had not been inspected for years, and gradually its resistance had
been worn down. The illness, the anger, the alcohol and the abuse
had undermined its delicate circuits. It had finally broken down
and, in attempting to carry out Toby's final order to lift, had
strangled him. The machine had been drunk.

"I'm afraid the machine is dying too," said Neddelia. "*Now* can
we have that drink?"

Pawl was relieved by the knowledge that he was not, except by
the longest stretch of circumstance, responsible for his father's
death. "Smile, Pawl," said Neddelia, almost reading his mind. "It
could have come yesterday, or a week ago, or next month. He was
lucky that you were here. But the one certain fact is that you are
now Master of Paxwax and I want to be among the first to
congratulate you. Shall we go?"

They strolled into the sunshine. Pawl carried a decanter of Seppel
juice and his notebook. There were many questions he wanted to
ask Neddelia. She carried the glasses and her black case. They
stamped flat an area in the long grass and lay down.

"Just like the old days," said Neddelia.

To Pawl it was not like the old days. He remembered the nights
they had spent under the star-flecked domes of Lotus-and-Arcadia,
where colours wheeled in the sky. He remembered the artfully
perfumed air and the birds whose song and volume could be tuned
to suit the mood.

A fly buzzed in Neddelia's face and she swatted it away. There
were never any flies on Lotus-and-Arcadia.

She stretched out. Lying on her back, her full height and the
strength of her body were apparent. "It is really rather nice," she
said after a few moments. "I have to admit that these primitive

planets have their own kind of charm. I doubt if I could stand it for long."

Pawl poured them both a drink and handed Neddelia her glass. Then he opened his notebook. Neddelia eyed him.

"Questions, questions. Always questions with you, Pawl Paxwax. I have a better idea. Read me one of your little songs. A love song. I'll close my eyes and pretend it is addressed to me and not that wretched Dama you were so attracted to."

"It is not wise, Neddelia."

"Wise. Ha, what a pompous man you have become. You were attracted to me too, weren't you?"

"You know I was."

"Yes, and I used to make fun of you. You were always so serious. So moody. So *deep*. It was the only way I could control you."

"Did you need to control me?"

"Somebody had to. You were quite dangerous . . . and very rude, sometimes. I liked that. Come on, read me something. Something gentle. I promise not to laugh."

Pawl leafed through the pages of his book. It was filled with fragments, odd ideas, notes, questions. "Here, how about this? I wrote it on Lotus-and-Arcadia."

> Burn the forest,
> You'll not kill him.
>
> Beat the thicket,
> You'll not start him.
>
> Cover the wildland with dome and glass,
> You'll not trap him.
>
> He'll still be there,
> Waiting,
> Crouched like a wrestler,
> Staring out of grass and pools,
> When you least expect him.
> Bid him greeting,
> The Green Man.

Neddelia screwed up her face and her curved fangs made strange shadows. "Mmm. Don't like it. Don't like burning and killing. I said a love song."

"It's a song above love."

"Ha! Some love. Some song."

Pawl leafed on. "Well, how's this then?"

> I thought it was dying, the beetle,
> That crawled into my room,
> After knocking on my window.
> I thought. . . .

"Spare me," interrupted Neddelia. "Or shall I leave now? I want something to warm the cockles of a lonely heart."

Pawl found some lines he had never finished. "Try this."

> Rough as a dog and famished too,
> I find sweetness in the cup you bear,
> You brought me fruit in winter
> You bring me love I will not share.

Neddelia sat up and looked at Pawl. "There's my man. That's what I came to hear." She lay back and looked up over the grass and out to the clouds. "Who for?"

"I can't tell you."

"Fruit in winter. That is a nice thought, a fine thought. But beware of love that you cannot share, for it will consume you. Pawl, are you happy? Do you know where you are going? Are you in love?"

"I don't know how to answer such questions."

"Well, the new Master of Paxwax should think about them every day."

They lapsed into silence. Twice Neddelia began to speak, and both times she stopped. "It's hot," she said finally, and loosened the zip of her red suit. "I've had enough of verses and death for one day. Let us drink and be merry. Tell me why there aren't any people here."

Pawl described his homecoming. He told her about the flooded grave, and the fallen statue in the ruined garden and the madness of his father. "He killed them. Made the island a place of terror. The dog is a killer too. Centuries ago they used it for executions. There are probably other graves. I don't know. I'll find them. Do I shock you?"

"I'm hard to shock."

"Even so."

"I've seen more of the Families than you have. You would hardly believe some of the things I have seen. Compared to the Lamprey, your world was democratic. But all the Families are cruel. It is the way of power. Will you be any different, I wonder? You have a cruel streak."

"I don't want to cause suffering."

"Well, threat and worry can break even the strongest of minds. You have a strong mind. Stronger I think than your father's. But even so, the best of intentions can begin to founder. When you feel spies in the bushes . . . when you become afraid to leave your Homeworld in case something happens . . . when criticism becomes treason . . . your universe will shrink to a few acquaintances and they will be sycophants. Any threat from outside will be countered in the most radical and ruthless way because any other response leaves too much to chance. You will even become suspicious of your friends. Do you believe me?"

"I don't know."

"I work in the real world, Pawl. Come close. I am suddenly cold."

Pawl lay down beside her and she slipped her arm easily under his head and cradled him. "You know, if you wish to be free you must become the aggressor, my dear. Imagine now; how do you react if I tell you that my ship, standing over there, has particle generators capable of cutting this planet in half? That while we were upstairs, my crew occupied your silly little island. That our every word is recorded. That at this moment as you lie here you are in the cross-sights of an energy pistol and that at a signal from me you will be executed. How do you react?"

Pawl sat up and stared at her and his amber eyes brightened. "How can I react? You leave me few options."

"Well, you could write me fancy words swearing eternal love."

"I could. . . ."

"Do you think I am joking?"

"I don't know."

"You could beg for mercy."

Pawl nodded.

"You could try to overpower me. . . ."

"Or I could stand up and walk away and take my chance that you were bluffing."

"Do you care to try?"

Abruptly Neddelia reared up and raised her hand. Pawl froze. For seconds he held his position, and then Neddelia laughed.

"I am joking, of course. It is a game. A mind experiment. You always used to like those. Don't worry. The particle generator is asleep and the crew have orders to remain in the dark ship. But what I am trying to tell you is real. I know you like to think in pictures, so face what is real. Your future, Pawl, is freedom within a walled garden."

Pawl relaxed and lay down beside her.

"Can you live in a walled garden?"

"No."

"Then kiss me and remember your words."

Pawl kissed her and Neddelia lay back silent. She looked up at him. "What are you thinking?"

"I am thinking you are a great romantic."

"All sensitive people are romantic. It is compromise that makes us cruel. Do you think I love my life? I do not. Let me tell you. What do I have? What do I see? What am I? I am a proud woman who tests dead bodies. I was taught to compromise from the day I was born. It was always, 'The Family', and I never began to think for myself until it was too late and *I* was compromised. If I'd had any choice in the matter I wouldn't have been born into the First. I'd rather be a quiet girl on a quiet world. Ordinary, really. Free to follow my heart. Free to fall in love with a man who could match me. Have children. Bring them up to hate the Families and stand on their own two feet."

"You could still break away," interrupted Pawl. "It's not too late and you have the means."

"The means, aye, but not the will. Not any more. Well, not alone, anyway. That would be too difficult. Didn't I tell you I was a coward too?"

Pawl laughed but Neddelia looked at him with unsmiling eyes.

"I'm serious, mighty Master of Paxwax. I've learned to face what I am. Let me tell you. Two of your hours from now I shall be on Lotus-and-Arcadia and hopefully drunk and steeped in a satin bath which will make me feel like a virgin again. And I shall take a fresh lover or two and feel reckless, until the call comes and I have to put on my red suit and set off to some petty Homeworld where a father has murdered a son in his anger or children have committed matricide. And I'll sort them out, catch the lies, and watch the greed and envy; and I'll endure their fawning because I am of the First.

"And my brothers, what do I see in them? I see them running just to stay in the same place or besotted or worn out with fear and intrigue and suspicion. Fear and suspicion are more corrosive than any illness . . . they kill the spirit. What are we, all of us? I'll tell you. We are cockroaches scurrying in a burning box, and there is no health in us. There, how's that for an image for you Mister Master of Verses?"

"Very graphic."

"Thank you."

"And very true. I don't want to be a cockroach."

"Then don't." Neddelia knelt up in front of him and placed her hands on either side of his head. "Be yourself. For the sake of all of us who have compromised, be yourself. Let me tell you something. I can only say this once . . . perhaps it is the Seppel juice, perhaps because I hope I will never see you again but . . . you are the purest thing I have ever known. Please don't fail me. Be yourself. Be a Master."

Then she leaned forward, opened her mouth and scratched him gently under the jaw with the points of her tusks.

The effect on Pawl was like an electric charge and Neddelia giggled wickedly. "There, that always used to get you going, didn't it?"

"I am not made of stone."

"No. You always used to remind me of a horse caught between bridle and spur. *There.* Messy and foolish and full of conceit, but *there.* Mine while you were in my arms. We will always be friends. Let us drink to that. I feel as if I've talked for an hour."

They recharged their glasses and sat back looking at one another. Pawl hoped that Neddelia was not beginning to feel too amorous. That nibble had un-nerved him and shown him how susceptible he was.

She lay back and looked at him, smiling as though she could read his confusion. "Tell me the name of your lady-love."

Pawl remained silent.

"Come on, tell me. You are in love, aren't you? I can tell. You are much less fun than you used to be and that is always a sign that a man is in love . . . either that or he is feeling guilty."

Still Pawl remained silent.

"Well, suit yourself. I'll find out soon enough. But do you mind if I give you some more advice?"

"I would like to hear your advice."

"Marry soon, put an end to speculation. You have suddenly become the most eligible man in all the Families. A great prize. My family will be fishing for you . . . one of my high sisters. You could probably even have one of the Xerxes matrons if you set your mind on it. And as for the lovely Dama, with the snow-white limbs and heart like an ice cube, you could probably arrange to have her as a concubine." She watched closely when she said this to see if Pawl made any reaction. "So what say you, Master of Fortune? Choose quickly. Choose carefully and realize that whatever choice you make you will be wrong. You will be hated by the less fortunate and distrusted by those above you. I do not envy you."

"Is there no way out?"

"Look inside yourself. Are you a rebel?"

"I could be. God knows, I don't like what I've seen about me."

"Well then." Neddelia laughed. "Oh, I'm dreaming Pawl, I'm dreaming, but you could jump over the garden wall."

"How so?"

"Pack a bag and climb into my ship. Come away with me. We need never be seen again. I can take us anywhere. I have more than enough for both of us. We. . . ."

Pawl started to laugh but stopped when he saw the streaks of pain on her face. "As I said, Pawl, I was dreaming. Laugh away. Laugh at me, Pawl. Laugh at me. I need to be hurt to stop my silliness. Why did I think for one minute that . . . I must be a fool. Either that or I'm in love with my own destruction. Because that's what you are . . . a destroyer. Why did I ever think. . . ."

"Please Neddelia. . . ." She stopped him with her hand.

"No. I haven't finished. Do you have any friends? Real friends?"

"A few."

"Well, now is the time you are going to need them. Up above your blue sky is darkness. We try to push back that darkness with our dreams of love . . . but that is all they are, dreams, and they fail, and all that is left is pain and bitterness. Expect no kindness. The chill of space is the only reality."

"I think you are wrong."

"Ha. Dream away, poet. Give me its name. Its colour. Its scent.

I would love to know it. I would love to trust it. But there is nothing. Nothing. Nothing."

Neddelia looked at him and then threw the contents of her glass into his face. "You bastard. What is it in you that gets me going like this? What power do you have over me? I was a happy woman looking for a reunion when I landed and now I'm . . . I don't know what I am. Why don't we kill all men? You're not worth the pain you cause us."

She sat still and silent for a few moments and then she said, "Time I was going."

"Please stay with me a few minutes longer. Don't leave me in bitterness. Talk to me," said Pawl.

Neddelia adjusted her red uniform and zipped it up to her throat before replying. "Very well, I will stay a short time longer. But when I choose to leave, I expect no discussion. Understood?"

"Of course."

"Well then?"

Pawl filled their glasses before he spoke. "Simple words, Neddelia. I have spoken with Lar Proctor; can I trust him?"

"He is a king rat."

"He gave me advice."

"I'm sure he did. He likes titles and fancy names. He believes his own lies and that makes him wholly dangerous."

"How so?"

"Does a fool become learned because he wears a scholar's gown? The title never dignifies the man. Pawl, if you want space to breathe you must play him at his own game. Smile at him, stroke his vanity, but tell him nothing of what you are thinking."

"Whom should I fear most?"

"The Lamprey and the Xerxes. But all the Families would like to see you fall. Toby made few friends."

"Can I trust you?"

"No. Yes. I don't know." She smiled a dry smile. "Oh, I suppose I'll try to help. I'll watch you, but don't expect great things from me. I am a humble Death Inspector and the news I learn is little more than accurate gossip. I am far from the source of power."

"What do the Families respect?"

"Power."

"Anything else?"

"No. Just power. It is an alliance of fear."

"How can I be secure?"

"Secure? That is easy. Marry a high ranking bride. The Eleven thrive on alliances. Make a secure alliance in the Eleven and you will be part of them. And now it is time to be going. The Inner Circle will be arriving soon, like crows round offal. I keep my dealings with them to a minimum. I shall contact Uncle Lar as soon as I am aboard my ship and you can expect the death announcement to be made quickly. If I were you I would close down your Homeworld for a while. When the announcement is made everyone will be trying to contact you, offering condolences, trying to sniff out what changes you propose. Put the Paxwax on automatic. Talk to no one until you know what you are going to say."

"I'll do that."

Neddelia nodded. "Wise man." She faced him and then leaned forward and her lips brushed his. "God speed, Pawl. I hope that whoever it is that you love has a skin of silk and a heart of iron. She will need both." She began to move away. "Don't bother to walk with me. I can find my own way. Get on with building your own life, Master of Paxwax. Shine, Pawl. Shine. For all our sakes. Get some life into this place. Real people. Not ghosts and mechanical dogs. Children and laughter. A real wife. Perhaps *you* can find another way out of the garden. Remember I'll be watching. Ciao."

She turned and walked away from him towards her ship without a backward glance.

Pawl stood and watched the great ship lift and dwindle in the sky. When it was little more than two black dots he saw it contract. Then there was a sudden flash of silver light and it was gone.

Already, Pawl knew, it would be materializing above the strawberry domes of Lotus-and-Arcadia.

He turned and ran back as quickly as he could to the main buildings. He pounded up to his father's rooms and brought the vivante to life. Time was suddenly against him.

"Acknowledge all calls but take no messages. Standard formula. Say that the Master of Paxwax will reply in due course. Understood?"

"Understood." The machine hummed as it went over to automatic. Now no one, not even Laurel Beltane, could contact him.

17

ON THALATTA

Semyon Beltane held the message in his hand and shook it angrily.

"And what am I supposed to make of this? 'THE PAXWAX FIFTH ARE HAPPY TO GRANT CONCESSIONS AND LOOK FORWARD TO A CLOSE ALLIANCE WITH A MUCH RESPECTED MINOR FAMILY'. It comes from the Paxwax Homeworld itself."

Despite her father's anger, Laurel could only smile. "It's all right father. Don't get so upset."

"Don't get so upset? What do you mean, girl? All my life I have tried to protect the Beltane Family from getting involved with the Eleven Great Families and now this arrives. What have you been doing? Have you begun to direct the affairs of this family from your residence on Lotus-and-Arcadia?"

Laurel bit back a tart reply and calmed herself by looking out through the portal of her father's galleon and studying the white clouds which towered like castles on the horizon. The galleon was floating a few hundred metres high and the low islands passed beneath them like the half-emerging backs of sand lizards.

"The message doesn't mean what it says," she explained, speaking slowly and carefully.

"Then what does it mean?"

"I'll tell you if only you'll stop shouting and listen."

Semyon Beltane sat down and placed the message squarely in front of him on a low table.

"Very well, I'm listening."

Paris, who was leaning against one of the walls and who had followed the exchange with growing agitation, interrupted.

"Look, you two. Will you stop it? All you've done since that message arrived is row. Laurel is home. Let's be happy. All I want to do is enjoy myself. So the Paxwax want to know us better. So what. Who cares? Tell them we're not interested."

"Go back to your house, Paris," said Semyon. "You don't understand."

"Huh." Paris sat down against the wall.

"Well, I'm waiting," said Semyon, facing his daughter.

Laurel wished she were somewhere else, wished the whole question of Pawl Paxwax did not have to be introduced this way. She could see no way of telling her father without hurting him.

"Can't we leave this? Just take my word that the message has nothing to do with property claims or Way rights or trade tariffs."

"I'm waiting."

"All right." She took a deep breath. "That message is from Pawl Paxwax. He is on his Homeworld."

"So?"

"So. We are in love with one another. I can't help that."

Silence. Semyon chewed his lower lip. If anything he looked angrier. "Do you mean," he said finally, "that he is trying to buy us off?"

"I said that we love one another." Laurel saw the expression that shaped Semyon's face when she said this. It was a mixture of derision and disgust. "And that is what I mean. That is what the message means. The close alliance means marriage. Pawl and I intend to be married."

Semyon stared at her. "And what does Toby Paxwax think of this? Have you asked him?"

Laurel blushed. "I think that is what Pawl means when he says, 'The Paxwax are happy to grant concessions. . . .'"

"Does he? Gracious of him."

"It's not like that, father. I know it sounds all wrong. But it is not like that, really."

"No. I'm sure it's not. Toby Paxwax always has his price."

"I'm sorry. I knew now was the wrong time to. . . ."

"Wrong time. Right time. Who cares? The Paxwax Fifth are big and dangerous. We must be concerned about what Toby Paxwax thinks of us. But did his son ever think to ask me? Was he ever concerned with what *I* think?"

Laurel didn't answer.

"No. And that is the measure of the man who you say loves you. The Paxwax are rogues. Only a fool would trust them."

18

ON ALL THE HUMAN WORLDS

THE SENIOR PROCTOR, OF THE PROCTOR FIRST FAMILY, ANNOUNCES WITH DEEP SADNESS THE DEATH OF MASTER TOBY PAXWAX OF THE PAXWAX FIFTH. HE IS SUCCEEDED BY HIS SON, PAWL PAXWAX, WHO IS HENCEFORTH MASTER OF THE PAXWAX.

TO PAWL IN THIS HOUR OF HIS GRIEF WE SEND OUR DEEPEST COMMISERATION. TOBY LED THE PAXWAX FIFTH WITH HONOUR AND KINDNESS. WE SHALL MISS THE STRENGTH OF HIS EXAMPLE AND THE WISDOM OF HIS COUNSEL.

WE ALSO GRIEVE AT THIS TIME THE PASSING OF LAPIS, ELDEST SON OF TOBY PAXWAX AND BELOVED BROTHER OF THE MASTER OF PAXWAX.

19

ON SABLE

On Sable, the Homeworld of the Shell-Bogdanovich Conspiracy, Helium Bogdanovich lit his pipe carefully and rolled over in his bath. He slid down as deep into the water as his pipe would permit and allowed the small gills on either side of his throat to open and flutter. Bubbles rose to the surface.

Clover Shell, his wife, slid into the water and paddled over to him with only her nose out of the water. They had both just heard the news. "Are you brooding about Pawl Paxwax?"

Helium removed his pipe from his mouth and placed it on a floating tray. "Well, the news *is* worrying. We know so little. I hoped Toby would abdicate in favour of Lapis. We could have worked with Lapis. I liked him. But Pawl I don't know. A moody, intemperate boy by all accounts. But responsibility can work wonders."

"It can make or break."

"True."

"Do you think you should *do* something?"

"Mmm. I heard a rumour. Came from the Felice. God knows how they hear these things, but it concerns the Xerxes and the Lamprey. Seems they are hatching something against the Paxwax. It's only a rumour but. . . ." He rolled over and Clover splashed water on his back.

"Act now," said Clover. "I feel it is right. There is a great deal at stake. After all, our families have worked closely for generations. I think Pawl would appreciate a helping hand. Arrange something."

Helium bobbed his large head and plunged completely under the water. He swam to the far end of the bath and pulled his bulk out of the water. He shook himself, sending up a fine spray. His gills closed neatly and the short hair which covered the whole of his body fluffed out as the water drained away. "What about an honour roll just to show that we have our eyes open?"

"Capital, and I'll compose a garden for him. It is bad for a young man to be alone."

When her husband was gone, Clover placed a call to the Longstock Eighth Homeworld. She spoke with Livil Longstock, her old friend and one of the senior wives in the Longstock household. Livil was Dama Longstock's foster mother. Clover was Dama's natural mother. The secret was well-guarded.

"Any news from the Paxwax?" asked Clover directly.

"Not a word. Their Homeworld is blacked out. What is going on there is anyone's guess."

"Helium tells me their Way Gates are all on standby alert, but that's only natural, given the news. I'm just wondering if old Toby had a chance to tell Pawl before he died."

"Terrible news. Shocking news. Dama's told me a lot about Pawl. He sounds a nice boy – a bit strange, a bit wild, but then. . . ."

"We were all wild once," finished Clover. "Well, calm yourself. If nothing has been said by the Paxwax Homeworld in the next few days we start to take action. I'll ask Helium to have a word with

Pawl. He's very good at that sort of thing and we are standing by just in case the you-know-who take it into their minds to try any tricks. Everything'll be all right. You'll see. And how is Dama? Is she still enjoying herself on Lotus-and-Arcadia? Did she like the Minzel trees I sent? I thought they'd do so well on a dry cold Homeworld like yours. They can't stand the heat here. Remind her to bleed them after the first shoots show or they won't flower, they'll just ramble all over the place."

The two women continued chatting until Helium returned and threw himself heavily into the water. The wave splashed up the walls and poured down again.

"Well, that's that then," he said. "If the Wong or Xerxes or Lamprey start moving through our stations they'll have to sign the honour register and we'll know something is happening. They'll know we're on their tails. Oh, and I've left a little message for Pawl. He's probably busy now. I imagine the Death Inspector will be with him. No messages are going in or out of Bennet, but it'll get through to him. Now where's my pipe?"

Clover paddled across the pool and retrieved the tray from one corner, where it was bumping against the side. "Here we are, safe and sound." She opened the tray and placed the pipe in his mouth. "Now lie back and I'll light it. I'm much happier now that we have done something."

20

ON AN

On An, the Homeworld of the Wong Third, a gentle breeze scattered petals of cherry blossom, made wind chimes tinkle at the corners of pavilions and stirred the red curtains in the Imperial chamber.

Emperor Wong Lungli was asleep. He lay on his back under a golden canopy. His white beard was combed out straight and rose and fell as the old man breathed. The light from a thousand longevity lamps played across his serene wrinkled face, restoring vitality.

At the entrance to the chamber an agitated conversation took place in whispers. Finally Sun Laohu, the Prime Minister, entered on his knees and approached the low bed. Still on his knees he took the old man's hand and began to massage it gently at the wrist.

Emperor Wong Lungli's eyes fluttered as he rose to consciousness, and opened.

The Prime Minister spoke hurriedly and had to place his ear close to the Emperor's lips to catch his faint reply. At the end of the conversation, the Prime Minister bowed and left the room as he had entered.

The old Emperor sighed and drifted back into sleep.

Within minutes the Way Gates throughout the whole of the Wong Empire closed. All movement stopped. Any Way travellers trapped in transit were reconstituted. They became Guests of the Emperor, a euphemism for those under house arrest, and were given every amenity except news and freedom to travel.

"When will the Way Gates come alive again? We demand to know," stated irate travellers.

"When the Emperor pleases," came the bland reply from impassive officials. "Rest now, please."

21

ON OK

On Ok, the Homeworld of the Freilander-Porterhouse Confederation, Savera Porterhouse was making love. The news was broadcast in her bedchamber. She pushed her panting lover to one side, slipped a girdle round her waist and hurried down to the main communication room.

Other members of her family were already assembling. They listened in silence. When the broadcast was finished they played it through again.

"Good God. Poor Pawl. It must have been a hell of a fight," said Savera to her young brother Anwar. "A lamb to the slaughter."

"At least it takes the pressure off us a little," replied Anwar.

"Send greetings to Pawl. Wish him well. If the Paxwax come in on our side we'll finish father and mother off once and for all. It is worth a try."

"Will do."

Tell him Lapis once said he would help us when he came to power."

"Did he?" Anwar's eyes shone, for to him Lapis was a great hero.

"Not in so many words. But I am sure that is what he meant. Now get to it."

"Will do. What are you going to do?"

"Relax," snapped Savera. "This war is getting me down."

22

ON FESTAL

On Festal, the Homeworld of the Longstock Eighth, the family gathered and arranged themselves formally, silently, in the vast padded communication chambers. Like the patriarch he was, Daag Longstock sat on the high throne and stared stonily down.

There was not a sound. Noise of any kind was forbidden in the chill rooms of the Longstock household.

When everyone was present he nodded to the vivante controller, who turned to the machine, touched its switches and tuned it. Lar Proctor appeared. His message was reduced to a whisper.

When he had spoken the machine went dead. If the Longstock felt any reaction they did not show it.

Finally Daag Longstock drew a deep breath. He signalled to Livil Longstock, who hurried close to him.

"Order Dama back from Lotus-and-Arcadia immediately."

That was all he said.

When he indicated that the assembly was over, the members of his family withdrew without a sound.

23

OF THE OUTER FAMILIES

When the Masters of the Sith, the Felice and the Paragon heard the death announcement they hurriedly gathered in a secret vivante conference.

Singular Sith, towering in his furs and horned like a bull, spoke for all of them when he said, "The Inner Families will fight. There has been good blood and bad blood spilt. We must confederate and wait. Victory will not go to the strongest, but to the best-prepared."

"Amen," said Laverna Felice.

The Felice were a vast family of dolls. A genetic accident at some point in the past had meant that for several successive generations their family had grown smaller. Laverna was little more than a metre high, though all parts of her physique were in proportion. The Felice were great engineers and conceded nothing to the other Families in terms of intelligence. If anything they were more belligerent. Laverna, by repute more than a hundred years old, raised her black aquiline face and stared at Singular Sith. "I do not know this man Pawl. Much will depend on his nature. Is he a chip of Toby? I admired Toby." She transferred her steady gaze to Cicero Paragon. "Toby was consistent."

Cicero Paragon shrugged and his fat body quaked. Above him

hung a chandelier such as Toby had worn. Cicero had good legs but his weight had long since rendered them feeble. "My youngest son knew him. An unpredictable boy evidently. Sometimes cold, sometimes friendly, always reserved, but dangerous too. Apparently he didn't mix much with the crowd on Lotus-and-Arcadia. Spent a lot of his time with a girl from the Beltanes. She was half mad . . . used to collect colours. Anyway, he was always quite a hit with women."

"How was he dangerous?" asked Singular Sith.

"His tongue. Used to make up silly rhymes. Recited some at a party once and it ended in a fight. Apparently they had to knock him out. He was trying to kill one of the young Proctors."

"Sounds promising – " this from Singular – "was he seen much with the famous and beautiful Dama?"

"They were together for a time."

"And?"

"That is all I know. My son did not like him. Avoided him."

"Well, it seems that we shall have interesting times ahead," said Laverna. "And what of poor Lapis?"

"Killed by a Spideret, so I hear," said Cicero.

"Dark beasts, too clever by half, we should have stamped them out long ago. I don't tolerate any in the Felice Domain."

"They have their uses," replied Cicero. "They can do things we can't. I use plenty of aliens. Protect them. Show them who's boss. Don't be too hard and they'll eat out of your hand. Most of them."

Laverna shuddered. "I think we have underestimated the aliens. At the next meeting of the Eleven I intend to move that we begin a purge. I am uneasy."

Tension was evident between Cicero and Laverna. And how could it be otherwise? Cicero Paragon looked upon Laverna as an exotic which in an earlier age he might have fed on. He assessed the worlds in terms of his lips and stomach. Laverna Felice, petite in every way and who, standing on tip-toe, would hardly have reached as high as Cicero's girdle, saw Cicero as an embodiment of Luxury. She wanted to relacquer her skin every time she talked to him. Only mutual interest held them together.

Singular Sith moved to defuse the tension.

"Well, let us agree that we will work together. We must be united in the face of the Inner Families. Unity means security for all of us. Let us not spread the discussion wider. We have enough on our plate just coping with the Paxwax."

Laverna and Cicero both nodded. They agreed to keep open communication and discover all they could about Pawl.

24

ON MORROW

Lastly, on Morrow, the news of Toby's death caused amazement.

Dame Jettatura ran down one of the branch corridors, her white hair streaming out behind her like the tail of a horse. She turned a cartwheel and then a double somersault and burst into the communication room where Clarissa, her feathers up and standing in a stiff corona round her head, was bending over the vivante console. Rose sat, her legs spread and her lustrous eyes concentrating on the image of Lar Proctor, who was speaking.

"TO PAWL IN THIS HOUR OF HIS GRIEF WE SEND OUR DEEPEST COMMISERATIONS. . . ."

"Is it true?" Jettatura was breathless.

"True."

"Then why are we waiting? The boy is a nothing. We should take him now, while he is reeling."

"WE ALSO GRIEVE AT THIS TIME THE PASSING OF LAPIS, ELDEST SON OF TOBY PAXWAX AND BELOVED BROTHER. . . ."

"We hold all the cards now. Oh. I feel it, don't you? Fate is playing into our hands. Come Clarissa. Cool and calm. Take the moment."

Clarissa placed a hand to her head and with an act of will forced herself to be calm. Her feathers ruffled as they subsided. "Yes, you are right. Now is the moment, but it is all so sudden."

"Just think," said Jettatura, her pink eyes bright with excitement, "within hours we can be beyond Portal Reclusi. We can take Elliott's Pocket from three sides and snip the Paxwax in half. Then we will let the Lamprey flow. Oh."

Rose watched her two sisters and sighed and stood up. She

waddled over to them, her hands raised. "Let us pause. Just for a short time. Something inside me is worried. You know they say that women with a baby inside them can feel danger. Hold. Hold. There must be a better way than this . . . cruelty."

"Cruelty, ha!" snapped Jettatura. "Revenge is cruel. Birth is cruel. Life is cruel. Do not talk to me about cruelty. Do you think the Paxwax would treat us lightly if they were in our place? Oh no, my fine sister, they would not." She turned away.

Clarissa looked at Rose. She had detected a strange note in her voice, and Rose so rarely offered an opinion. "Do you have something further to say, Rose? Do you have a new idea? Come on, speak up."

Rose was grateful for Clarissa's prompting. She faced her sisters squarely. "Yes, Clarissa – and you too, Jettatura – please listen to me. I have a new idea. Last night I lay awake. I was thinking about Lapis. I had expected an ogre, something that stank; and met a man, just a man. A man who is vulnerable as all men are. There is only a wildness in him. And I thought . . . and I thought. . . ." She began to blush. "I thought, how would I feel about him if he was the father of the child I carry?"

Clarissa and Jettatura stared at her aghast. It was many generations since a Xerxes had known a man, still less conceived a child by one.

Before the two sisters could say anything, Rose hurried on. "And when I thought that, the baby moved, and I thought the waters were about to break and I nearly called you. But I felt happy too. Happy. The Xerxes de la Tour Souvent and the Paxwax . . . why not?"

There was a long silence and finally Jettatura spoke. "You were always the crazy one."

Having begun, Rose was not to be stopped. "And now this has happened. Toby is dead. A young man we none of us know is Master of Paxwax. The rightful Master is below in the dog-hutch. Toby's death could be a new beginning. Isn't it worth a try?"

"The Paxwax grow from a line of vipers. They will sting when they have venom. History proves it," said Clarissa, but Rose ignored her.

"And I am thinking still. Neither Lapis nor Pawl would look at me, but you are both beautiful . . . you are . . . you could. . . ." Rose's voice trailed away, stifled by the enormity of her own thought.

"Say it," said Jettatura, "speak your mind fully." Her voice had a flat, dead, dangerous quality.

"I am thinking that you two should marry Lapis and Pawl."

In the silence which followed this remark, Lar Proctor began repeating the death announcement. Jettatura stood up and struck the vivante console with her fist. Then she rounded on Rose. At first it looked as though she might hit her. Instead, she placed her arms in front of her with the palms of her hands pressed together. She said, "Enough of this foolishness. You know very well, Rose, that Clarissa and I are as sterile as boys. *You* are the only fertile one."

"Even so," said Rose.

"Even so nothing. The Paxwax want children. They are at the end of their line." Jettatura turned away.

"And I – " said Clarissa. Blood had mounted into her pale face – "I am almost old enough to be Lapis's mother . . . and Jetty. . . ."

"Enough!" screamed Jettatura. She crossed to the door and when she spoke again her voice had regained its tight, clipped quality. "Call the Master of Paxwax now. Deal with him as you would with Toby. Call me when you have spoken to the Paxwax."

When she had gone Clarissa turned to Rose.

"That was a silly thought. An impossible. You have been dreaming."

Rose looked at her defiantly, the look of one who knows that there is nothing to lose. "Do you have a better thought? Do you?"

Clarissa did not reply, and there the matter ended.

Clarissa delayed calling the Paxwax for a few hours while she composed herself. She hardly dared admit it to herself but Rose's words had unsettled her. The very idea of a liaison with the Paxwax, unthinkable until stated by Rose, was both repulsive and thrilling and it took a long time before Clarissa, standing before Dame Rex's beady eyes, felt herself grow calm.

Then she acted with deliberation. She mounted through the tree to her private quarters. There the little men in white smocks who attended her bed chamber were waiting for her. She had her finest robes brought out and displayed. She selected a gown of purple and flame. It was the gown she had worn on the day her mother died, the day she became leader of the Xerxes. She set some of the little men to burnishing the Xerxes emblem, although its crystal and steel segments shone.

She gave herself to a private luxury, preening. Two of her attendants with long fingers began to work at her feathers, brushing against the lie, probing down to where the shaft entered her skin, working the shaft like the most delicious scratching, blowing on the barbs to separate them, combing the feathers with their fingers, tugging at the fine down until Clarissa gasped and felt herself floating.

When every pen had received attention, Clarissa was dressed and the emblem placed upon her shoulders. She felt glorious and imperious and every inch a queen as she rode down to the central communication room.

Jettatura was waiting like a statue carved from white wax. She had the vivante cube which held the image of Lapis Paxwax. Rose was not present.

Clarissa dismissed the attendants, and when they were alone Jettatura set the vivante cube in the transmitter. Its image could now be sent directly to the Paxwax Homeworld.

Clarissa took a deep breath, observed with pleasure that colour had mounted into Jettatura's pale cheeks, and tapped out the Paxwax call sign.

They waited while the co-ordinates locked. They saw the vivante space darken and come alive as time weakened between the two Homeworlds and the great symbolic codes leaped into the dark to join. They saw the space brighten as the Paxwax Homeworld linked with theirs. But there was no image, just a monstrous wall of gleaming motes and a voice which spoke with dry precision, a voice scrubbed of emotion. "Your call is received and noted. At this time the Paxwax Homeworld is closed to all communication. Your call will be returned by the Master of Paxwax as soon as it is convenient. Meanwhile, no other calls will be accepted until this call has been returned. The priority is acknowledged."

It was a formula. Clarissa could have dictated it herself. Until the Paxwax opened up, there was no way anyone could communicate with their Homeworld.

The two sisters stared at the vivante space, which collapsed into random motes of light as the Paxwax broke contact.

"Well, so much for nothing," snapped Jettatura. "I should have thought. You should have thought. Of course he's closed up, tight as a lid on a sewer. What think you, my sister? We shall just have to wait."

Clarissa was aware of her finery, of the weight of the emblem. "I feel rather foolish," she said. "I can't sit about dressed like this just waiting until Pawl Paxwax, damn him, deigns to call. Shall we re-think our stratagem?"

"No."

Any further conversation was cut short by the bright twinkle of a warning bell, a communication from the Way Platform above Morrow.

"Are we expecting anyone?" asked Jettatura. Visitors were not common on Morrow.

"Not that I am aware of," replied Clarissa, and touched the communication panels.

Immediately they were joined with the Way Platform, where the Xerxes attendant stared in surprise. She had not expected to see the ruling sisters in person.

"You have a message?" asked Jettatura.

The attendant nodded. "Lorca of the Inner Circle has just Gated through."

"Her business?"

"Friendly relations in view of the Paxwax news." The attendant was clearly reading from the Way form. She had not yet allowed Lorca to exit from the Way Gate. "Shall I allow her to come down?"

"What does the Inner Circle want now?" muttered Clarissa.

"Protocol. Protocol. A bit of wheeling and dealing. You know how active the Inner Circle get whenever there is a transfer of power. Get her down. Treat her nicely. Make concessions to show good faith, and then get her off the planet."

"You talk to her," said Clarissa, "while I get changed. Then I'll attend to any ceremonies."

Clarissa removed the vivante cube of Lapis and hurried from the communication room. Jettatura gave her attention to the Way attendant.

"Allow Lorca through. Show her every courtesy." The Way attendant nodded and turned away from the screen while she operated some controls. Behind her the door to the Way Gate swung slowly open to reveal Lorca of the Inner Circle, dressed as ever in the dark gown with the heavy hood and wearing the pale mask with its ubiquitous smile. She walked forward to the communication console and inclined her head when she saw Jettatura. Then she threw back her hood and removed her mask and shook out her grey hair. She smiled warmly.

"Dame Jettatura of the Xerxes de la Tour Souvent, it is a pleasure to see you again. I bring greeting from the Inner Circle."

"Greetings to you, Lorca. Welcome return to Morrow. Your rooms, as ever, stand ready and waiting."

"I trust you have heard the important news?"

"We have."

"My visit concerns that. I felt it essential that I come in person. There is much to discuss."

"We will talk when you have settled in. Was the transit through Portal Reclusi arduous?"

"No worse than before. But I am not getting younger. I would appreciate a few hours' rest."

"Of course. Come down straight away. Feel at home on Morrow."

Lorca moved out of sight.

The familiar face of the Way attendant came into view. "Shuttle activated. Arrival time, forty minutes." The screen cleared.

Jettatura left the communication room and ushered the regular attendants back to their positions. An impressive number of communiqués had built up during the short time that the sisters had been there. A priority call was waiting from the Lamprey. "Tell them we are in conference with the Inner Circle," said Jettatura. "Tell them we will return their call as soon as we can. They will understand." She hurried from the communication room.

Alone in her rooms on Morrow, Lorca crouched on the floor, her arms tight round her legs and her face pressed against her knees. Every muscle was strained. She was sweating as she rocked back and forth. The snake which lived in a special cradle between her shoulder blades flexed, joining the brilliance of its coiled nerves to the concentrated energy of Lorca's mind.

Lorca disliked telepathic contact. It left her feeling unclean, but in the present situation there was really no alternative.

She sent her mind out. Her thought was a spangled dewy web trembling in a breeze – a distinct call sign. Far below in the roots of the tree, the Spideret that hung above Lapis sensed the imagery and joined with it. It sent a web of its own which enveloped Lorca.

The two webs twisted together like shadows on a cave wall, and in an instant merged.

Communication was total and immediate.

In that instant the Spideret knew its mission and Lorca learned of the vivante cube that the sisters had recorded of Lapis Paxwax. A vivante cube! It needed to be found and destroyed, so that the Xerxes might have no hold over the Paxwax whether in appearance or reality. Lorca felt sick from the intimate contact with the Spideret, but knew that she needed to push wider.

She felt through the great tree on Morrow; gently like snow falling; with great care, like a blind person baiting and then setting a mouse trap. She felt the distinctive aura of Dame Clarissa, who was in her robing room changing.

Dame Clarissa's mind was irritated, prone to sudden anger, and Lorca had to be careful in case she became trapped in Clarissa's anger and revealed herself.

She was close when Clarissa struck one of her little attendants about the ears and sent him bowling across the floor. Clarissa shrugged and the magnificent purple and flame gown slipped from her shoulders and buckled on the floor. She stepped from it, admiring the colour and her own slim legs, and in that one moment, while Clarissa's mood lifted, Lorca was able to glance into her. She could not read her – that would have been impossible – but she was able to catch a thought of Lapis. She amplified that thought and Clarissa lifted her fingers to her lips in sudden worry. She glanced over to a small table where she had placed the vivante cube and felt relief when she saw it. Lorca knew all she needed to. She was set to withdraw and yet something of the fragrance of Clarissa held her: a brief awareness of luxury, a feeling for sensuous power, a glimpse of riches beyond the dreams of a humble parasite guardian in the grip of the Inner Circle. She experienced the feeling of lace next to naked skin, the coolness of silk, the deep, toe-curling warmth of a thick carpet under bare feet, and wine in the blood.

Clarissa stretched. Her plumes rose and Lorca arched with them. Then the Spideret was with her again, picking at her, pulling her back, plucking from her mind with a brute singleness of purpose the image of the vivante cube.

The Spideret withdrew, leaving Lorca ill on the floor. Her worm coiled with her, massaging the nerves in her neck. Oblivious, high in her private rooms, Clarissa continued dressing.

*

At the base of the stone tree, in the darkness above the dog-hutch, the Spideret spread its legs wide and stared down at the sleeping Lapis. In its mind it transformed him. He became a brother and comrade, one worthy of honour, and the enemy would not have him.

It stretched its legs until they were almost straight, like the points of a starfish, and then it closed to a hairy ball and dropped silently and swiftly. Gently it woke Lapis by rolling him back and forth with one of its feelers. Lapis stirred and his eyes opened. Crouched by the side of his cot, the Spideret helped him sit up and then it did something that Lapis had never seen before. It climbed on to the bed so that its body was over him and the tight hairy folds of its abdomen began to expand and stiffen. Revealed, as though branded on the creature, was the sigil of the Inner Circle.

Then it began to stroke him with its short front feelers, weaving a complicated message. "I don't understand," said Lapis, and at that moment twin mandibles darted forth and pierced him in the soft glands just below his jaw. His chest heaved briefly. Red foam appeared in the corner of his mouth. His eyes turned back in their sockets, and Lapis became still.

The Spideret rose on stiff legs. From an orifice close to its mouth it began to spray him, covering him from head to toe in a thick mucus which contracted as it dried. Lapis was embalmed. The Spideret rocked in ecstasy above him, its feelers weaving and rubbing over one another, and then it ate.

The ceremony it had selected was that for a fallen warrior. As it consumed Lapis it felt its body knit for battle. Its colour changed slightly from brown to red as the hairs on its body thickened and stiffened. *Honour to Lapis*, it thought, as it cut and tore, and soon he was gone.

The Spideret climbed slowly. At the centre of its web it hung, wide-legged but relaxed. It turned slowly in the wind that blew through the ancient tunnels.

Inside it powerful life was active. Juices dissolved Lapis. The fighting spirit of Lapis entered the Spideret. Lapis became energy, and when the Spideret felt charged, it moved.

It scampered across its web to the edge of the dog-hutch, disengaged and dropped to the ground.

Silently it ran across the floor to the iron gate which closed this section of the tunnel. The gate was charged, the Spideret knew, but by flattening its body it was just able to squeeze under.

Beyond the gate the tunnel in the stone curved and became the guards' quarters. Bright lights shone and voices reached the Spideret as it held to the shadows. It listened, detecting the positions of the strong female warriors who guarded the prison and the small men who served them.

It attacked silently, climbing round the walls, until it was above a table where three guards were eating. There should have been four guards, but it was too late for the Spideret to worry about that.

It dropped. One guard it slashed, the second it stung, and the third stared in disbelief as the giant spider crouched on the table, gathered itself and jumped and spat. The venom sent her crashing back, clawing at her eyes before she could draw her gun. Quickly the Spideret smothered the little men who tried to ward it off with their stumpy fat arms.

For a second the Spideret debated whether to wait for the fourth guard. It dismissed the thought. Time was flowing. Surprise was its ally. Discovery would come soon enough.

The Spideret ran to the end of the hall, where it found the access door to the communication chute. It tore open the door and revealed the narrow pressure tunnel which snaked upwards through the tree. With straddled legs it began to climb.

Once a transit sleigh hurtled past the Spideret and it flattened itself against the wall. The sleigh brushed its back, opening up a thin wound. The suction in the wake of the vehicle dislodged the Spideret but not before it had managed to secure. It dangled for a few moments, bumping against the wall, and then it gathered itself and began to climb once more.

As it mounted through the tree the tunnels became more complex and the junctions more frequent. More sleighs passed. It learned how to listen for them and then, when the way was clear, climb with all legs to the next niche. Briefly, lodged safely in the crook of a fissure, it spun a thought, the image of the Inner Circle mask. Lorca's mind responded and the Spideret knew where it was. Two hundred metres further and it would be in the area where the Xerxes sisters lived. Then it would turn down the narrow side chute which served Clarissa's rooms. Clear in the Spideret's mind was the small table upon which the vivante cube rested.

It moved on, and as it moved it heard alarm bells ring in the depths of the stone tree.

Lorca of the Inner Circle heard the same alarm as she stepped from her quarters and began the short journey to the conference room. Female guards in their trim blue uniforms, which Lorca had always considered merely ceremonial, hurried down the corridor, pausing only to give the briefest salute to the member of the Inner Circle. All the guards were armed.

She entered the conference room, where Clarissa and Jettatura were waiting for her. It was an ancient room and had not been carved by the Xerxes. Once, in the far long ago when the tree lived, it housed a pulse which drove a river of sap down a side branch. The walls were smooth like the inside of bark and still exuded a faint resinous aroma. It was a restful place fit for quiet and thoughtful discussion.

Neither Jettatura nor Clarissa was restful. Clarissa paced while Jettatura tapped her long fingernails against the top of the conference table. Both stopped when they saw Lorca. Lorca observed that their colour was high and both ladies' eyes were bright.

"Welcome, Lorca of the Inner Circle. I trust you are rested."

"Rested and refreshed. Your generosity as ever leaves nothing to be desired, but is there something wrong? I see the guards, passages closed, people running. . . ."

"Nothing wrong," said Clarissa, "only. . . ."

"Practice. Drill," interrupted Jettatura, taking over from Clarissa, who was faltering. "We spring it on them – " she indicated the door vaguely – "every so often. Keeps them on their toes. Keeps us prepared. You never know what emergency may arise. We live in troubled times. We would have cancelled the drill if we had known you were coming."

A senior guard appeared at the door. She spoke in Morrow-tongue, and whatever her information was it had its effect on Clarissa, for her quills suddenly lifted like the tail of a peacock and she sat down hurriedly. Seeing Lorca's amazement, Clarissa forced a weak smile.

"Just drill," she said, "but we try to keep it as realistic as possible."

The Spideret was at the entry port just outside Clarissa's chambers. Moments earlier a steel door had irised shut behind the Spideret, closing off the tunnel and trapping one of its anterior feelers. With the feeler gone its senses were not so acute. It could not tell whether or not there was life beyond the transit door.

Taking a strong position on the wall by the door, the Spideret seized the lock in its mandibles and began to work it backwards and forwards. The metal began to tear as the lock worked loose. With a final pull and a twist the whole locking mechanism came away and the transit door fell into the room.

The Spideret entered with a rush and its legs scratched at the highly polished floor, seeking for purchase. No one was there. Incredibly, no one was guarding the transit chute leading directly into Clarissa's rooms.

The Spideret scuttled across to a corner and looked round, its eyes turning quickly on their stalks. The room was little more than a vestibule. A mirror embellished with gold orphrey work covered one entire wall. Ancient pottery jars with brilliant crimson and blue glazes stood against the other walls. From these came perfumes which acted like an astringent to the finely-tuned nervous system of the Spideret, making its eyes retract.

Facing the broken transit door were tall blue and white doors which the Spideret guessed led directly into Clarissa's quarters. Despite its weakened senses it could hear beyond the door. Someone was coming. Hurrying, with loud footsteps. The ornate twin handles began to turn.

As the door opened the Spideret leaped and crushed the blue uniformed guard under its abdomen. She screamed a bubbly scream. Then the Spideret was in. It bounced round the walls, spitting and cutting with its mandibles at full extent. Its legs blurred as it ran, finding easy purchase in the rich embroideries and silks which hung on the walls.

Seven were in the room. Five died in the first surprise attack. One lay injured and bleeding on Clarissa's bed, the blood welling from a mandible gash beneath the heart. One named Latani Rama, personal guard to Dame Clarissa, escaped and slammed the door leading to the rest of the rooms.

The Spideret worked quickly, searching through the chaos of the room to find the small table. It was on its side in a corner. Close to it was a tumbled box of jewels and among the jewels was the vivante cube. It was cracked already, but to make certain that there was no possibility of it being used or reconstituted at a later time, the Spideret crushed it to fine powder.

Its job was done. Any hold the Xerxes might have had over the Paxwax was ended. What now? For the first time since leaving the dog-hutch the Spideret felt the tension in its fibres relax. It was not a conscious action, just a simple response to tiredness. The Spideret wanted to hang in a web over flowing water and feel the wind rock it while it drank the dew that formed on the web lines. But there could be no such relief.

Escape was impossible. But not to try and escape was equally impossible. Not to try would have been an insult to Lapis and all the Spiderets that had died fighting as long ago as the Great Push. In dying the Spideret would carry as many with it as it could.

There was a noise behind it and the Spideret turned. A whole section of the wall was darkening and blistering. Wisps of smoke and small bright flames erupted along the cracks.

When the wall began to crumble the Spideret jumped, hoping again to win by surprise. It jumped blind, its eyes retracted and its mandibles advanced to take the shock.

Scorched but not severely burned, it landed in smoke. Particle beams cracked as it ran at random, zig-zagging across the room and into a narrow corridor. A guard facing it fired, but the shot was hurried and the Spideret moved so quickly. It bit and plunged on. Before its eyes was a mistiness.

There was a door, and behind the door a squeaking. The Spideret broke through the door and into a dormitory where slept Clarissa's little male attendants. They were crouched in corners, under beds, against the walls.

The Spideret killed ruthlessly. What matter they were defence-less? The blood lust was on the Spideret. All it saw was enemy. Two-legged. Forked. Cunning. Weak. The cause of all misery. It wanted to glut on slaughter.

Sudden consciousness of pain reached it. It felt its body lifted by a great force which slammed it against the wall. Red fog plumed in its mind, redness fretted with blackness, and beyond the blackness, the thick anchor strands of a giant silver web. It had only to reach and climb.

Latani Rama watched from the door leading into the dormitory as part of the Spideret exploded, spreading its life round the walls. She held her particle pistol with stiff arms as she watched the Spideret slump. Incredibly, after a direct hit the creature was still moving. The charge had not reached the seat of its consciousness.

Latani Rama watched helplessly as the Spideret dragged itself on five legs through the far doorway. She could not fire again until the energy in her pistol built up. *What do you have to do to kill these things?* she wondered. Her pistol tingled in her hand. It was ready to fire again.

She picked her way through the mess in the dormitory. It was not difficult to follow the path of the Spideret. Its body was dragging and leaking on to the tiles in the passageway.

She entered part of the working quarters of the Xerxes tree. There were no carpets here, just stone passages and stairwells starkly lit by overhead lights. Every noise seemed loud. Latani Rama could hear the Spideret somewhere in front of her. It had entered a side passage.

She followed it down a stairwell and into a long straight corridor. Briefly she saw it at the end of the corridor. There were no doors and the lights stared down coldly. She knew this passage, and there was no exit. The Spideret was trapped. It would be waiting where the passage bulged out into a blind doorless chamber against the tree wall.

She began to advance, carefully, silently, her humming pistol held in a two-handed grip in front of her. Halfway down the corridor she paused. The Spideret crossed and then recrossed the opening at the end of the tunnel. It still seemed quite agile.

Latani Rama realized that it was tempting her to fire, tempting her to take a risk. She smiled grimly, the salute of a warrior, and walked slowly on.

Suddenly the Spideret came into full view round the corner. It was scurrying towards her. It was running straight. Latani Rama held her ground, legs braced, and fired just as the creature swerved. One leg was burned, but still it came.

Latani Rama turned and ran. She was faster than the Spideret but at the foot of the stairs she slipped on some of its slime. The Spideret was closing. The pistol was useless. For a moment she was assailed with panic and thought to throw the pistol at the creature. But then the logic of her training came to her aid. The steps were a barricade. The Spideret which could now only crawl could scarcely climb.

She ran up several steps and turned, just as the giant Spideret lurched to the foot of the stairwell. It stopped and looked at her. Only half of its head remained. Its eyes could no longer rise and lay bedded, like a cluster of dull grapes, but they shifted when

Latani Rama moved and she knew that the Spideret could still see. It was losing blood. It was dying before her. Perhaps she would not need the particle pistol. But then the Spideret's body shuddered and it reached up with two of its long legs and seized the rail and started to climb.

Latani Rama retreated backwards up the stairs and her eyes never left the Spideret. She felt the tingle in her hand when the pistol was recharged. At the top she made her stand.

The Spideret climbed slowly. The stumps of its legs churned the air. It tried to spit but the bladders that powered its venom had been destroyed in the first hit. Venom dribbled like cream.

Latani Rama held her ground. She held her fire until she could see the small feeding mandibles beneath the dull eyes.

And when she fired, her final shot was decisive. At this range the particle beam scythed the Spideret in half and it slumped and fell and tumbled down the stairs.

Latani Rama looked at the remains. She had studied on Terpsichore and death held no horrors for her, but she was shaken. She had felt the will of the beast that now lay tangled below her. *What manner of creature is this?*

Lorca of the Inner Circle pretended not to hear the called orders in the corridor outside the conference room or the alarm bells that clamoured without cease. She attempted to concentrate on Jettatura and Clarissa and spoke politely about unity and trust. But she knew the moment when the vivante cube was crushed and felt the death of the Spideret. It was a release. It was as though a screaming inside her head had suddenly ceased.

"So," she heard herself saying, "we of the Inner Circle will use our influence to calm the antagonism between your two families. We believe that Pawl will prove a competent and considerate Master, and only ask that you, as heads of the fourth most powerful Family, call upon our diplomatic services whenever you require them. The same message is being carried to all the Great Families by representatives from the Inner Circle."

Dame Clarissa smiled tightly. "As ever," she said, "we Xerxes want peace."

At that moment, the door leading to the conference room opened to reveal Latani Rama, blood-spattered and with her pistol still in her hand.

25

ON VERITAS

Songteller had no known vices and few interests outside his work. All his adult life he had spent in close consultation with fast brainy machines or in poring over small print or in riddling the complex clauses of contracts. But even Songteller needed a break occasionally and for this purpose he maintained a small boat on one of the lakes on Veritas. Being Songteller, of course, the boat was equipped with advanced communication modules and so he was never really far from his work.

When Songteller heard Lar Proctor delivering the death announcement he gave it not a second thought but continued with his plans. He had contacted Dame Clarissa and told her he was leaving and she had told him warmly that he was welcome to come to their Homeworld but to maintain secrecy. Songteller was no fool. He did not tell Clarissa everything he knew but merely hinted that there were other secrets that would be of interest to the Xerxes. He knew that his security depended on his usefulness.

So there he was, down on the jetty, preparing to cast off his boat, on a dark moonless night. A second figure, small like Songteller, and wearing a thick overgarment, hurried aboard the boat and went quickly below.

The boat made way out on to the dark lake, leaving a phosphorescent wake behind it. The waves slapped peacefully against the side of the boat. High above, the stars flickered and held their place. Somewhere up there invisible and silent in the darkness, the Way shuttle dogged the small boat.

In the middle of the lake Songteller cut the engines and dropped the anchor. Then he went below to join his companion.

He was a man whom Songteller had selected many years earlier precisely because in size he resembled Songteller himself. The man was unmarried and had no close relatives. He worked as a grease monkey servicing the shuttle and it was an easy matter for Songteller to reschedule his work so that his absence would be unnoticed or at least not seem exceptional.

Below decks the man stared at Songteller not with fear but with curiosity and awe. Why, he wondered, had one so eminent as Songteller wanted to speak to. . . .

Songteller killed him efficiently. He sprayed toxic gas into his face from a small aerosol. Minutes later, when the gas had dispersed, Songteller removed his nose plugs and lugged the body into his cabin.

Then he summoned up the main computer using a special code. A friendly voice greeted him, deep, resonant and avuncular.

"Good evening, Songteller. How can I help you?"

"Establish code XX 1010."

"That is the delete code."

"I know."

"Delete code XX 1010 has a delay imperative of only twelve hours. May I suggest you employ code XO 2121, which will effectively remove the material from my memory banks but shunt it to an indefinite holding bank."

"Establish code XX 1010."

"Delete code XX 1010 established."

"Good."

Working solely from memory Songteller began to enumerate a long series of contract codes. As each was named it was deleted from the central computer as though it had never existed. Methodically Songteller eradicated all the independent contracts he had negotiated with the Xerxes and the Lamprey. He excised parts of contracts which involved Way Rights and many of the strange little contracts which the Xerxes had asked him to negotiate with some of the Minor Families.

The work took a long time, for as each contract was erased he double-checked to make sure that no telltale wordings remained.

"Finished," he said, at last.

"Well, that was interesting. There was a certain logic to the erasures, I note."

"Yes, unavoidable. Now include this call under Code XX 1010."

There was a pause and then the computer link went dead. The call had never been made, at least as far as the central computer was concerned.

It was time for Songteller to leave.

With the cabin lights off he changed clothes with the stiffening body and placed his identification bracelet round its wrist.

He summoned the shuttle. Within minutes it hovered above the silent ship. His last act before abandoning the ship was to place a small incendiary grenade beneath the vivante.

Three minutes high, Songteller looked down and saw a plume of flame erupt on the dark sea. It turned the caps of the small waves red.

Songteller passed through the Way Gate unobserved. At this hour the Way Gate was on automatic and the Way Guardian accepted without question his identification. He was simply a technician going off-planet with full authorization.

He Gated through to Portal Reclusi.

But Songteller was not used to practical subterfuge and found himself breathless and panting as he stood under the particle shower on Portal Reclusi. He selected garments appropriate to a seasoned Way traveller and stepped outside.

Only a Pullah, its olfactory organ extended like a giant feathery fern, was aware of Songteller as he emerged from one of the remote Paxwax Gates. The fine hairs on the "fern" twitched and it uncoiled a few inches as he hurried past, head bowed and secret. The Pullah smelled fear. Once that scent would have made it swell to twice its piebald bulk and rise up on its bulgy pseudopodia like a grotesque inflated toy. Once it would have been dangerous. It could roll and squeeze, and the black tufted hairs that sprouted on its body were able to inject a neuropathic substance which led to paralysis. But now it was harmless and it allowed Songteller to pass without so much as a huff. It was gelded. And the multiple centres of its consciousness were cauterized so that even the elementary pleasures of topography were denied it. Its job was to clean gutters and gather refuse. It was good at its job and never complained. This Pullah, like thousands of its brethren, kept the walkways of Portal Reclusi clean.

Hunched in his white transit suit, Songteller hurried to the end of the deserted Way corridor and boarded the escalator which would carry him out of the Paxwax sector.

At the end of the escalator run he joined a handful of other travellers who were hurrying to leave and within minutes he was out of the Paxwax domain. He fought down a panicky desire to run. He feared the gentle tap on his shoulder or the polite calling of his name. He felt conspicuous and clumsy. Adroit at computer finesse and subtle argument, he had none of the skills of the street.

Facing him was a wide flight of stairs. Beyond the stairs were flashing lights and music, muted for the moment by acoustic panels. In time of strife these stairs could lift to become a smooth wall. He saw that there was a long queue of people waiting to enter the Paxwax Gate system, and that each person was being carefully scanned. There were many guards too.

Songteller climbed the stairs, stepped over brass lined grooves in the pavement and walked out.

Before him was Portal Reclusi.

26

ON PORTAL RECLUSI

Except for Central Changeway, Portal Reclusi was the busiest Way Gate station in the entire galaxy. At this unique point in space-time the empires of the Wong, the Shell-Bogdanovich Conspiracy, the Xerxes de la Tour Souvent, the Paxwax and the Proctors all touched. But all the Great Families, including the remote Sith and Felice and Paragon, held gates here. From Portal Reclusi you could get anywhere.

It was a great flashing satellite, bigger than many moons, and it maintained its own precise orbit among the stars. Turning with it in a complicated but controlled dance was its powerhouse, a ravenous tiny black hole, with a corona like the orange legs of a crab. Portal Reclusi, with its thousands of Gates, needed prodigious energy.

Songteller looked down into the main concourse. It was like looking down into a fairground. People milled about everywhere. Lights flashed and music poured from loudspeakers. It was a place of bustle. Hucksters of all kinds plied their trade. Tents and booths rubbed shoulders with the ornate palaces of gamblers and money changers. Here you could buy anything . . . anything. There were no restrictions. There were no police. Criminals wanted in five empires here found sanctuary, though they could never leave. Fights were common. Death was common. Vice was a way of life and churches and brothels fought an open war for patronage.

From his vantage point on the rim, Songteller could see right across the concourse. He could see the great cavernous openings which led to the Families' Gates. All seemed to be open except the Wong, which was dark. A metal screen forbade access to the Wong Gates.

In the centre of the concourse was the Living Statue, a renowned work of art and a great tourist attraction. It was a clock, and every hour on the hour it went through its motions. A warrior emerged and fought a Giant Hammer to its death.

Above all stretched the fabled dome of Portal Reclusi. This roof and the animated statue were all that remained of the days when Portal Reclusi was a rich man's hideaway. The roof was a brilliant mosaic. It told the story of humanity, from the days when man first stepped into space to the final battles of the Great Push. In the centre was a naked man with arms spread. He was enclosed within a circle and the apex of the dome was precisely at his navel. Spreading from his loins was a spiral of colour which, turn upon turn, gradually filled the entire dome. Within the spiral were segments and each segment told a story. The pirate John Death Elliott was there, burning an innocent planet. The defeat of the Spiderets, the annihilation of the Lamphusae, the capture of the Hammer-hold, and the destruction of the Limbus empire were all there. Even the humble Gerbes and Pullah had their place in the vast mosaic. The roof was said to have taken over fifty Central years to complete. As Songteller glanced up and ran his eye over the bright ribbons of colour he saw a Spideret, at this distance no bigger than a fly, patiently cleaning and rubbing and polishing.

No time to waste. Songteller climbed down the steps leading from the rim and into the concourse. This was the first time he had made this journey alone. On every other visit to Portal Reclusi he had had an honour guard which carried him shoulder-high in a closed chair. Now he was alone.

He stepped into the concourse, trying to emulate the confident stride of the couriers who made this journey many hundreds of times in their short lives. But it seemed as though the crowd was waiting for him. A woman pressed an orchid into his hands. It had claws like a crab and exploded in perfume as it tried to copulate with his thumb. He paid for it with Paxwax currency and received no change.

A strong man with an oiled bald head and a tattooed dragon on his chest pushed him out of the way as a sedan chair passed. In the chair a voluptuous youth with carmine lips leant out and winked at Songteller. Songteller stepped back in astonishment.

He trod on the toes of a small woman who was burrowing through the crowd like a rodent through straw. She screamed an obscenity and elbowed him and people turned to stare. Songteller apologized and moved away as quickly as he could.

Partly carried by the crowd and partly as a result of his own pushing, Songteller found himself moving deeper into the concourse. He came into an alley filled with the tables of fortune-tellers and the coloured banners of psychic doctors. A beautiful woman with raven black hair and a golden snake coiled round her neck and full bare breasts with hard nipples leant out towards him and placed a red dot square on his forehead.

He moved on and found himself pushed into a small courtyard. In the centre of the yard was a white alabaster slab on which was placed a vivante machine. Round the slab were stools and couches. Many men and women were seated, visitors by their apparel, and a girl with red ringlets tugged Songteller by the tunic and led him to a seat.

It was a pornographic vivante, a fantastic opera in which a young man was zipped, stormed and glutted by a tribe of women who finally bent down a pine tree and tied him between the tree and the earth. Covered in blood, the frenzied women then turned to the audience and beckoned them to join. One seemed to look straight into Songteller with smoky eyes. In embarrassment he stood, and quickly found himself possessor of a copy of the vivante tied in a gift box. Again he received no change.

He left the courtyard in as dignified a manner as he could by squeezing between the rows of stools and benches. But he was goosed as he pressed through. The flimsy transit gown gave him no protection.

Back in the street he let himself be carried along past restaurants with broiled delicacies on display and wine shops which smelled of musk. Pickled Spideret eggs hung like garlic. Tenderized rind of Pullah lay in slabs. The stamen of the Parasol, candied and packed with almonds, was ready and gift-wrapped.

*

Eventually he found himself at the centre of the concourse. He sought a seat in the sparse parkland which surrounded the living statue. People were gathering. It was almost the hour.

The hour began with bells: a staccato ringing of thimble bells as the Giant Hammer, its skin made of discs of gold, came alive. It reared up, pawing the sky and with its tentacles flailing. Its great sting opened and closed like a parrot's beak. Opposite the Hammer stood the Warrior, his legs braced and with a pneumatic bolt nocked in his bow.

The bells rang louder, the sting arched and the Warrior fired.

Skimming on taut wires, the bolt entered the mouth of the Hammer and the Hammer fell to its knees. It thrashed and beat its sting. Then it lifted on its back four legs, towering over the Warrior. He fired again and the beast sank with jerky abrupt movements until the Warrior was able to place his heel on the sting. That marked the end of the hour.

Children shouted and people clapped as though at a live performance. Songteller did not clap. Opposite him, on the other side of the living statue, he had seen two Paxwax guards who were serving their time on Veritas. They had been on home leave and were clearly enjoying the delights of Portal Reclusi before the final Gate back to Veritas.

Songteller slipped into the crowd. All his worries had returned. He lost sight of the guards as he worked his way towards the Xerxes Gates, but then as he turned a corner he almost bumped into them.

A shop doorway with a bright bead curtain offered itself and Songteller plunged in. He was in a puppet shop.

There were puppets everywhere, dangling from the roof, hanging in corners. On one wall were hung members of the Great Families. Dame Clarissa was there, her feathers tight and scalloped like a helmet. Old Toby Paxwax, minus his chandelier, hung pretty much as he had in real life.

A tall, thin man with a neatly trimmed beard came from a back room. Following Songteller's gaze, the man took down a puppet of Dame Jettatura and ran his fingers through her hair. "Real hair," he said. "You feel it. You buy."

Songteller shook his head and glanced through the bead curtain. The man watched him shrewdly. "You hiding? You safe here. You buy. I make you dolly. Make anyone. You give me the picture."

He hung Dame Jettatura back up on the wall. "Make dolly of you if you want. Five minutes. You sit in studio. No one see. No eyes."

Songteller took the hint and found himself ushered into a back studio. There he sat while the man tinkered with waxes, dies and plastic. In ten minutes the head was finished and Songteller paid for it. It was expensive.

The coast was clear. There were no guards in the streets and Songteller set off as fast as he could in the direction of the Xerxes gates. In his hands he held a box and in the box, resting on red satin, was an effigy of his head.

There were no more delays. Songteller reached the perimeter of no-man's-land and stepped on to a moving walkway which carried him up to the rim of the concourse outside the Xerxes Gates.

The Xerxes maintained over a thousand Gates in continuous operation and the entrance was busy with travellers.

Songteller presented himself to the Way Guardian and gave his name and destination.

There was a delay. Finally the Guardian asked him politely to enter one of the side offices to take a vivante call direct to Morrow. The procedure was irregular and Songteller felt his bowels turn to water. The call was already programmed and the face of Dame Jettatura appeared even as he sat down. She looked immaculate, cool and businesslike.

"Songteller, how nice to see you. I hope you are well."

"Thank you, I am well. I am on my way to your Homeworld. I spoke to your sister. She said she would help me. She said. . . ."

"Dame Rose rarely deals with matters such as these. I am surprised that she. . . ."

"Not Dame Rose. Dame Clarissa. She said I would be given clear transit. Once there I agreed to talk freely."

"Ah yes. Clarissa did mention that. She said you had some important information. Information that we would be glad to hear. I hope it is as important as you pretend."

"It is."

"Then tell me now."

"I will speak when I am on your Homeworld."

"Don't you trust us?"

"It was agreed."

"Well, I am afraid my sister has changed the agreement. She wants to know now."

"Delay will not change anything. Just let me be safe."

"Now."

Songteller began to sweat. His nightmare was coming true. He was being squeezed and he had no freedom to move. "I want peace. I want security. I have served you well. Why deny me now?"

"We deny nothing, and you will be safe. Events have moved more rapidly than perhaps you know. You have our protection. But we cannot delay by even a few hours. What special information do you have?"

Songteller gambled. "It concerns Pawl Paxwax's intended wife."

"Ah, Dama Longstock we presume."

"No. He plans to marry a girl called Laurel Beltane. That was why he and Toby argued."

No flicker of surprise showed in the pink eyes of Jettatura but it was several seconds before she spoke. "Beltane. One of the lower families."

"The Fifty-Sixth, I think."

"I see. Good. Your information is most helpful. Is that all you have to tell us?"

"Yes. I made a clean escape."

"Good. Well, I won't delay you. You need to rest. Journey by Way Gate can be so tiresome. Thank you, Songteller, for all your help. Your way is clear."

The image of Jettatura faded and Songteller found himself facing the dull metal of the vivante cubicle.

When he next presented himself to the Way Computer there was no delay and he was directed to Way Gate 49.

It was at the end of a corridor. He entered, identified himself and was showering when the doorway to the mirror room slid open and a woman entered wearing the white garments of a Way traveller. She was holding a particle gun which she aimed at Songteller, and without a word fired. The murder was quick and clean. He fell with burn marks on his chest and face.

Two other women entered the chamber and bundled the body into a standard Way sack used to transport non-perishable goods. They dragged the sack into the mirror chamber and dumped it on the low bed. Then they withdrew.

The lights began to spin and seconds later the sack disappeared.

Moments later it appeared at a distant garbage station at the edge of the Xerxes empire. Pressure built up in the cabin and when

the floor opened, the Way sack containing the body of Songteller
was ejected into space.

27

ON BENNET

The clamour of the warning bell brought Pawl from his doze. The
Way Gate above Bennet was active. The Inner Circle had begun to
arrive.

Pawl ran out of the shadows of the house and into the late
evening sunshine. He stared up into the pale blue sky and could
just make out the black speck of the shuttle descending.

Within the shuttle stood Odin, his basal sucker clamped firm to the
metal floor. He was alone.

Ever since he emerged from the Way Gate, Odin had been
sampling the planet's psychosphere. He felt the great organic mind
of the red algae and understood its contentment. It was a species at
home, unambitious for more than its proper place in the sun.
Equally he sensed the easy rhythm of the Maw as they drifted,
consuming the algae, processing them in their vast crucibles and
ejecting nutrients which the living algae fed on.

As the shuttle lowered, Odin focused his mind on the small
island. It teemed with life. The birds and insects were a glaze of
gleaming motes. Odin was aware of Pawl but shunned direct
experience of the man's mind. Odin could feel a latent power in
Pawl and feel his ignorance too. Concentrating, he could even
detect where Pawl had walked, for there the grass was incandescent.
Odin turned his mind away and listened to the simple chatter of
the sheep.

Through a bird's eyes Odin could study Pawl. He saw him
standing, shading his eyes as he looked upwards. He saw Pawl's

long hair blowing in the wind. He saw Pawl raise his hand and wave to the descending shuttle.

For a brief moment Odin allowed himself a glimpse of Pawl's mind. It was like a mirror reflecting the sun. Odin perceived the singularity of Pawl and threw the shutters up.

The bird began to labour. It had food in its crop which it needed to disgorge. It had young ones with gaping mouths. Odin released the bird and it flapped clumsily for a few moments before flying away to the neighbouring woods.

The shuttle settled and Pawl strode towards it through the long grass. When the doors did not open he banged with his fist on its side.

Within, Odin knew he must be careful. He had seen enough of Pawl to know something of his power. For protection, Odin built a symbolic barrier about him; all the symbols were drawn from his nature.

The shuttle wall cracked open and lowered to the ground. Warmth, the evening sunlight, and sweet air swept in. Standing waiting, like a figure in a portrait, was Pawl Paxwax with uncoiled hair, eyes like flint and crooked awkward legs.

Here is what Pawl Paxwax, standing in the sunlight, saw as the shuttle opened. It was dark inside but something was moving, shuffling forward. . . .

Then it seemed to Pawl as though the whole of the shuttle brightened. It began to glow and then blaze. The hole in its side shone like a beacon and yet he was not blinded. It became a wave of sea water, green and glossy and foam-capped, which broke towards him but never became any larger. He saw the wave rear and hunch and turn on itself silently and crash into a million splinters of light which spun away from him.

Momentarily, in those spinning particles of light, Pawl saw his own face and then a voice spoke to him. "I am Odin, sent to help you." The light evaporated and Pawl found himself staring at a small stunted creature in black with stumpy raised arms and the familiar sardonic mask of the Inner Circle.

Pawl opened his mouth to speak but a sudden tiredness overwhelmed him. It was like a blow to the body and Pawl staggered back, away from the gaping mouth of the shuttle. One thought was in his mind: rest, sleep, relief from the bone-weariness which threatened to buckle his legs. He wanted to curl up there on the grass.

But something held him and lifted him up. He stumbled back to the house, to the door, to the small flight of steps. He climbed, pulling his body up with his arms.

In his room he turned and tottered to his bed and collapsed, face down on the cover. Merciful darkness covered him.

Here now is what Odin felt in those few brief moments of contact. He filtered Pawl's presence until he could only perceive him as patterns of colour. Pawl became a whirlpool of light. There was hardness and softness. Brilliance and darkness. Close-banded energy. Odin had rarely encountered such contradiction in one small being. He saw raw emotion flow into the air like a fountain of fire. Such emotion was overpowering. It was too much for a careful Gerbes.

The contact became painful. Odin felt his power begin to slip. The whirlpool was drawing him out. He sought for weakness. Saw Pawl's tiredness and magnified it. He tied a cowl of thought above Pawl and watched as Pawl's power began to wane.

When the man stumbled, Odin guided him home. He supported him and led him to his place of rest.

When Pawl slept, Odin withdrew, quivering and dry.

Oils erupted on his soft skin and trickled down his whole trunk. Sensitive to the small creature's needs, the black garment constricted about him, preserving his vital moisture.

Odin waited. He was not a strong creature, and the effort of sustained telepathic contact in the absence of gentle response left him withered and old. Nowhere on Pawl's world was there balm. How unlike his own world, where bands of energy, springing from the rocks and the crests of waves, swarmed like snakes of silver light and no creature who was aware ever felt alone.

Odin felt desolate, and deep within him his "stone" throbbed and chafed.

He waited. Only time could heal. He would become strong again. Perhaps in time he would learn to draw strength from Pawl.

Time passed.

Evening gathered and shadows crept across the long grass. Eventually, when the dew was gathering, Odin moved. He relaxed

the tension in his great central muscle. He lifted the lip of his basal
sucker and rose up on fine red tendrils which rippled as he glided
down the exit ramp.

He drank from the rich grass, and then he sought sanctuary. He
sensed the shape of the house and entered. He glided down
corridors and was aware of the central staircase which led upwards
to where Toby lay. Stairs were difficult and Odin made his way
slowly, lowering his centre of gravity and feeling for each step with
the lip of his sucker.

He avoided the passage which led to Toby's rooms and pressed
on higher. He felt age in the stones about him. Thousands of years
had elapsed since the mason's hands shaped these hard slabs. He
found a circular room with small high windows. The floor was cool
and damp and here Odin settled. He hunkered down and his black
gown gathered on the floor.

Secure, he contacted the shuttle and liberated it.

The shuttle rose and began to ferry members of the Inner Circle
down to the ground. It worked all night. Soon the whole of Pawl's
rambling house was alive with parties of dark figures. All had their
jobs.

28

ON MORROW

Dames Clarissa and Jettatura were dining alone. The circular table
which separated them was piled high with fruit but neither sister
seemed interested in eating. They were preoccupied. Clarissa toyed
with the spread flesh of a peach and Jettatura tapped her two-
pronged fork on the side of the plate.

On a small silver tray close to the table lay the crushed remains
of the vivante cube.

"Let us grant," said Clarissa, speaking for the first time after
several minutes of silence, "that the activities of that Spideret do

seem to have purpose. It still does not follow that the Inner Circle
are aware of our plans. I think the presence of Lorca and her
obvious friendliness demonstrate that. She saw nothing . . . well,
almost nothing. And what she did see we explained."

"You place a great value on coincidence," replied Jettatura. "I
mean, I can accept the spider thing killing Lapis. Who knows what
goes on in their strange minds? But the vivante cube? That argues
a wholly different intention. It is almost as if it was instructed."

Clarissa smiled a wintry, tired smile. "Such things are not
unheard of. Ceremony takes many forms. In some cultures images
are given the same respect as the original object. Don't ask me
why, just accept that this is so. The Spideret, following some logic
of its own, for they are creatures steeped in ceremony, chose to eat
Lapis. Following the logic it also had to consume the image."

"But it didn't, it crushed it."

Clarissa threw her knife down. "Jettatura, you are sometimes so
literal-minded. Crushed, consumed, it amounts to the same thing.
Understand the ceremony."

"I don't."

They stared at one another tight-lipped across the table. "Well
then," said Clarissa, "what do you propose? That we abort? Drop
the plans that have taken years of youth and care to put together?
That we withdraw? Tell the Lamprey to suck eggs?"

"No," replied Jettatura, "I say we attack now. Forget any fine
plans. Strike while we still have advantage."

"And I say no."

"What do we gain by waiting?"

"Jettatura, the Great Families are jumpy now. The moment we
move, unprovoked, they will ally against us."

"So what? If we move quickly the prey will be dead before they
can take action, and the Families are not sentimental."

"The Shell-Bogdanovich Conspiracy have already put their Gates
on alert. The Wong have put up the shutters."

"Ha. The Wong are watching the tide and as for the Shell-
Bogdanovich . . . fat old Helium calls an honour roll whenever he
wants to feel important. He has smelled something in the wind,
that I grant you, but believe me, Clarissa, when the grapes are
crushed he will drink the wine with the rest of us."

"Well, you are right about that," conceded Clarissa.

"So why delay?"

"We yet have one major . . . nay, massive advantage."

"What?"

"You told me yourself. Songteller's news. The Beltane girl of the Fifty-Sixth."

"Yes, well, the boy's a stupid headstrong fool. He will learn sense."

"He will not. He will defy the Code. He will offend the Eleven. The Eleven will unite against him and we will strike first. We will strike with authority."

"Ha."

"Don't mock a moral advantage."

"Ha."

"What do we really want? Territory? Not really: we want to see the Paxwax humbled. We will take from them what is our right. We will disperse their Empire. But with style. I see it so clearly now. So clearly."

"And if he doesn't declare himself for this Beltane woman, what then? What if he reverts to Dama Longstock?"

"He won't. You see, Jettatura, I have been studying Pawl Paxwax. He is a strange man but I think I can read him. In his heart he *wants* to attack the Eleven. He places his emotions above the Code. There is a rebel in him, as there was in his mother, and it will bring his house down about his ears. Be calm, Jettatura – you are normally good at that. In this, be ruled by me."

29

ON BENNET

While Pawl slept and Odin stooped, the members of the Inner Circle were at work. They searched every inch of the grounds and opened every room and dome and closed passageway. They clambered down shafts deep below the main buildings and came to where the main power packs glowed. They climbed on the walls and roofs, noting damage and weaknesses. They attended to Toby

Paxwax, cleaning and dressing him and preparing him for burial. They clucked over the ancient vivante transmitter, wondering that it still functioned at all. One member threw back its sleeves and revealed ropy tentacles. With these it cracked open the wall above the tank which contained the Pandora snails. It reached into the orange broth and removed them one by one, placing them carefully in a large cupped box which it then sealed and carried out to the shuttle for transport. The rats it set free.

As the general state of the Homeworld was revealed, technicians were called in. They Gated through with their equipment and shuttled down to the ground.

Gradually, as the night wore on, parts of the house began to come alive. Old cables were stripped and dragged outside. New cables were laid. A warning was called as power was fed into the staircases and walkways. They lurched. Some stopped with a grinding. Others squealed and then began to flow. Picture walls flickered and then became solid and glowed with colour. Light spangled the outside walls and brightened the walkways and court-yards. So much needed to be done. Centuries of neglect were revealed. Everything was catalogued. Everything was noted.

The headquarters for the Inner Circle operation was the vivant-ery, a spacious room filled with narrow shelves. On the shelves stood thousands of dusty vivante cubes. They contained the history of the Paxwax, almost back to the time of the Great Push.

Seated at a portable vivante was the leader of the Inner Circle technical team. She had discovered the original plans prepared by Sceptre Paxwax and she pored over them, deciphering the inten-tions of the original architects.

Dawn came and passed.

Music blared and was then cut short. Water gurgled and then spurted in the herb enclosures. Dry soil soaked it up. In the Combat Chamber, the images of different worlds flitted about the walls. In dusty corners, Spiderets with plastic legs stretched and scuttled.

During all this Pawl slept.

Once he woke briefly when the lights in his room blinked on and off in rapid succession. Odin stirred at that moment, for he had created a psychic bridge with Pawl, and he transmitted thoughts of warmth and comfort and love, and Pawl rolled over, muttered to himself and slept again.

*

Hours later he came fully awake and sat up. He could hear sounds all about him. He jumped out of bed and looked through his window. In the courtyard a team of black-robed members of the Inner Circle were busy pruning the trees and lopping down the branches which rested against the walls of the buildings. Others were on the roof adjusting the giant vivante aerial.

What the – ? thought Pawl. He shook the sleep from his head, and stretched. While he was mystified, he also could not ignore a massive hunger that was gnawing at his inside.

He pushed open his door and came face to face with the glimmering mask of a member of the Inner Circle who was busy tearing down some of Toby's secret wiring.

It was hard to tell who was the more surprised, but the representative of the Inner Circle stopped his work and beckoned him and then led him down to where the flow ways poured in the corridors like molten glass. Gliding together, the member of the Inner Circle led Pawl to the vivantery and ushered him through the door.

Pawl was just too late to catch sight of the face of the Inner Circle architect, for she replaced her mask as he entered.

"What is happening? Who are . . . ?"

"Repairs. Necessary repairs." The voice was thin and nasal but easily understood for all that. "We began work immediately."

"Who are you?"

"Isn't that obvious?"

"Yes, but. . . ."

"There is much to be done."

Pawl stared out through one of the low vivantery windows. He could see the pink side of a dome. Creatures were straddled there, mending holes with long sheets of pink laminate.

"Who is in charge? I demand. . . ."

"I am in charge of technical repairs. But there is another who is in charge of everything else."

"Who is this other?" asked Pawl, but the member of the Inner Circle only shrugged.

"We are very busy. Would you like me to show you some of the repairs?"

Pawl nodded and then shook his head. "Yes and no. I want to eat first."

The member of the Inner Circle tapped the vivante keys and whispered something in a language that Pawl could not understand.

Then the pale mask turned to him. "Food coming now. You eat, then we go take a look."

The food was acceptable. Fruit, eggs and a sticky porridge. Pawl would have eaten raw meat, he was so hungry. But as he chewed and swallowed, Pawl had the strange sensation that he was being watched. The architect had her back to him and was busy tracing nodal energy points. She paid no attention to him. Several times Pawl glanced over his shoulder, but of course there was no one there.

High above him, in the damp circular room, Odin stretched and coiled the fibres which covered his body. Odin had followed Pawl and observed his reactions. Odin was deliberately allowing Pawl to feel his presence, in the same way that a trainer gradually allows an unbroken horse to become aware of weight on its back. Soon Odin would have to make himself known to Pawl, but not yet. Not yet.

"Do you know my brother Pental?" asked Pawl, wiping his lips.

"I have seen him," answered the architect, sitting back.

"And?"

"And what? He is not here. He is a full member of the Inner Circle. He no longer has dealings with Families and such."

"I thought he might have come."

"He is no longer interested. Do not think about Pental. You are the Master of Paxwax. *You* must think about the future."

"Mmm. Why are you helping me? I mean, don't think I'm not grateful, I am. But why?"

"We of the Inner Circle have been watching you for some time. We want to give you every help we can. We do not want to see war among the Families. Now, if you are finished, I will take you exploring."

Together they wandered through the buildings. Everywhere there were teams of workers.

"You need to get new humans here. We will get things going. But then we will depart."

They entered an old part of Sceptre Paxwax's Folly. They faced a quadrangle of moist soil. A diseased orchard had been torn up. New trees, apple, plum and pear, were already on their way.

"Have you given any thought to where you would like to live,

Master of Paxwax? A master needs a home. You can't live in that
stinking little room. Besides, it is already being pulled down . . .
the walls were rotten."

Pawl looked about. Peeping above a garden wall he could see
the top of the Red Tower. Sceptre Paxwax had lived there at the
height of the Paxwax glory. "I would like to live in the Red
Tower," said Pawl.

"Curious," said the architect. "That was my guess. I have already
begun the renovations."

Later, as the sun was beginning to set, they re-entered the old
building.

"We have prepared a room for you for the time being. It is not
grand, but it has everything you will require." The architect threw
open the door to what had once been, as Pawl remembered, the
main dining room. There was a long polished table made from the
trunk of a single tree. To one side was a bed and the grandfather
clock. At the far end of the room a fire winked in the grate. It was
a real fire and its light danced round the walls. Lying in front of the
fire was Punic; one of its legs was trembling.

"There is little we can do for the dog, I am afraid. All its circuits
are deteriorating."

As Pawl entered Punic lifted its head and its tail thumped on the
floor, but it did not rise.

In a corner was a brand new vivante. "We considered this an
essential piece of equipment. I do not know how your father
managed with the old one. It is now junk. Everything is connected
up. I think you will have a busy evening, Master Pawl. There
are many calls awaiting your attention." The architect began to
withdraw. "I will leave you, Master Pawl. I hope we do not disturb
you with our noise. We shall be working all night. Oh, and
tomorrow you must bury your father."

The door closed.

Immediately Pawl inspected the room, moving chairs, glancing
into alcoves, peering under the table and the bed. Again he had
the uncanny feeling that he was being watched.

But he found nothing.

On a small table by the fire stood a decanter of Seppel juice and
a glass. Pawl whispered a word of gratitude to whichever member
of the Inner Circle had thought to supply him with this comfort.
He drank and warmed himself at the fire. A gust of wind rumbled

in the chimney. Outside the walls the weather was returning to its
normal pattern and the whole of Bennet Island was becoming
subject to the natural seasons of the planet. It was early spring.
Winter was still in the night air.

Pawl eyed the vivante. Above its dark plate glowed a misty
green shower of particles. He drank one more glass of Seppel
juice, throwing his head back and downing the drink at one gulp,
and then he settled in front of the machine.

The priority calls were arranged in order.

First and most urgent was a call from Veritas.

Songteller was dead. Pawl saw the remains of his small boat,
burned right down to the waterline. He saw the charred remains of
the body and the bright identity disk. He spoke to the chief security
guard on Veritas and the man seemed frightened. Pawl heard
himself say, "Songteller must be given every honour. I shall visit
Veritas myself. Meanwhile, let standing orders prevail. All dealings
with the Paxwax Empire are frozen. There is no danger to the
Paxwax. Tell everyone." He saw the man relax. Orders were again
being given. The man saluted and then his image faded.

It took Pawl a long time to accept the news: Songteller dead.
Pawl felt neither regret nor worry. In some ways he was glad.
Songteller had known about Laurel. *Perhaps it is all for the best,* he
thought, *but I wonder how I shall conduct the Paxwax without him.*

He could not dwell on that thought.

Other messages were demanding his attention. Pawl noticed that
second priority was given to the Xerxes.

Now, I wonder what the ladies want? he thought. *I must prepare
myself for them.*

30

ON MORROW

"Rose is sick again. She is in buoyancy now. She worries so much. All this. . . ." Dame Clarissa spread her hands to suggest everything. "She was never strong, even as a girl."

High above, Jettatura did not reply but took the bar of her trapeze firmly in her strong hands and eased herself off her platform. She swooped down, white hair streaming, and her toes cut the air a few feet above Clarissa's head. At the height of her swing she drew herself up on the bar until she could balance on her hips, and in this position, like a swallow, she flew down and back up to her platform.

Though she affected a lack of interest, Clarissa had to admire Jettatura's style: her trim elegance, her firmly-shaped body revealed by the close-fitting leotard. The different temperaments of the two sisters were revealed in so many ways. Where Clarissa communed with her ancestors, Jettatura sought the solitude of her gymnasium. Where Clarissa disliked exercise of any kind, Jettatura would push her body to the limit. Clarissa loved to lie in a rose-dew pool where she could float with her feathers spread; Jettatura took joy from the particle shower and she never allowed anyone to touch her hair. *The baroque and the classical, two approaches to reality. But where does that leave Rose?* wondered Clarissa.

Jettatura prepared to swing again.

"Will you come down off that thing. I want to talk to you about Rose. I am worried about her."

Jettatura took hold of a rope, swung free, and with her legs round the rope slid slowly down to the floor.

"Very well," said Jettatura, reaching behind and scooping up her hair. She coiled it and secured it with a three-pronged pin. "We will talk in my audience room, but I am not happy at being interrupted . . . for whatever reason."

*

The room was of polished wood, bright and clean, the colour of honey. There were no carpets and no wall-hangings, just the grain of the wood.

They sat at polished chairs on opposite sides of a smooth circular table. *More like enemies than sisters*, thought Clarissa.

"Is the child inside her well?" asked Jettatura.

"Seems to be."

"Mm, well I think we ought to take it out, now, before it comes to any harm. It would be much safer in the artificial womb."

"Rose would. . . ."

"Rose would have no say in the matter. She is silly enough as it is and is getting sillier by the day."

"The rules of our family are quite clear: all leaders must be natural born."

"Rules were made to be broken. Look at you. You were premature by weeks. They used forceps to drag me into the world and I think mother's labour with Rose . . . well I think it was the main thing that killed her. Do you remember how she looked? Do you? Her head going back and forth and slamming into the pillow . . . and all that blood and the sweat. Is it worth it? For what? And when she saw that little bulgy-eyed. . . ."

"Jettatura," snapped Clarissa, "I forbid you to speak like this."

"Well. Well, who would have guessed that that deformed creature would be the only one with an active womb."

The two sisters stared at one another. "Do you . . . do you still keep trying?" asked Clarissa finally.

"Of course. But I am told my ovaries are like walnuts. And you?"

"Yes, but I have come to dread the implantation. I am told the sperm is live but . . . well, I am older than you and I do not wait for miracles." Clarissa stood up.

"I think we need to take action about Rose. For all our sakes," said Jettatura.

"But we will wait a few more days. Meanwhile, try not to put any pressure on her. No bullying. Try to be warmer, gentler."

"Very well."

In the room a soft bell started to chime and both sisters looked up in surprise. The bell was to announce an incoming call. Partitions in the ceiling slid back silently and the local vivante machine lowered.

"If that is the Lamprey again tell them, tell them. . . ." Clarissa

sought in her mind for the words she would like to tell the
Lamprey. "Tell them to have a bath and then I'll speak to them."

But it was not the Lamprey. Holding in the vivante space was
the star emblem of the Paxwax.

In all the excitement with the Spideret and Songteller, and then
the concern about Rose, Clarissa had completely forgotten the call
she had placed to Pawl. It seemed an eternity ago. It belonged to a
different age. She was not prepared. Her bright red feathers began
to lift.

"Calm yourself," said Jettatura. "Remember he knows nothing."
She stepped to one side of the vivante, out of its range of vision.
"Handle it with grace. Just wish him well. Tell him we long for a
new order." The room darkened.

Clarissa stroked her feathers and they settled. She sat more
upright and slightly turned. She touched the controls.

The vivante came alive. A million small silver worms crawled
and then Pawl's sharp features appeared. He stared out at Clarissa,
unsmiling.

"Greetings to you, Dame Clarissa of the Xerxes de la Tour
Souvent. You have a priority call to my Homeworld. I am replying
to that call."

Whatever Dame Clarissa was expecting, it was certainly not this
calm and self-possessed young man who now spoke to her.

Pawl had been busy since receiving the call from Veritas. A
particle shower had brought colour to his cheeks and toned his
muscles. He had changed his clothes and now wore a dark blue
hunting jacket with high collar, tight wrists and loose sleeves. Over
his shoulders was the Paxwax emblem, glowing like water-gold.
His long dark hair was plaited into a crown of snakes and the ropes
of hair were held in position by two long silver pins. A fleck of
make-up to the sides of his eyes made his eyes seem more
prominent. The eyes which stared out at Clarissa were golden like
the eyes of a lion. Though Clarissa had seen pictures of Pawl, she
was wholly unprepared for the animal vigour which now confronted
her. It seemed that at any moment he might lean forward through
the vivante space and touch her. It was impossible, of course, but
the thought made her recoil.

"Oh. Yes, thank you for returning the call. We wished, all of us,
to congratulate you on becoming Master. We hope that our families
can work together."

"Thank you, Dame Clarissa, I am grateful for your good wishes.

I too hope we can work together in trust. But was that all you wished? The coding made me think it was a matter of life and death."

Pause. Silence. Clarissa could think of nothing to say. Jettatura was signalling something from the gloom beyond the vivante. "We . . . er . . . we must have made a mistake," she heard herself say and cringed inwardly at the weakness of her reply. "We certainly did not want to worry you at this time of great stress. We will not detain you longer." Clarissa reached for the cut-off switch.

"Wait," said Pawl. Clarissa looked at him in astonishment. He was leaning forward. "Before he died my father spoke to me about his dealings with your family. For the distrust between us, I think he was much to blame. I do not have the same mind as my father. I hope we can begin a time of friendship. Please think carefully about that. Goodbye."

It was Pawl who broke the contact.

The bridge which linked them across space/time evaporated. Clarissa stared surprised as Pawl's face faded.

"So that's him," said Jettatura, coming round the machine. "He looks like an animal. God alone knows what the Paxwax have bred with in their time. There is no purity there. Did you notice those jeering eyes?"

"Yes, I noticed them," said Clarissa. The vivante console folded itself and began to retract into the roof and the room brightened. "An animal, like you say. He has his father's arrogance. He may even be more dangerous than his father. Toby was a fool. This young man is not. It will be a pleasure to lift that Paxwax emblem from his shoulders. I am glad to have seen him."

"Indeed."

"Was I all right?"

"Elegant and enigmatic. Two of your virtues." Jettatura gave a little laugh. She seemed to be in high spirits. "Still," she continued, "I am glad that Rose was not here. I can believe that the Paxwax youth has a certain charm. A naïveté. Rose responds to such." She laughed again, a bright tinkling laugh. Clarissa looked at her in surprise. "Oh, you have to admit, Clarissa, that we Xerxes do act with a certain high drama. I see that he is wilful and our victory will be so much sweeter if our enemy traps himself. Do we have any vivantes of his lady love?"

"We can obtain them."
"We must."

31

ON BENNET

Pawl sat at his vivante for a long time after the call had ended.
Alarm bells were ringing in his head. He had noticed Clarissa's
nervousness and the way she glanced to the side as though looking
for support. There had been someone else with her, Pawl guessed.
And why had she lied to him about the priority of the call?

Something strange *was* going on.

Dame Clarissa Xerxes de la Tour Souvent.

Pawl had never seen the lady close-to before. She was somewhat
younger than he had expected and there was a distinct glamour
about her. Perhaps it was the feathers . . . *I wonder what it would
be like to stroke them?* Pawl smiled at the impropriety of the
thought, and then dismissed it.

There was much to be done.

For the next several hours Pawl sat at the vivante and communi-
cated with the Masters of the Great Families. He introduced
himself, tried to be pleasant, fielded questions and generally gave
the impression that all was well with the Paxwax. His only surprise
was that Helium and Clover of the Shell-Bogdanovich Conspiracy
were more friendly and open than he had expected. Obviously
they had held his father in high regard.

Finally he pushed the vivante away from him and stretched. His
back was stiff and his shoulders felt as though he had been carrying
sacks of lemons. He lifted the Paxwax emblem off his shoulders
and placed it in its black wooden box.

Enough of being a Master for one night.

He took a brief tour round the house, skimming on the flow

paths which ran like liquid marble, and then returned to his room.
He felt much more relaxed. There was one more call he wanted to
make. He dragged the vivante across the floor and set it up by his
bed. Then he lay down and tapped out the co-ordinates for the
Beltane Homeworld.

Pawl watched the vivante space become smoky as the co-
ordinates matched and locked. The space cleared and Pawl found
himself staring straight into the face of Laurel Beltane.

"Made it," he said. "How are you, love? Are you alone?"

"Of course. I've been waiting for you to call. Watching all the
incoming signals."

Pawl nodded. "I know. This is the first time I've had to myself
since . . . well, since I got back here."

They looked at one another for a long time in silence and then,
for no reason that Pawl could understand, Laurel began to cry.

"It's nothing," she said, as though answering his thought. "It's
just that with everything that has happened, I'm so relieved to see
you. So happy to hear your voice. You've no idea what it has been
like here. Waiting. I wish I hadn't been so stubborn and had come
with you."

"I'm glad you didn't. What a mess. You wouldn't believe. . . ."

"You didn't kill him, did you?" The question interrupted Pawl
and was stated carefully.

Pawl shook his head. "No, I didn't kill him. I wanted to, but
it doesn't make much difference. I imagine space is wild with
rumours."

"It is. The most incredible things. I didn't know what to believe."

"Well, believe me now. Toby died of old age and bad living. I
am Master of Paxwax and I love you."

Bands of tension which had held them apart dissolved with those
simple words. They reached towards one another and then laughed
when their faces and hands slipped through one another. Their
images were no more substantial than air.

"Lie back, silly man, and relax. Tell me everything. I want to
know everything that has happened since we said goodbye on
Lotus-and-Arcadia."

"I don't know where to begin."

But he did begin. He talked freely, letting his thoughts ramble.
He described the deserted Homeworld and the bodies he had
found in the pool. He spoke about the madness of his father and
the night he had spent alone while his father created images. He

told about Neddelia and the coming of the Inner Circle. There was something there he couldn't remember, something about a wave breaking. The memory would not come clear.

"So what is happening now?"

"Well there is an army of the Inner Circle here. They are cleaning up. Rebuilding."

"And you are the only person there?"

"Yes. So far."

"What's going to happen?"

"I'll get new people. Or rather *we* will. We're going to make this the finest and brightest Homeworld in the Great Families. The Inner Circle will help. They don't want to see the Paxwax fall."

Laurel was silent. Perhaps more clearly than Pawl she could see the difficulties ahead. "And what about the heads of the Families? What do they think?"

"They don't know. At present the Paxwax is a facade. We present a bold face. Business as usual. But I have my defences up. It was quite funny tonight, you know, talking to the Masters. All they wanted to know was whether or not I was going to continue to honour existing treaties. The Freilander-Porterhouse wanted me to take sides in their civil war."

"What did you say?"

"I told them to get lost."

"You are beginning to speak like a Master," said Laurel and laughed.

"And what about you?" said Pawl. "Have you told your father about us yet?"

"I didn't have any option."

"What do you mean?"

"He received your message. Wanted to know what it meant. He got very upset. I had to tell him about us in the worst way possible."

"And . . . ?"

"Well, things are quieter now."

"I'm glad. He will come to understand. I will speak to him."

"If he will speak to you."

"What?"

"You must see things from his point of view. He is a good man. Our family is small but stable. We lack for nothing, really. We have a comfortable Homeworld. A modest, fruitful space. We are well-placed for trade and our planets prosper. We threaten no one and have no real enemies. I know I am not a renowned beauty, but I could have my pick of a thousand suitors, all sound men, and none of them would disturb the order. My father fears change. He is content with things the way they are. He says, why do I talk of love in a world of politics? He says, why do I walk beside a man who will never be happy? He says, why do I tie myself to the big chariot, for when the big chariot falls, everyone who accompanies it is dragged into the mire. Worst of all, he thinks you will cast me off as your father did with his wife."

Pawl nodded. "He sounds a wise man, your father. The Paxwax are not noted for their fidelity. He does well to doubt." The words were meant as a jest but Laurel did not laugh.

She moved closer. Her face held an expression that Pawl had rarely seen. "Do not say *that*, Pawl. Do not say *that* even in jest. I love you beyond everything I have ever known. I have faced what this means. I know the price I shall pay. I know the risks. One day you may desert me. Men are like that, aren't they? But never joke about it. Because if I can't have you, I'll have no man. I can't help it. That is the way I am." She sat back and some of her intensity left her. "You know, if I didn't love you, I would hate you. I am glad that I am on the right side of the fence. My love makes me the strongest woman. You have all my strength."

"If you hated me I would shrivel."

"No," said Laurel Beltane. "I would die. That is the way with love and hatred. One is life and one is death."

Love had come so easily, like rest after swimming. When Pawl first met Laurel Beltane, with her delight in crazy colours, he met someone who made him, for the first time in his life, feel simple. Amid the banalities and mind-softening sensuality of Lotus-and-Arcadia, he had found something to live for. Together they had created a little corner of heaven. And now what had happened? Just when the worlds seemed a brighter place, fate had stepped on him.

"Sometimes, Laurel," said Pawl quietly, "you know you frighten me. You are so clear. So strong. If I lose you I'll . . . I don't know. I'll. . . ."

"Well, you're not going to lose me. Come on, cheer up. What else have you been doing? Have you written any songs?"

"One. I wrote it by the stream." Pawl felt for his notebook and read her the verses. "What do you think?"

"I like it. Me and water. Send it to me."

"Come and get it."

"Soon, love, soon. But don't stop writing songs, Pawl. You know, sometimes I feel that you are so close to me, in the same room even. I think when you write songs, something in you reaches out and touches me. It makes me feel warm and protected. Do you understand?"

"I understand."

Again they tried to kiss, but this time they kept their images a few inches apart. Their imaginations did the rest.

Behind Laurel there was a growing brightness. "Dawn is breaking here," she said. "Can I show you some of my Homeworld?"

Pawl nodded. He glanced at his own window. Outside it was still pitch black.

Laurel cleared one wall of her room. Behind her shimmered an opalescent light. The house was drifting past some mountainous dark islands and behind them the sun was rising. The dawn sky was a clear hard blue. Two other structures drifted with them.

"What are those?" asked Pawl.

"That is where my father and brother live. They are still asleep, see: there are no lights. Later I will swim across to eat with them."

"You'll be tired."

"I won't. I'll be happier than I've been for many a long day."

A breeze moved the curtains and carried with it the sound of distant breakers.

"Beautiful," said Pawl. "Beautiful. So calm. Is it always like this?"

"Somewhere on our Homeworld it is always like this. Just a matter of finding it. Sometimes we travel to the North where the sea is grey and black and there are mountains of ice and the kelp is as thick as your body and stretches for miles. That also is beautiful. The ice groans like cattle and there are birds with long thin wings that fly into the wind. You can see storms walking like giants. We ride the storms and when we are tired we lift the houses high. Just now we are enjoying the shallow seas where it is always warm. We are drifting with the breeze. I love my Homeworld, Pawl."

She yawned. Tried to stifle the yawn, but it had its way.

"Rest, love," said Pawl. "You have seen me through a hard night. We will talk every day."

"How long before I can be with you?"

"As soon as I've got this Homeworld on its feet. Sooner, if the going is hard. I feel you are near me. We are the best-kept secret in the universe, I think. When I am secure I will challenge the Eleven and they can roar to their heart's content. They will not shake me. Tell your father that. Tell him I will speak with him whether he wants to hear me or not. I will leave him in no doubt."

"Take care, love."

"I will."

There was a swirl of garments and Laurel stood naked before him. She came close to the vivante, so close that Pawl could see the fine down on her skin. "I love you, Pawl. I want you."

"I love you, Laurel." There was great fierceness in his words.

Seconds later they broke contact.

They had reached the limits of vivante communication. To have remained longer would have been foolish.

But for Pawl his dark room remained alive with her presence. He felt light-headed and delirious. He wanted to sing and shout and run and fly all at the same time. He wanted to call her again but resisted the temptation. There was a sweetness in the pain he felt.

Where's my bloody book? He found it on his bed. He started to scribble.

Song to Laurel

You came to me in a crazy time,
Travel-dazed and trailing my anchor,
Love, love me and never change.

You outshone the lights of Lotus,
You made the nights on Arcadia your own.
Love, love me and hold me firm.

If I could climb through space I would,
Swing on the stars to be near your side.
Love, love me and never change.

Fresh as the rain and bright as the sun
That rides the heaving backs of waves,
Love, love me and hold me firm.

Come to me in passion with strong arms
And let me lie in your warm dark sea.
Love, love me and never change,
Love, love me and hold me firm.

Words, words, words. Simple words on a page. By what strange alchemy did they take brute emotion and transform it into knowledge?

Pawl lay very still in his bed. He was aware of the chemistry inside him, his tumult.

He began to drift. As he relaxed, he imagined himself floating on water. He felt his love flow through him and thought of it as a tumbling torrent of silver. The songs were just another shape of love. In a song his love gained strangeness and charm, form and force. Like a flying arrow of light it split the dark and the shadows ran like frightened ghosts.

Pawl flew out of himself like the arrow. He found his way to Laurel. Was she lifting her head? Was she thinking of him as . . . ?

Pawl's breathing became regular and deep.

Odin was moving. It was time for him to make himself known. The small creature had drunk Pawl's emotion.

Odin rode the stairway down, undulating easily over the steps. He glided along the flow way and came to Pawl's door. The door opened easily and silently.

Pawl was dreaming of fishing. In the dream he was standing in a small boat, casting a black net out into the clear water. Suddenly a giant shape moved through the water under the boat. It lifted the boat on its back and just as he was about to fall he woke up.

He came awake suddenly with no muzziness. His yellow eyes blinked as he turned. He saw the door swing silently open. Beyond was darkness and in that darkness something advancing.

Before Pawl could move or cry out, a presence uncoiled in his mind. It was a warmth, a *thereness*, a living entity, complex and bright. It did not threaten. There was something familiar about the thoughtshape that nestled inside him. He remembered a wave breaking, but that never made a sound.

Pawl called for the lights and as the room brightened Odin advanced. Pawl stared at the small black figure in the pale mask and tried to remember where he had seen it before.

"Who . . . ?" he began. But fireworks erupted in his mind before
he could articulate the sentence. And a voice spoke to him. It was
a voice just about to break into laughter. A voice that was neither
male nor female but had something of both.

"Who are you?" Pawl's question was whispered.

"I am a friend," said the voice.

"Do you have a name?"

"Many names."

"Give me one. For a thing is only known when it is named."

"Call me. . . ." Pawl stared as red flukes began to creep like
worms through the eye-holes and mouthpiece of the mask. They
fluttered and felt the air, feeling for him. "Call me . . . this."

Pawl had no word for what he saw.

"You will remember me by this sight. Call me Odin. What you
see is me. Is Odin."

"Odin." Pawl tried out the word in his mouth. As he spoke the
worms began to retract until the mask was again a simple unadorned
face. "Odin." He tried out the word in his mind feelingly.

"Here, Pawl," came the bright and bubbly voice, "see how easy
it is."

Odin watched Pawl's emotions. He felt them like a prickle of
heat. When an emotion threatened to become too extreme, he
damped it down. He controlled Pawl's revulsion when he saw the
red flukes. Odin had to be careful for he was very vulnerable. He
controlled Pawl's astonishment. Through his voice he offered calm
and care.

Odin was a simple creature and his nerves ran straight to the
seat of his consciousness. Like most telepathic creatures he had
few mental defences and relied mainly on the tact of whoever was
communicating with him. Among telepaths this was understood.
But Pawl was not a telepath and his thought was direct and harsh.

Facing Pawl he tasted the moisture from his body and absorbed
the musk from his glands. Oils of his own flooded down within the
dark gown.

A question was rising in Pawl.

"Who are you? Why are you here?"

"I come from the Inner Circle. I am here to help you."

"You're an alien."

The word alien was like a red-hot dart. In other circumstances it might have seared Odin. But he absorbed it, neutralized it, removed from the thought its barbs of contempt.

"You might call me an alien. I might call you an alien. Among my own people I am called a Gerbes." The word meant nothing to Pawl. Another question was rising.

"How do I hear you?"

"I am speaking with my mind."

Immediately Odin saw mental barriers spring up in Pawl. Pawl knew something about mental defences. He had learned disciplines on Terpsichore. "Do not fear. I will not harm you. I am here to help. Let me help you."

Pawl looked at the small, dumpy creature. There was something pathetic about it.

"How can you help me?" he asked. And no sooner was the question shaped than there came a roaring of laughter inside his head.

"Many ways. Many, many ways, oh Master of Paxwax. I can be your father and brother and friend. There are many ways I can help you. But for the moment you must rest. Remember me." The image of the red flukes danced in Pawl's mind. "I am always near."

"Rest?"

"Yes, rest. We both need rest. You will rest and I shall watch. Given time we shall come to know each other." Odin began to withdraw. Pawl felt the voice fade in his mind. And yet something remained, a residual scented warmth.

Pawl watched the figure glide to the door and out into the darkness. The door closed.

Pawl thought of the red flukes and the name Odin. Immediately Odin was there. "Yes, Pawl. Can I help?"

"No," replied Pawl. "I couldn't help myself. Where are you going now?"

"Outside. I can feel your tiredness and I can feel the plants in your garden breathing. They are getting ready for the day. I will join them."

"Are you a plant, then?"

"No. I don't know what you would call me. I am a Gerbes. A lover of sea and air, like you."

The mental barriers Pawl had erected he maintained. He could feel no threat and, considering that this was the first highly intelligent alien that Pawl had ever been close to, he felt a curious elation. That of course was suspicious; that could tell of manipulation.

Lingering in the room was a smell of oils, a moist smell that was not quite of the earth. Gradually the fragrance faded. Pawl stretched out and despite himself fell asleep.

As for Odin, he felt his own kind of pleasure as he glided outside. He was well satisfied with this first meeting. He now knew something directly about the creature he was to be close to. A bridge was there.

He felt his way out into the grass. It was wet with dew. Tendrils, strong and pliable, issued from the sides of Odin's basal sucker and dug deep, sliding into the soil. Odin settled and fed.

32

ON SANCTUM

A Homeworld can not be reconstituted in a few days, and on Sanctum a council of leading aliens followed all developments. They tried to foresee problems.

The Spideret that was in charge of the council was emphatic. Small feelers close to its mouth wove a complex semaphore. A Gerbes, adept at translating, made the Spideret's feelings known to the other members.

THE BENNET HOMEWORLD IS NOT PROTECTED. IF WE WANT PAWL PAXWAX TO BE SAFE, THEN WE MUST SUPPLY HIM WITH THE FINEST EQUIPMENT THAT CAN BE OBTAINED. IF THE TREE IS RIGHT AND OUR FUTURE IS LINKED TO THIS PAXWAX, THEN WE WOULD BE FOOLISH NOT TO TAKE ACTION NOW.

A Pullah dilated its sensitive fern. THAT MEANS OBTAINING THE SEEDS FOR A BIO-CRYSTALLINE BRAIN. NONE OF US LIKE THAT IDEA.

WHY NOT? ARE YOU AFRAID OF ARTIFICIAL INTELLIGENCE? SOME OF YOU HAVE BEEN USING SUCH FOR YEARS.

IT IS NOT A HEALTHY FORM OF LIFE.

MAYBE NOT. BUT IT IS WHAT PAWL NEEDS.

IT WILL BE LIKE PLACING A BOMB IN THE HANDS OF A CHILD.

RUBBISH. OTHER FAMILIES HAVE BIO-CRYSTALLINE BRAINS.

NOT HIGH ORDER CRYSTALS. THE FAMILIES' BRAINS ARE IMPURE. THEIR ABILITIES ARE LIMITED.

EXACTLY. SUCH A BRAIN WILL GIVE PAWL AN EDGE. IT WILL GIVE HIM A FIGHTING CHANCE. COME ON, WE DO NOT HAVE TIME TO STALL IN DISAGREEMENT. DO WE WANT PAWL PAXWAX TO SUCCEED OR NOT?

The Spideret looked round the assembly. I'M WAITING.

One by one the aliens gave their assent. GOOD. NOW WE WILL NEED CRYSTAL BUDS FROM THE NOREA CONSTELLATION. THE INNER CIRCLE SHOULD BE ABLE TO OBTAIN THOSE FROM THE LAMPREY WITHOUT TOO MUCH DIFFICULTY. I SUGGEST WE USE THIS MAN TO INSTALL THE BRAIN. HE IS THE FINEST BIO-CRYSTALLINE TECHNICIAN I HAVE HEARD OF.

The Spideret selected a vivante cube and pressed it into the machine. Immediately the image of a man appeared. He was thick-set like a wrestler and had a tangled black beard. Tattooed on his forehead was a large black cross which showed that he was a convict held by the Proctor First. HE MAY NOT LOOK IMPRESSIVE. BUT HE IS THE BEST MAN FOR THE JOB. A STRANGE HUMAN. HE WAS CAUGHT STEALING CRYSTAL BUDS FROM THE PROCTORS. HIS NAME IS BARONE. ARE WE AGREED?

Again the creatures gave their assent.

Within minutes a message streaked across the galaxy to the penal mining camp where Barone was held. He feared the worst when he was summoned by the black hooded figure of the Inner Circle.

NOW, WHAT ELSE? said the Spideret. THE BENNET HOMEWORLD IS EMPTY. IT NEEDS PEOPLE. HUMAN EXPERTS. WE CANNOT STAY THERE FOR LONG. IF THE FAMILIES THINK WE ARE TAKING TOO GREAT AN INTEREST IN PAWL PAXWAX THEY COULD BECOME SUSPICIOUS. WE MUST FIND UNCOMMITTED HUMANS. I HAVE BEGUN TO PUT TOGETHER A LIST OF NAMES. I WOULD WELCOME OTHER SUGGESTIONS.

NEED THEY BE MEMBERS OF THE INNER CIRCLE?

NOT NECESSARILY. ODIN WILL BE OUR SENTINEL ON BENNET.

With surprising speed a list of over two hundred names was drawn up. Cooks, gardeners, Way technicians, mechanics, guards . . . every profession the Homeworld needed was listed.

BUT YOU KNOW, said a Diphilus, sparkling, PAWL WILL NEED A FRIEND. SOMEONE HE CAN CONFIDE IN. THERE IS A MAN I HAVE HEARD OF. HE IS CALLED PERON. HE IS A STUDENT OF HISTORY. A LIBRARIAN. ONE WHO IS INTERESTED IN ALIEN CEREMONIES. I THINK HE WOULD HELP YOUNG MASTER PAWL.

INCLUDE HIM, said the Spideret.

BUT HOW DO WE KNOW THAT PAWL PAXWAX WILL ACCEPT THE EXPERTS WE PROVIDE?

THAT, said the Spideret, IS ODIN'S PROBLEM. HE MUST MAKE THEM ACCEPTABLE.

AND THE XERXES, asked the Diphilus. WHAT OF THE XERXES?

THEY ARE QUIET FOR THE MOMENT, answered the Spideret. WE DO NOT KNOW WHAT THEY ARE PLANNING. BUT LORCA IS NO LONGER WELCOME ON THEIR HOMEWORLD. NO EXPLANATION WAS GIVEN. THEY ARE SUSPICIOUS. WE ARE WATCHING THEM. WE WILL TRY TO DIVINE THEIR PLANS.

33

ON JEUPARDI:
HOMEWORLD OF THE LAMPREY

That the visit was occasioned by duty did not make Clarissa feel any better as she gazed down from the Way Gate to the dung-coloured Homeworld of the Lamprey.

She and Jettatura had feuded for days, each suggesting reasons why the other should go. In other circumstances, Rose might have been the emissary, but Rose was still sick, and in any case her pregnancy precluded such a possibility. So finally Clarissa capitulated and agreed to go.

The visit was necessary. Ever since the change of plan, the Lamprey had been jittery. Conservative by nature, they were suspicious of change. They felt slighted, kept out of the centre of things, and only a personal visit (itself a rare event among the Great Families) could calm them. So here was Clarissa.

She travelled secretly, of course, with a small but powerful retinue, and all the Way Gates were closed as she passed. Even Portal Reclusi was brought to a brief standstill.

Slowly the shuttle dropped. The dun earth revealed shapes: rectangular pits, low buildings, the dark stain of irrigation ditches. There were rows of solar panels strung on gantries of metal. There were the half-buried roofs of vegetation houses. Everything was angular and functional. Nowhere was there the bright relief of colour; only the brown, the black and the grey.

The shuttle landed. When the doors did open, she found herself confronted by an honour guard of the Saints. A blind, and therefore senior member of the Lamprey Family complete with his guide and amanuensis was waiting to lead her through.

The Saints stared in front of them with the dead eyes of the totally obedient. At Clarissa's side the Lamprey shuffled on flat sandal-clad feet, his hand advanced and resting on the shoulder of his guide.

After the honour guard had stamped and slapped their hands against the generator packs of their particle guns, Clarissa was led below.

She entered an iron lift which carried her under the surface of the planet. The floor was stained and dirty and the air had an oily, recycled flavour. Clarissa held herself stiffly erect and breathed only through her nose as the lift descended.

Waiting for her in a dim cloister was Everett Lamprey. He ushered her to a stone bench. Seated, she suffered him to take her bejewelled hand between his dirty palms. Clarissa cringed but she kept her voice sweet. "What a pleasure to be with you, Everett. May your ancestor be praised that you are well."

"Joy to you, my child." Clarissa sat quite still while the blind man's hand explored the softness of her hand and wrist and then darted to her face and touched her forehead, nose and lips. "I read health in you."

"We have much to discuss." Clarissa glanced round the vast dark cavern. Thick pillars which seemed to bear a heavy weight disappeared into the gloom in all directions. Beside them stood lower members of the Lamprey Family like brown wooden statues. "Can we discuss matters here?"

"Nowhere safer. There are no enemies on Jeupardi. We are all curious to understand the change in your plans."

And this was it, Clarissa realized. Without ceremony or nicety, old Everett with the sewn-up eyes had introduced the main reason for her visit. He clapped hands and the other members of his family shuffled closer.

"We found it necessary to change our plans. Lapis died before we could make a vivante of him."

"Ah."

"Then came the news of Toby's death and this young creature, Pawl, became Master."

"We thought to strike then. A baby cannot defend itself."

"Yes. Yes. My sister Jettatura was of your opinion. I argued against it. You see, we discovered that he intends to defy the Eleven, to defy the Code. I advised that we wait. Wait until he defies the Code, then strike. Our action would have the sanction of the other Families."

"Mmmm." Everett Lamprey placed his fingers to his lips. The other members of the family whispered together. "We also heard," continued Clarissa, lifting her voice slightly, "that he was maintaining an amorous relation with the First Family. But he does not intend to marry her."

This was the big lie. Clarissa and Jettatura had pondered it carefully. The Lamprey were vicious, but they were not gamblers. They would not chase the baby cub if the mother bear were near. The Lamprey were silent, their closed eyes directed to the darkness, their ears trained on Clarissa. She continued. "Now you know as well as I do that the Proctors would not be averse to an arrangement with the Paxwax. The Proctors are top heavy and they know it. They would like to share a bit with one of the more vigorous families, especially one that would offer no threat. What more logical than the Paxwax?"

A babble of conversation broke out, but Everett Lamprey stopped it with a word and Clarissa continued in silence.

"When the Paxwax breaches faith with the Proctors, then is the time to strike, with no risk to ourselves."

Everett Lamprey gathered his rough garment more closely about his thin body. "This is news. We presumed he would make a liaison with some daughter of the Longstock." He darted his finger at Clarissa's face. "What is the name of the girl he plans to marry?"

Inwardly Clarissa breathed a sigh of relief: the lie had been accepted. "A slip of a thing called Laurel Beltane."

"Never heard of her." One of the Lamprey turned and shuffled away.

"There is no reason why you should have heard of her. She belongs to the Fifty-Sixth."

At this the Lamprey jabbered again.

"Where is her Homeworld?"

"On the edge of your domain. It is called Thalatta, an alien name by the sound of it."

"How long before he intends to make his move?"

"Soon."

"How do you know?"

"Songteller was our spy." That secret brought Everett to his feet. Clarissa was sad to let that piece of information go, but truths, she knew, could often be used to sell lies.

"You are a subtle lady. And Songteller told you all?"

"Everything. He was completely our man."

"And where is he now?"

"Dead now."

Everett Lamprey reached down and felt for Clarissa's arm. "We have talked enough for the now. You must rest. Later you will join us at the chapel for a festivity. Treasure will escort you to your room."

A shapeless figure that could have been a man or a woman stepped forward and beckoned. With a gracious incline of her head Clarissa allowed herself to be led away.

Later, in her stone-floored room, beneath a hideous tactogram of the Lamprey ancestor, Clarissa sat and pondered. She could imagine the activity that her words would have started. The Lamprey would be checking. Spies on a thousand worlds would be about their business. Perhaps even now a Lamprey agent was trying to get down into the Beltane Homeworld. The Lamprey communication hall would be like an ants' nest that has been stirred with a stick.

Conversation during the late meal was restricted to pleasantries. Everett Lamprey excused himself early on the grounds that he had to attend a vigil of the younger members and Clarissa was glad to return to her room.

When the Lamprey attendants had left, she stretched and allowed her little men to preen her feathers. Latani Rama checked the rooms for the fourth time to make sure that no listening devices had been secretly installed. She found none.

The gloom, the oppressive walls and the constant presence of dirt and smell weighed heavily on everyone. The little men were skittish and one drew blood at the base of a feather.

Latani Rama spent the long night awake close to Clarissa, and only when the bells rang announcing a new day did she allow herself to relax.

An entertainment had been arranged: Clarissa was to watch the training of a death squad. The small party moved to the surface of the planet and Clarissa found herself on a high parapet which looked down over a parade ground. Standing on the parade ground in full battle dress was a detachment of the Saints. At a signal the detachment divided into two groups. One group occupied a low stone building with slit windows. The other group took up position in bunkers at the perimeter of the ground. The Paxwax flag rose on a mast from the low fortress.

Everett Lamprey stood close to Clarissa. She could hear him whispering into a throat microphone. She knew that embedded behind his ear was a speaker. He seemed to follow the games as though he could see them. "You may start the games, Clarissa Xerxes de la Tour Souvent," he whispered, and Clarissa raised her hand.

Immediately a wave of particle fire from the low fortress made the ground shimmer. A group of Saints who had stepped out from their protective barrier fell as though sliced with a scythe.

The battle began in earnest. Dab bombs turned sections of the fort to dust. Legions of the Saints attacked over the bodies of their dead comrades.

Weight of numbers prevailed, and within a short time Saints of the attacking force were crouched under the fortress walls and tossing grenades through the narrow windows. The building shook with the detonations and the blocks from which it was made shifted. Smoke poured from the lower windows.

The Saints attacked again, hurling themselves through the

breached walls. One appeared on the roof and he cut the Paxwax banner down with one rake of his gun.

A cheer began from the Lamprey family members assembled on the roof and the cheering became deafening when the surviving members of the force which had occupied the fort were marched out. They were lined up on the roof; there were only five of them. Clarissa clapped, believing she was saluting their courage, but as though that was a signal, the helmets were removed from the soldiers and one by one they were decapitated.

Clarissa understood the charade. It was a warning saying, "Look at the forces we possess. Look at their mindless obedience. They will go where we direct."

Later Clarissa pinned a medal on the arm of the commander of the attacking forces. It was a woman. She had clear blue eyes, baby eyes, eyes that looked at the world with innocence.

"We hope the sight of our Saints in action has impressed you," said Everett Lamprey, stepping forward. "That was an occupation force. Thousands of such units stand ready at the fringes of the Paxwax."

"Knowledge of your strength gives us confidence," said Clarissa.

"They are a moral force. They will burn out resistance. They will eradicate every mark of Paxwax occupation and when the planets are cleansed, we will establish a new order."

Clarissa smiled and nodded and used every ounce of her will-power to keep her quills from rising.

At Everett's insistence they dined together alone.

"We have considered the information you brought us yesterday, my child, and we find you have acted with wisdom. Our shock troops need only an hour's warning. We are strong in Elliott's Pocket and in the Great Rim. We can isolate the Paxwax from the Longstock, Sith, Felice and Paragon. The Freilander-Porterhouse are nothing to us. But we cannot close the line where the Shell-Bogdanovich meets the Paxwax."

"That," said Clarissa, crisply, "is our region. Have no fears for the Shell-Bogdanovich."

Everett Lamprey nodded and waved his hand. "Eat, my child. Eat. You need your strength."

Everett broke an egg into a bowl and drank it down raw. Part of the albumen was trapped in his whiskers and dribbled down the front of his tunic. That, Clarissa knew, was the image of Everett Lamprey she would carry to her grave.

Two hours later she received a communication from Jettatura informing her that Rose was close to her time and that she must return immediately. It was a prearranged message designed to allow Clarissa to leave without delay. Her reply to Jettatura told her all that she needed. "I will be at her side when she needs me."
  Jettatura nodded and her image faded.

Quickly Clarissa packed and set out on her way to the surface where the shuttle was waiting. All the Lamprey had assembled to bid her farewell. They stood in a circle and sang while Clarissa waved.
  The shuttle closed and lifted, climbing up into the darkness where the Way Gate turned.
  As it dwindled in the sky Everett placed his hand on the thin shoulder of his next eldest brother. Together they walked underground. "And still I ask, can we trust that woman?" he murmured. "I fear we cannot. We must be ready, when the push comes, to advance further than they expect. Perhaps even to Morrow itself."

34

ON BENNET

Bennet was bustling.
  Pawl and Odin stood together on a low hill and watched the activity. The shuttle finished unloading its cargo and began to rise for another journey. It worked round the clock as tons of supplies were moved on to the small island.
  Pawl was aware of Odin at all times. Since that first meeting the creature had settled just outside his consciousness. He was like a

radical idea that will not go away, and Pawl had accepted him as such. Pawl had only to think of the fine red tendrils and Odin would speak in his mind. Pawl was no longer afraid of the presence, but he still maintained his defences.

This day they had climbed the hill together. Pawl knew that his defences kept Odin at bay and could feel Odin's frustration.

Unbidden he felt Odin's presence nose its way into his mind. He heard the creature speak.

"This could be the happiest Homeworld among the Eleven Great Families."

"I intend it shall be." Pawl mouthed the words, half-whispering them: he still found it difficult to make simple unambiguous thoughts. "But what do you know of other Homeworlds?"

"A little. I have travelled somewhat. We of the Inner Circle have wide access. But this much I do know. No Homeworld is happy unless secure."

"Your meaning?" Pawl had already guessed Odin's meaning but he wanted to draw the small creature out; there was still so much he did not know about Odin.

"I mean, quite simply, that your house will not be at rest until you have children . . . heirs to the Paxwax . . . offspring who are registered and recognized by the other Great Families. You are the most vulnerable man alive."

"And if I choose to remain single?"

"Then there will be war. That is the way with your people. The Paxwax will be mauled and torn apart. The other Families will squabble for bits. Some will emerge stronger. Perhaps some of the lower Families will be elevated to the Eleven. But the Paxwax will be finished."

"Does that concern you?"

"It does."

"Why?"

Silence. Pawl finally accepted this as an answer. He had discovered that for Odin, silence was not merely a way of avoiding an issue, rather it was a way of stating something . . . that the limits of a particular conversation had been reached.

"Perhaps you will live to find out," whispered the small creature. Pawl was amazed at the depth of pain that was carried with the thought. The idea arose in Pawl that perhaps there was no subterfuge in Odin. Perhaps the creature was simple and straightforward.

"You are here to protect me?"

"Correct."

"Are you protecting me now?"

"All the time and in many ways."

"Why?" Pawl waited for a few seconds. "Come on, Odin, no silence. This is important."

It was as if Odin had sighed. "I am of the Inner Circle and the Inner Circle is concerned with stability. We have watched you from your birth . . . not me personally . . . I was always humble . . . spittle on a stone . . . but the Inner Circle saw the failure of the Paxwax . . . the way it shrank, the absence of wise counsellors . . . the Inner Circle decided to help . . . I was chosen . . . I have many abilities and am, in all that concerns you, a good – " For a few seconds Pawl's mind blanked out. An alien concept, raw and unmodulated, had slipped through. It rested like a live sea urchin, filling the space of his skull. Then it evaporated. "I am a good person," Odin continued.

"In my mind I journey to every part of this wild planet. I look for enemies in the shadows, in the hearts of those who are about you, in every visitor who asks permission to land, and make no mistake, I find them. Some I have killed. Others I have sent away. None I detect can live. It is not difficult. But the greatest enemy I think is in you." Here Odin turned and his pale mask stared sightlessly up at Pawl. "If you wish to survive you must become less vulnerable and the only way to be less vulnerable is to have a successor. Your father knew that. Why are you so unclear?"

"I am not unclear," said Pawl. "And I do take action." For a second the image of Laurel flitted in his brain.

It was as though that were a cue. With the gentleness and deftness of a child sorting pebbles, Odin reached into Pawl's mind and drew forth an image of Laurel. It was a private memory, a night-time memory: Laurel naked and alive, squirming like an otter as she received him inside her.

Pawl cried aloud at the violation.

Words failed him as anger flooded through him. He sought a weapon and found nothing. It seemed as though all the air had been sucked out of him through his nose.

"Your secrecy was becoming a barrier," whispered the gentle voice of Odin. "She is a fine woman. The right woman. You should love her. You should call her to you without delay."

But Pawl was not listening. He was slumped back on the hillside.

"You sickness. . . ." he gasped. "By all that moves I will kill you for that."

"Listen to me," said the voice of Odin. "*Listen to me.*" The voice was suddenly like stone. "I want to help you. It is the foolish man who does not know his friends." Pawl sat and listened. "I will help you with your love. That is also why I am here."

"You mean you will help me against the Eleven?"

"Yes."

"Why?"

Silence. And then faintly, "Because in my way I too am a great lover."

Pawl stood up and dusted off his clothes. His first anger had faded but he still felt dirty, as though raped. He was confused. Whom could he trust?

Close to the conglomeration of buildings the shuttle was descending. Men were gathered to receive and transport the goods. For a moment Pawl saw the house as a meaningless interlocking of lives. "Why bother? Who cares? To hell with the Paxwax. To hell with the Eleven. To hell with all slimy creatures that fear to show their faces."

He began to make his way down the hill. Odin slowly followed.

From the distant Mendel Hills there came a deep boom which rolled over the land. The quarries were open again. Soon cartloads of crushed marble would arrive to surface the paths.

"I will think about what you have said," said Pawl. "And I shall watch you closely."

"Watch as much as you like, Master Pawl," replied Odin. "I know that there is nothing I can say that will make you trust me . . . and yet you can . . . you know so little of other intelligences. You are like a man who lights a lamp in a dark room but never thinks to open the curtains. If you knew more you would not doubt. You see, I cannot lie. That is the way with us Gerbes. We may not always know the truth, but we cannot lie and that is why I am sometimes silent."

Pawl did not answer. He limped down the hill. Odin toiled behind.

At a gateway Pawl halted and waited for Odin to catch up. Beyond the gate was a maze with neatly trimmed bushes. Pawl rested on his haunches in the sunshine. With yellow eyes he watched the small black-gowned creature toil up the lane towards him. Despite his anger he had to admire the determination of the creature, the Gerbes. He wondered what it looked like without its gown.

"Tired?" he called.

"Yes, but still game," came the reply.

"You say you have killed for me?"

"Yes."

"Often?"

"When necessary."

"Tell me."

Odin arrived at the gateway. "Tell you. All right. Two days ago. One came to the Gate. Said he was an architect. Wanted to land. But he was Lamprey in mind. We stopped him."

"We? You and who else?"

"The Way Gate."

"You mean you and the Way Gate can communicate?"

"In a fashion. Listen, Pawl, you say you do not trust me, but what I am about to tell you few other men know. The mechanism which transmits you from here to another Way Station is analogous to thought. So close, indeed, that I can communicate with it on a simple level. Of course, the thought of the Way Gate is mechanically generated and that is what gives it its steadiness. It lacks imagination. But it can respond to suggestion."

"So you of the Inner Circle control the Way Gate system?"

"Not completely. But we have influence. No one can control the Way Gate. Of its nature it must remain independent. But if a Way Gate becomes unhealthy it transmits its unhealth and we are able to intervene."

"So if you wanted, you could close a whole world or an empire."

"Theoretically."

"Theoretically, nuts. You could. You know you could." Pawl stood up. "Why do so few people know this?"

"Most people are not curious. If a thing works they accept it. If it works for many generations it becomes a law of nature."

Pawl thought about this and grudgingly agreed that Odin was probably right. He moved on, walking up the path, which led to a green waterfall and thence to the maze at the entrance to Sceptre Paxwax's Folly. He halted as another question entered his mind. "So you stopped one who claimed to be an architect. How did you spot he was a danger?"

"The mind cannot lie. At the moment of transition, when the entity is spread out in space and time, all motives are clear. I

ordered the Gate to reject any entity in whose mind there were
complex relations with any other Family. It is very simple. I
ordered it to disseminate any creature that had the intention of a
killer."

"Disseminate?"

"Mmm. Not reassemble. Leave in particles. Let scatter in space.
The balance of matter remains the same and the spiritual question
is nicely settled. If the intent is to kill then what matter if it is the
killer's life that is lost? I feel no guilt. Such balance is a law of
creation."

Pawl nodded. "Have many been disseminated?"

Silence.

"Damn your silence."

"It is not good to dwell on such things."

"Answer me."

"Since I arrived on this planet, I have been aware of twenty
executions. Is that clear? Is that adequate? And yet, in saying this
I have said nothing. It is all so simple, really." Odin's voice became
soft and gentle. "I hardly know where to begin. You have thought
so little. Experienced so little. Hold on to this idea. If you love all
life you must reject everything that is against life. I do not speak of
winter, for that is nothing but a sleep. I speak of that which
destroys without compensation . . . that which takes the spirit and
rolls it in the dust. Love is central to us . . . It is all so simple . . . I
am far simpler than you think. Trust me."

Silence settled between them.

Odin began to move away, gliding over the finely-cut grass. He
spoke for a last time in Pawl's mind. "I cannot read you, Pawl. I
cannot tell whether you are still angry and hurt or whether you are
thinking reasonably. We still have much to explore. You are trying
to be too strong, too alone. Give yourself time to think, and then
when you want to talk, call me."

An image of red feelers seemed to caress Pawl's face, and then
faded. Pawl watched Odin glide away. The Gerbes entered the
maze and was gone.

Pawl stood for several minutes after Odin had disappeared, trying
to sort out his feelings. Odin was an enigma to him. Obviously the
creature was powerful in ways beyond Pawl's comprehension.
Equally obviously, the creature was sensitive and seemed to have a
deep feeling for life. Pawl wanted to trust Odin, wanted to believe

him, and yet . . . the creature was an alien, subject to its own
instincts. What bridges could be built between the alien and the
human? *I'll find out about you, Odin,* thought Pawl. *I'll find
everything about you, then I'll talk to you. Either that or I'll send
you packing off my Homeworld.*

Any further thoughts were cut short by the arrival of Punic. The
great dog shambled into view. Riding on its back was a child.
    "Master Pawl, Master Pawl. I have a message for you." The
child dug its heels into Punic's flanks and the dog responded by
breaking into an uneven trot.
    "And who are you?" asked Pawl.
    "Adam Reuben, sir."
    "Ah yes. Your family is taking charge of the kitchen. I hope the
food will improve now. What is the message? Something to do
with provisions?"
    "No, sir. Barone is looking for you. He's very excited. He wants
you to come to the Red Tower immediately."
    "I see."
    "It's very urgent. He says the brain is ready to come awake."
    "Is it?"
    The child nodded, very serious. "He's been running all over the
place looking for you."
    "Then I'll go and find him. You go and look for him too, and if
you find him before I do, tell him I've gone to the Red Tower."
    "Will do." The Reuben child tugged at the fur on Punic's back
and the dog turned obediently and shambled off in the direction of
the maze.
    The Reuben family, five generations of them and all like pressings
from the same mould, had arrived a few days earlier. Already they
were changing the feel of Bennet Island.

Pawl approached the Red Tower through the arcades of Sceptre
Paxwax's Folly. All the muck had been cleared away to reveal a
vast mosaic of black and red tiles. The tower stood in a courtyard
and it dwarfed the side buildings.
    It had the form of a giant spiral. A long staircase wound slowly
up the outside like the thread of a screw. The staircase told the
story of the journey from birth to enlightenment. The way passed
through dark tunnels, under marble waterfalls, past enclosures
where mechanical monkeys jabbered, along the tail of a dragon,

then through the mouth of a toad and finally on to a narrow bridge
which led to the very pinnacle of the tower itself. All along the way
were texts in many different languages. The pinnacle was terrifying.
There were no protective barriers or walls. You stood, suspended
between earth and sky, with only the wind for company and a
howling drop on all sides.

So much for the outside. Inside were rooms. Sceptre Paxwax
had once held court there and the whole tower was a museum of
antique luxury.

The workers of the Inner Circle who had restored the tower had
been careful. The casual eye could detect no changes, but beneath
the tower great particle screen generators whispered like sleeping
giants. At the touch of a switch, or a shout from Pawl, their
screens could spring up, enclosing the whole of the tower in a
beehive of energy.

Anchored in space directly above the tower and resonating with
its form was a new vivante aerial. Its shape was that of a giant web
and it rippled, like patterns of sunlight under water, as it dipped
into and out of the proximate space/time, keeping harmony with
similar aerials across the wide bowl of the galaxy.

Waiting inside the tower, high in the living quarters, was Barone.
He was another newcomer to Pawl's Homeworld. He looked like
an all-in wrestler, with crushed ears and a shaved scalp and fingers
like bath taps, but he spoke about computers as though they were
animals that he lovingly trained. Pawl had liked him on sight.

"Been looking for you everywhere. We've almost reached critical. Come and look."

Barone led Pawl through the circular living room and up a white
ramp which curved against one wall. The ramp ended in a white
ceramic chamber shaped like a giant egg. Descending from the
ceiling as Pawl entered was a white vivante console. Cupped within
it was the black square of the vivante plate. Barone passed his
hand over the plate and it disappeared as though severed at the
wrist.

"Good, still just warming," said Barone. "I haven't fed it much
power yet. Now, what do you think?" He gestured expansively
round the walls.

Pawl wondered what he was supposed to see. "There, in the
trough. Can't you see? The buds."

Pawl looked closely. He had followed the building of the new
communications centre closely. He had thought the walls were just

that: walls, white and new. But now he noticed that between the surface of the gleaming plastic and the white back wall was a narrow trough. It extended right round the room.

Bedded in the trough at regular intervals were crystals, each no bigger than the nail of his thumb. In shape each was like the newly-opened flower of the white lotus. Petals were tightly enfolded in petals, each with its delicate sharp cusp.

"What are these?" asked Pawl.

"These will grow into one of the most powerful brains in the Homeworlds," answered Barone. "Perhaps *the* most powerful. It all depends how they respond. Certainly I've never handled such pure crystals before."

"Where are they from?" asked Pawl. "They're beautiful."

"The Norea Constellation. Have you ever been there?" Pawl shook his head. "Well, you should. It's in the Lamprey domain. I was taken there when I was a student. You could feel the balance in the air as you breathed. Stillness, perfect stillness. And when you looked out through the ports, there were the hundred suns of Norea. All around you. Equally spaced, equally brilliant. Fantastic. That's where the crystals grow. When they start to grow they're like grains of salt."

"Not like Elliott's Pocket," said Pawl.

"Nothing like Elliott's Pocket. No tension. No knots. Do you know, the Lamprey won't even allow a Way Gate within ten lems of the crystal farm in case it sets up a tremor. You are very fortunate to have obtained such crystals. They will serve you well."

"Why have you set them like this? Why in this narrow trough? Why not give them plenty of space to grow?"

Barone laughed, and his laughter boomed in the small chamber. "Well, Master Pawl, you may be Master of a great Empire and me only a common convict, but you certainly know nothing about bio-crystalline brains. Crystal growths have certain, very specific voluminal tolerances. Give them too much room and the cystine balance is upset. You don't end up with a brain, but with waking dreams."

"Waking dreams?"

"A technical term. You see, left to ramble, the crystals develop their own internal logic . . . the logic of minerals made animate. Hell, how shall I explain it? The crystals develop their own logic, not our logic. I saw a rogue brain once, on an abandoned station. It had broken out of its compartment and spread into what used to

be the living quarters. It had grown in the shape of a man.
Damnedest thing I've ever seen. Great white spears of silica for
the fingernails, great white bulbs for eyes. It was up on a wall and
one of the arms had grown right into the ceiling. We had to cut it
out with lasers. It must have thought that if it grew in our shape it
would become like us."

"Was it dangerous?" asked Pawl.

"Dangerous? No. It had just spread too far. You couldn't trust it
any more. I mean, if I'd asked it, 'Does two plus two make
four?' it might have answered, 'Only in an ideal world, such as
mathematics. At other times rarely.'"

"Meaning?"

"Meaning that it could no longer keep mathematics and morality
separate."

Pawl digested this. "Did it die after you carved it with the
lasers."

"Well, no, not really. They don't die, they just get simpler. We
budded it . . . took it back to singularity, and then we resold it."

"That seems cruel."

"Cruel? No. To leave it without work, that would be cruel. And
now, Master Pawl, if you are ready, it is time to put this brain to
work."

Barone crossed to a small control panel set in the wall low down
beneath the trough. He made adjustments and tapped keys, and
fluid began to pour into the narrow space between the walls. "This
is saline. Once the walls are full we can begin."

While the walls were filling Barone fetched a helmet and handed
it to Pawl. Fine bio-crystalline threads led from the helmet to the
wall. "You wear this for an hour. It concentrates the electrical
activity of your brain. The current from your brain will trigger the
bio-crystalline reaction. Your thoughts will bring this brain alive,
do you understand?"

"I understand nothing," said Pawl, as he placed the helmet over
his head. "Does it matter what I think?"

"Just lie back and relax," said Barone. "What you are will come
seeping through. Think anything, think dirty thoughts. Count to a
hundred. Look out over your world. Do whatever you want, but I
suggest you relax. You don't want to get it too active to start with.
But once it is alive, it will be part of you. This is the secret. It can
never betray you. It can never be used against you. And when you
die, it will die with you unless you order it to live on and

serve others. It will help you with your thinking and remember everything."

"Will it be able to write songs?"

"Probably not. But it might just achieve the desire to do so, and that is perhaps more important."

Pawl adjusted the pressure pads on the helmet, making it more comfortable, and then moved down into his living room, trailing the fibres behind him, and lay down on his bed.

"I will return in an hour or so," said Barone. "The walls are filled. Have no fear."

Left alone, Pawl wondered what he should think and found that he could concentrate on nothing. He noticed that as the seconds ticked past the pads seemed to grow tighter. He could feel the weight of the helmet. *As if I had horns*, he thought.

He thought of Laurel and wondered what she was doing, but it was hard to hold the thought. The face of his father bobbed into his mind and then faded without expression, like something lost under water.

He remembered what he had eaten at lunchtime. He thought about Odin and the conversation they had had that afternoon.

Suddenly Laurel was there again, pushing him back, strong as an otter, smothering his face with kisses, and just as quickly she was gone.

There was a ringing in his ears and for a brief second he saw double. Two grandfather clocks, a pair of crazy lamps. . . .

Lights appeared beyond the window. They were distorted and flowing. They formed a face. Old, dead Sceptre Paxwax, remembered from portraits, fat as a frog and with a broad peasant face that looked as though it could eat earth. Sceptre grinning through the window and then sliding away like a face made from rain.

How much of my life is seen through windows? thought Pawl, and the thought seemed brilliant and funny. Pawl started to laugh, to giggle.

He stood up and crossed quickly to the windows which ran round his room. He was surprised to discover that night had fallen. A stinging nausea gripped him and a pain which seemed to emanate from some deep recess in his brain. He gritted his teeth and breathed deeply and the anguish passed. He saw clearly again. Below him and about half a mile distant was the rectangular roof of the building where his father had lived. The courtyard where the phantom figures had thrown snowballs was bright with lights. Real children were kicking a ball.

He stared at the steady lights outside and slowly walked round the perimeter of the room. He passed the place where the external walkway crossed the window. Then he was facing the open countryside. His eyes found the beads of light which marked the lane where he had walked on that first day back on the Homeworld. Bright arc lights were blazing in the place where the bodies had rotted. They were all buried now under several feet of earth and pipes were draining the swamp. Replanting was in progress. In years to come a grove of cedar trees would stand there.

Beyond in the darkness were the Mendel Hills, faintly present as a shape in the quickening moonlight. There was a village in the hills, Pawl knew: a crazy place of burrows and towers and steep-sided barns. Gardeners once lived there, and the technicians who tended the vast network of pipes which fed the thousands of waterfalls in the countryside. . . .

Rebuilding was a joy. To create a new beauty. Life was not to be spent like some sad, frightened creature running from one thicket of worry to the next. It was for the living.

Pawl saw with a sudden dazzling clarity why he needed children. A child continues the traditions you start. A child is a guarantee that there is a future. Not just a way to hold together wealth but a way of holding together the promise of life. It was all so simple; why had he never seen it before?

Again Laurel popped into his mind, like a face at a porthole.

The hour was finished and Pawl lifted the mask from his head and set it aside. His mind was clear. He hoped that whatever communication was supposed to have taken place with the growing crystals had been successful. He peeped into the room that was shaped like an egg. The crystals lay in their bath of brine just as he had left them, but a change was taking place. Each of them was a focus of spreading whiteness, like a skein of milk in water. The whiteness was gathering into lattices, and the lattices were forming bridges, delicate arched structures. They were joining up. Activity was apparent all round the trough.

Pawl realized that reflected here was the activity of his own brain. The myriad charge and discharge of cells was here. In one way there was less, for no crystalline growth of cells could match the creative power of the human brain. In another way there was more, for no human brain could face the accumulated conclusions of logic and remain human.

He waited and watched.

After a few minutes Pawl heard a polite tap at his door and Barone entered directly from the vacuum chute. He looked nervous and excited. "All well?" he asked.

Pawl nodded. "I think so. I wore your helmet for an hour. It affected my thinking."

"Bio-feedback. Often happens. Not too unpleasant, I hope. Well, let's see how things are progressing." Barone crossed the room and walked up the ramp into the egg-shaped chamber. There he got down on his knees against the wall and studied each of the crystal growths in turn. When he had completed the circuit he stood up and beckoned to Pawl. "So far so good. None have blackened. All of them are sending out laterals. It will be interesting to see what patterns they take." He checked the vivante, making some adjustments, and the pump which controlled the flow and filtration of the saline. "No problems. Well, Master Pawl, I suggest we leave it to get on discovering itself. Don't try to communicate with it. The strain to respond might do damage. You know, we human beings carry a psychic aura. The bio-crystalline cells can sense it. In its formative stage, your very presence might. . . ."

"Don't worry. I'll leave it to itself."

"Tomorrow you'll be able to speak to it. Why not come down to the combat room? We could spend a few hours hunting. It's many years since I. . . ."

"You go if you like. Hunt yourself crazy. I've got a job to do. Some research. It'll probably take me most of the night."

Pawl was thinking of Odin, the Gerbes.

35

ON SANCTUM

CAN WE TRUST ODIN? It was the Diphilus speaking, glowing like red coals in a fire-grate.

IN THAT HE IS A FULL MEMBER OF THE INNER CIRCLE, replied the Spideret, suspended a few feet from the floor, WE CAN TRUST HIM, AND THE POPULATION OF THE PAXWAX HOMEWORLD SEEMS TO BE PROGRESSING WITHOUT ANY HITCHES.

I MEAN CAN WE TRUST HIS NATURE?

AAHHH, murmured the Pullah. THAT IS A DIFFICULT QUESTION, FOR WE ARE NONE OF US THE SAME TWO MINUTES TOGETHER. WE ARE ALL SUBJECT TO TIME. The Pullah inflated itself slightly and unfolded its fern. It sensed a discussion opening and wanted to make itself comfortable.

The feelers near the Spideret's mouth worked convulsively. WE DO NOT HAVE TIME FOR A SPECULATIVE DEBATE. WE HAVE TOO MUCH TO DO, AND TOO MUCH IS AT STAKE. IF YOU HAVE WORRIES – here it addressed itself directly to the Diphilus – SPEAK THEM PLAINLY.

I WAS MERELY THINKING THAT THE GERBES ARE SENSITIVE CREA-TURES. IN THE PRESENCE OF A STRONG PERSONALITY SUCH CAN BECOME UNSTABLE.

YOU THINK HE MIGHT BETRAY US TO PAWL PAXWAX.

THAT IS ONE POSSIBILITY, BUT THAT WOULD REQUIRE CONSCIOUS DECEIT. NO, I WAS THINKING THE GERBES MIGHT TRY TO GET TOO CLOSE TO PAWL, MIGHT TRY TO JOIN WITH HIM, MIGHT TRY TO LOVE HIM EVEN. THE GERBES HAVE A FONDNESS FOR LOVE.

The Spideret's eyes stirred as it considered. It glanced across at the Gerbes which was translating for them. The creature was stooped. Its mind was open. It seemed to be taking no interest in the thoughts that were passing through it.

The Pullah huffed. IT IS MY OPINION THAT THE GERBES IS SELF-AWARE AND MUST THEREFORE KNOW ITS OWN WEAKNESSES. I THINK THE CREATURE WAS WELL-CHOSEN. IN ITS FONDNESS FOR LOVE IT SHARES TERRITORY WITH THE HUMAN. YET IT IS UNDENIABLY ALIEN. A

PULLAH COULD NOT DO WHAT IT IS DOING. WE WOULD MERELY BE LAUGHED AT. WHAT COULD A DIPHILUS ACHIEVE?

The Diphilus glittered. I DO NOT THINK THE HUMAN WOULD KNOW WHAT TO MAKE OF US, AN INTELLIGENT CREATURE THAT IS NOTHING MORE THAN BANDS OF ENERGY. . . .

AND A SPIDERET WOULD BE SHUNNED ON SIGHT. MOST HUMANS HAVE A PECULIAR DISLIKE OF US. BUT STILL YOUR QUESTION WORRIES ME. THE LAST THING WE WANT IS FOR THE GERBES TO BE SEDUCED BY ITS VICTIM. SHOULD WE SPEAK TO THE TREE?

For the first time the Gerbes that was translating reared up. It transmitted to all of them directly. YOU DO NOT UNDERSTAND THE GERBES. IT IS TRUE THAT WE THRIVE ON LOVE, AND I HAVE NEVER BEFORE HEARD THAT CONSIDERED A WEAKNESS. BUT ODIN HAS ACCEPTED HIS FATE. ODIN WILL FIND NO RESTING PLACE FOR HIS STONE. HE KNOWS HE WILL CHAFE AND BURN. AND HE WILL STILL HAVE STRENGTH IN HIM TO LOVE HIS VICTIM. YOU, DIPHILUS, YOU SHOULD UNDERSTAND THIS. STRENGTH IS WEAKNESS, WEAKNESS IS STRENGTH. YOU, PULLAH, SHOULD UNDERSTAND THIS. AND YOU, SPIDERET, BE AWARE THAT IF ONE LIKE ODIN SO CHOSE, HE COULD MAKE YOU WALK ON TIPTOES INTO A FURNACE. HAVE NO FEAR FOR ODIN. PITY HIM, RATHER.

36

ON BENNET

Pawl was in the vivantery. With him was a pale-faced young man, whose otherwise handsome face was disfigured by a scar which ran from his lower lip jaggedly up to his ear. This was Peron. He had grown up in poverty, had educated himself and finally achieved a distinguished professorship. He was an historian with a special interest in the alien wars called the Great Push. What had drawn Peron to Pawl's Homeworld was the money he would receive and the knowledge that he would have access to a vast array of early vivantes. He had a private interest, one which he hardly ever talked about for it could have brought him into official disfavour: he was intrigued by alien ceremonies.

"The Gerbes, eh? You want to know about the Gerbes. Well, there is very little about them in the classical encyclopedias. They were never a warrior race and so did not make much of an impact on history. I know little more than their name. But you think Odin is a Gerbes. Well, well. Your catalogue system is practically useless and interest in aliens is noticeably lacking in your family. I shall have to dig and pray for inspired guesswork. I don't suppose you have ever seen it without its robe?"

Pawl shook his head.

"No, I doubt if any human being has. Look, I find it difficult to work with someone looking over my shoulder. I wonder if you would mind arranging for some food to be brought. Perhaps some Seppel juice. Research among dusty vivante cubes makes one very thirsty."

Pawl left Peron to his work. He spent a couple of hours in the kitchens talking with the members of the Reuben family and finally returned, bearing a covered tray and a carafe of Seppel juice.

The evidence of Peron's work was all about. Opened books, stacks of shelves of vivante cubes, all with spills of paper dangling from them. Peron himself was sitting back puffing on a pipe and staring glassy-eyed at the ceiling. "Quite a journey," he said when Pawl reappeared. "I'm not talking about you. I'm talking about me. But I think I have what you want. Perhaps more than you want. Forget about the food and start looking at these." He gestured to some books which lay open on the table.

The first book was an old bound copy. It was an illustrated dictionary of alien life and had been a birthday present to one of Pawl's ancestors. Some of the pictures had been crudely coloured by hand.

"This was where I got my first lead," said Peron. "I couldn't find the name Gerbes anywhere, so I leafed through this book and found this picture. Seem familiar?"

Pawl found himself facing a careful drawing of a creature that looked like a wheatsheaf. There was no face, or even legs, but the artist had been careful to show that the creature was anchored to the ground by a huge sucker. Pawl thought of the dumpy figure of Odin with his hunched shoulders and misshaped hood. Perhaps under the black gown there was something like this. It was a guess. The caption at the bottom of the picture read: *Quaam. Native of Cross Road, formerly called Calm Port.* "Quaam," said Pawl. "I've never heard that name before."

"Nor me. Anyway, I checked it out. There are only a few references. Cross Road is a dingy cold world at the far end of the Proctor First. Bad air, a lot of methane, a lot of rock and even more sea. The seas were originally mined by the Proctors for a kind of weed."

"What references are there to Quaams?"

"Only a few. They were never military. Never developed space flight – in fact, as far as I can see they had no technology. I was drawing a blank everywhere and then I found this." Peron held up a black cube. "This is one of the oldest cubes in your library. We are lucky it hasn't crumbled. I'd say this little cube is nine hundred years old. I found in it a solitary reference to Quaams under *Culinary. Seafood.*"

"Have you looked at it?"

"I have."

"And?"

"It tells you a great deal. Watch."

Peron placed the cube in the vivante machine and the room began to darken. It took a long time for the particles to coalesce, and even when the image was reasonably solid it still continued to flicker and fade.

Pawl stared at a man on whose forehead was stamped the crest of the Proctors. The man was obviously a bonded official. He was standing behind a black polished table and was slowly sharpening a knife. A voice boomed and tinny music swelled to a climax. "Welcome to number 47 of our series of cookery demonstrations: Secrets of the Imperial Kitchen. Today, Abraham Ahmen will discuss the preparation of one of the new delicacies which are finding favour in dining rooms close to Central, the Quaam." Again the tinny music swelled, and as it faded the scene changed to a wild, sea-battered coast. An invisible narrator spoke. "We are on the planet of Calm Port, recently brought within the Imperial Realm. This is the land of the mysterious Quaam. We are at the equator, but here the temperature rarely rises more than twenty degrees above the freezing temperature of water." The camera began to pan round, revealing smooth boulders like walrus backs. The sea raced in between the rocks, filling up the channels and pools and stirring the heavy arms of brown seaweed. Clamped firmly on the rocks were glossy creatures like domed pillars of melted wax. "These are aquatic Quaams. As part of their growth all Quaams spend time perched just above the high waterline, where they are exposed to the wind and spray. It is thought that this hardening process helps in their maturity. Mature Quaams dwell on the land."

The camera continued to pan and a low headland entered the picture. It was a headland of dunes. The only vegetation that could be seen was a line of low bushes like flax. The long blades of flax flexed and waved in the wind like feelers. Along the crest of the dune something was moving. The camera zoomed in revealing a shape like the letter X.

"This is a mature Quaam. It stands a metre high."

The shot changed. It became a close-up of the Quaam. Pawl found himself staring into a mass of coarse ginger hair. The hair lifted like small blind worms, as though tasting the air. Beneath the long strands of hair Pawl could see short stumpy feelers of a deeper red. They were like small fingers and gave an impression of strength. These were the feelers which Pawl had seen press through the eyes of Odin's mask.

The shot changed again. A man wearing a light contact spacesuit and an anti-gravity pack entered the picture. He was gliding beside the mature Quaam, which continued on its way down the headland seemingly oblivious of the proximity of the human.

"Mature Quaams are most often used in stews and to provide a high-protein ingredient in stock. Most favoured as a delicacy and most sought-after are young Quaams."

Again the picture moved to close-up. A human hand was feeling in the ginger hair of the Quaam. It tore a handful of the fur away from the body and threw it to one side.

"This fibre, which grows from a sub-epidermic layer of fatty tissue, is unsuited for culinary purposes and it is always discarded, though the enterprising cook can use it as the bedding for an attractive presentation plate."

The hand continued to feel through the fur and then pulled free a small Quaam. The small body, identical to its parent except for its size, rested across the palm of the intruding hand. It squirmed as it tried to escape.

"The Quaams carry their young on any part of their body and up to fifteen young Quaams may be found clinging to a single mature specimen – a ratio which should be well considered by any prospective farmer or hobbyist cultivator prepared to create the unique environment required by the Quaam."

The scene changed and returned to Abraham Ahmen, who now stood behind his black table with a set of three thin-bladed knives set out before him. In his hands he held a young Quaam. At his side was a skillet of warm water.

"I will now demonstrate how to prepare a Quaam for the table. It is important, for considerations of flavour and texture, that Quaams be prepared while alive. A few seconds' immersion in warm water will render the Quaam quite inert. The operation thereafter is completely painless. However, preparation of a Quaam should be carried out quickly, as the delicate texture of the meat quickly deteriorates."

He dipped the squirming Quaam in the water and within a few seconds it became flaccid. He quickly began tearing the fine hair from the creature and set it to one side.

"Removal of the hair while the creature is still alive tenderizes the meat. A creature will be revealed which is shaped like an X with the two lower portions joined to form a basal sucker.

"This basal sucker must be removed completely as it has a strong flavour and will taint any dish."

Ahmen held the small Quaam flat down on the table, selected the largest of the knives, and with a swift cut severed the basal sucker. Using the blade of the knife he brushed the sucker to one side.

"Now," he said, selecting the middle knife, "make two long cuts down the arm and opposite segment. The knife follows the direction of the tissue easily. The two cuts should cross in the middle of the Quaam. Place the fingers in the lateral flaps and ease the body upwards. It is white and covered with a fine oily membrane. You will find the skin separates easily from the inner animal. Once it starts to come away, ease the body through the cross-cuts. Try not to strain or bruise it as this will disfigure the flesh when it is cooked."

At the table, Abraham Ahmen eased the skin back from the white underbody until it suddenly flopped out. It lay, pulsing slightly like a new-born puppy.

"There." He smiled at the camera. "Now, there is a right side and a wrong side to the body of a Quaam, and this is most important. Press the body lightly until you can feel a ridge of cartilage under the inner skin. This should be removed with one cut. Slice cleanly and straight, using your smallest knife. Be firm. Cut right down to the cartilage."

Holding the body firmly Abraham Ahmen located the ridge. He cut and the knife rose and fell on the cartilage. The incision was clean. He prised the flesh apart and inserted his thumbs. He worked them back and forth and then limbered them upwards, prising to the surface a shape which at first looked to Pawl's eyes like a purple, mottled plum. The "plum" slipped free and landed on the surface of the table with a thump. Ahmen picked up the smooth egg-shape. "We call this the *stone*. All Quaams possess one, even the very youngest. Its biological function is not known. Some theorists believe that the stone helps in the Quaam's digestion." He placed the, stone to one side. "Finely polished, these Quaam stones make beautiful pendants."

Briefly, the picture changed to show dignified men and women wearing Quaam stones in their hair, about their wrists and round their necks. Then it returned to the de-stoned Quaam lying on the black table.

"The Quaam is now ready to be cooked. Speed is essential, as the flesh begins to deliquesce quickly upon removal of the stone. Slice the body into thin steaks. Place the steaks into a greased tin and cook gently until. . . ."

Pawl drew his hand across the controls of the vivante machine and the flickering image faded. The lights in the vivantery came on.

"Make you hungry?" asked Peron. "No? Well, I have more for you to mull over. The Quaam did not remain a delicacy for long. Here." He handed Pawl a printed magazine with the pages folded back. Pawl read. "Attention is drawn to a detail which indicates the rapidity of alien evolution. The Quaam, once favoured as a delicacy, have gradually become toxic. This is seen as a rapid evolutionary adaptation in response to their culling. In order not to arouse evolutionary antagonism, it is suggested that all alien species be exploited with caution and kill quotas be established with regard not only to the survival of the species, but also the *threat* presented to the species."

The article continued but Pawl read no more.

"Apparently, if you ate a toxic Quaam you developed swellings on the neck," said Peron. "These could result in asphyxiation through compression of the trachea."

"I'm sure you are right," said Pawl. "Thank you for your research. You have done well. Have you found anything on the philosophy or the life beliefs of the Quaam?"

"Not a word," said Peron. "The few authorities which mention Quaams are concerned only with the physiology. I must admit that it is interesting that a Quaam – a Gerbes, that is – is so adventurous as to join the Inner Circle. Especially when you consider that they have such a low level of civilization. How do they communicate? Have you any ideas, Master Pawl?"

Pawl shook his head.

On his way back to the Red Tower, Pawl thought of the days on Lotus-and-Arcadia, when he had stuffed himself with delicacies without ever thinking of their origin. He remembered bird tongues and scorched Lamphusae, scooped while still threshing and shovelled by the hundred into steaming vats.

Waiting for him at the base of his tower was Barone. "I couldn't sleep," he explained, hopping back and forth like a guilty schoolboy. "Thought I'd just wait here until I saw your lights come on."

"How was the hunting?"

"Good. Well, not bad. I couldn't concentrate. Kept on wondering how things were developing upstairs."

Upstairs the brain was gleaming.

Behind the clear walls silver plants had blossomed and were now pressing their delicate, featherlike leaves against the walls. Their branches grew into one another and swarmed round the walls and over the roof, filling the entire narrow space between the walls. Nothing moved, and each parent crystal shone like a nugget of magnesium.

Barone stood with his hands on his hips and surveyed the sinuous shapes. "Never two alike," he muttered. "I've seen brains like spires, like rods of glass, like piles of plates, like scales even . . . and now a jungle. God knows what you've got between your ears Master Pawl, if you'll forgive the expression."

"Is everything all right?" asked Pawl.

"Seems to be. There's balance and harmony in the growth. No ugly clumps or blisters. It might even. . . ."

As Barone was speaking a long low sigh filled the room.

"What's that?" asked Pawl.

"Hush," said Barone, his fingers to his lips. "It's going to start speaking. It is aware of you."

Again the sigh rang in the air but this time it had more shape. It could have been the name "Paaaaawwwwl".

"Are you coming awake?" asked Pawl.

A moment's silence and then there came a blare like trumpets, followed by the deep rumble of an earthquake. Both Pawl and Barone instinctively ducked and then a voice that was infinitely sweet, infinitely deep and seemingly very distant spoke. "Master Pawl. I am hungry," it said.

Barone's laughter hit the walls and filled the room. "Hungry! Ha. I'll give it something to chew on."

He placed two fingers between his lips and whistled as though calling a dog. Part of the ceiling wrinkled and contracted and then lowered with the silent sliding grace of a snail's antenna. Cupped in the white plastic material was the velvet blackness of the vivante. This vivante was now the main input for the bio-crystalline computer.

Working quickly, Barone touched switches, established bridge circuits and muttered instructions. A pyramid of brilliant, flickering images grew in the vivante blackness.

"What are you doing?" asked Pawl.

"I'm bleeding the old computer in your father's room, for one thing. This – " he pointed to a pulsing red sphere at the very heart of the vivante darkness – "this is your direct link to the Way Gate. And this – " he pointed to a braided helix of blue, yellow and green strands – "this is information pouring in from all round your Homeworld."

"Impressive."

"Not really. The brute you've got here can do ten times this and more, just as easily as you can read a book and scratch your nose at the same time." He looked round the egg room. A faint violet tinge had come into the crystal's light. "I've fed it enough information to keep it quiet for a while. It is learning to discriminate." He looked at Pawl and shook his head and then laughed again. "Hungry, indeed! Try and deny the paternity of your child, Master Pawl. It already thinks in analogies. It is time to give it a name."

"A name?" asked Pawl.

"You will find it easier to live with. Something short. Punchy . . . names are hard."

Pawl thought for a moment. "I'll call it Wynn," he said.

"Wynn." Barone tested the word in his mouth. "Wynn. Yes. I like it. A name full of hope."

Clearly and forcefully, Pawl thought of Odin's red tendrils and immediately felt a warm presence in his mind.

"Come and talk to me, Odin," said Pawl. "Come as quickly as you can."

Pawl did not have to wait long. Odin was close to the Tower when he experienced the call. He was enjoying the weather.

He glided into Pawl's living room with beads of rain still clinging to his black hood. Pawl did not waste time. "Odin, you say you wish me to trust you."

"Yes P – "

"Then I have a few questions to ask you. And I do not want silences. Do your people . . . are your people known to my people under the name Quaam?"

"That was one of our names, but I have not heard it for many years. It is an ugly name to us, a name filled with horror and pain and guilt."

"Guilt?"

"Those against whom a crime is committed always feel guilty. Guilty because they were there and should have foreseen and prevented. I do not like the name Quaam. Once we were known by a much older name. Gerbes. It was given to us by an Earthman. It is wholesome. I like that."

Pawl thought for a while before his next words. Finally he said, "Odin, I will trust you if you will show me your face."

"It is not a pretty sight for your people."

"Even so."

"Even so."

Odin raised his stumpy arms and Pawl saw long tendrils of red fibre snake from the armholes of the black robe. The fibres curled about the mask like threads of wool and loosened it. The mask came away. Beneath it Pawl saw a nest of worms. The worms waved as they uncoiled, flexing. Some pointed straight towards him and at their ends were small holes, like mouths. Others felt up round the opening of the cowl. Pawl reached forward and touched one of the tendrils. He expected it to withdraw but it didn't. Instead it curled round his finger and squeezed.

"That is the first time I have been touched by an alien," said Odin.

"That is the first time I have touched an alien," said Pawl. He withdrew his finger and was aware that it retained a trace of slime . . . no, not slime, his mind corrected itself, moisture only: water, salt water, tears.

"Can you see?" he asked.

"Not as you see."

"Can you feel?"

"I can feel."

Unbidden, the memory of the human hand holding the baby Quaam entered Pawl's mind. And then the knife, and the cutting. The tendrils of Odin's body retracted with one movement, and for a few seconds Pawl felt an empty loneliness and silence.

"I'm sorry," whispered Pawl. Slowly he felt Odin return. "Do you carry little ones?"

"I have three," said Odin.

Silence. Pawl stared at the writhing red mass that was Odin's face and then he sighed and sat back. "Hereafter, when I am alone, I want you to be like this. Enough of masks. Now let us talk of other things."

"Content," replied Odin and the ivory-white mask slipped to the ground with a clatter.

"Tell me, what is the stone you carry inside you?"

"Ah that," said Odin. "I think you would call that my soul."

37

ON THALATTA

"I'm going for a swim," said Laurel Beltane, shrugging off her robe. "Join me, Semyon. We'll swim out to the Guardians and hunt for Dapplebacks. We'll cook them for breakfast."

She dived cleanly into the waves and emerged seconds later, swimming vigorously towards three pinnacles of rock which rose sheer from the sea about four hundred yards from the drifting house.

They had been arguing again, and it was this which gave rise to Laurel's abrupt tone. She did not want to argue with her father. She understood her father, but still the question of her marriage was a minefield between them.

Semyon Beltane watched her for a few moments and then set his own dark-green tunic aside and with a short run dived after her.

Laurel Beltane was a strong swimmer, but her father swam with the extra strength and grace and economy of a natural amphibian. He overhauled her close to where the waves smashed against the rugged sides of the Guardians. Both trod water. Laurel shook herself, sending a shower of droplets from her close-cropped head. The cool water had brought colour into her face and her eyes sparkled. "One, two. . . ." she began. Both swallowed air and dived. They met under water.

A large Dappleback was browsing among the sea lettuce, its tentacles splayed out, gripping the rocks.

Both saw it and both pulled deep to reach it.

Semyon Beltane was first. His black hand closed firmly on the creature's back and his fingers sought the knot of nerves that would paralyse it. Its tentacles writhed and then floated slack in the water as he squeezed. Holding the creature to one side he struck out for the surface. His daughter was waiting for him. She thrashed her feet in the sea, splashing him in the face. "That was mine," she said.

Swimming on his side, her father drew away from her and

headed for the small shingle bank which fringed the tallest of the
Guardians.

"Let me have one triumph at least," he called as he pushed
through the thick kelp and found a footing in the stones.

"Ha," she said, and dived again. Moments later she broke
surface, holding another Dappleback. She had not stunned it and
its tentacles wrapped round her arm like wet rope. "Catch this,"
she called, as she shook the creature loose and threw it at her
father. It landed close to him and he stunned it with a rock.

By the time Laurel threw herself down beside him, her father
had bitten deep into the backs of the two creatures and they lay
tangled and dead. Slowly their colour changed. The red and white
dappled markings faded to a dull brown.

"You are going to miss all this when you marry into the Paxwax,"
he said. "On this world you are at home."

"There are seas there too," she answered.

"Not as good as this, I am sure. The name for our world means
'sea' in an olden tongue. Here you belong, on Thalatta. There you
will be a transplant."

"It would be the same no matter where I went."

Her father was silent. Then he turned over and faced her. "Did
you tell him about me?" he asked, fanning open his webbed hands
and lifting his wrinkled otter's face.

"I told him you were not a pretty sight as humans go. And I
showed him a vivante. I told him some of our children might be a
bit strange. And Pawl told me about his father . . . you are no
worse than him. In any case, Pawl wouldn't win a beauty contest.
But none of it matters. Faith, dad, and love. Those are the words.
You taught me that when I was a little girl, and I have lived to
prove the truth of it. Come on. Enough of philosophy and doubts.
Let's go and cook these beauties. And afterwards we will visit the
island and drink wine all day. What say you, father? You're not
too old to have a good time with your children, are you?"

From the floating house came a shout. On one of the high
balconies a figure was waving. When he saw he had their attention
the figure dived, and performed crazy acrobatics in the air. He
entered the water with a loud splash.

"Your brother is in good spirits."

Laurel Beltane nodded. "I think he and Pawl will get on well
together."

Father and daughter entered the water and began to swim slowly back to the house. Paris broke surface close to them and blew out noisily. He pulled himself as high out of the water as he could and beat his webbed feet and then crashed back down in a welter of spray.

Paris was the image of his father. "Dapplebacks," he said. "I'll get the charcoal blazing." He churned the water and streaked away to the house.

"When do you expect to be called to the Paxwax Homeworld?" asked the Master of Beltane, casually, rolling over on to his side and trailing the Dapplebacks.

"When Pawl is ready. He has a lot to do."

The father did not reply but swam on in silence.

That afternoon, after a late siesta, the three Beltanes crossed the short stretch of water to the island of Saprosma. The name came from the tall, bushy trees with a pale aromatic bark which covered the whole of one half of the island. Saprosma was the main administrative centre and the only island on the whole of Thalatta which supported a large population. It was artificial but so artfully contrived that it blended with the natural landscape.

It was not one of the "portrait" islands, or clover- or heart-shaped monstrosities which were once in vogue among the Home-worlds. This was a functional island, planned for agriculture and fishing, and located where the climate was most gentle. It raised its hills and peaks at one of the foci of the planet's energy lines.

Many centuries ago, when Thalatta was first occupied and named, it was designated a quarantine planet. Here were sent the first sufferers of Ivory sickness. At that time the planet was held by a family called Diaz, now long fallen into obscurity, but it was they who established the island and set up the vast hospital and sani-tarium complex. Since those days, and despite a change of Family, the hospital had remained intact.

It did not dominate the island but was lodged there, discreet, its steep grey roofs just visible in the hills among the Saprosma trees. The sanitarium burrowed into a hillside, rose in terraces beside a lake, and occupied the whole of the central valley in a series of lodges.

The non-medical community, who managed the island's affairs and agriculture, lived in small towns round the coast. Their houses were little more than sleeping-holes, for the activities of the island were conducted in the open air. Meals were communal in dining halls. Hotels and guest houses catered for the great number of visitors who came to see relatives confined in the sanitarium and these provided the clientele for a vast number of cafes, taverns and wine houses. Life continued in a relaxed way, like a contented hive, on the island of Saprosma.

The largest inn was called the Ferry and it was run by Milo, a native Thalattan with webbed feet and hands. When the Beltanes visited the island they always came to the Ferry. There they mingled discreetly with off-worlders and only the Thalattans knew them. Milo was the Beltanes' spymaster.

The inn overlooked the harbour. The pale water shone in the afternoon sun and small flies danced in whirligigs, riding the warm air. Occasionally the surface was ruffled, where a school of silver-sided dartfish turned in a flurry escaping some predator. But the main occupant of the harbour was a giant orange squid which made an easy living eating the scraps tossed to it by the visitors. Its tentacles could be seen, coiled among the seaweed, flexing and occasionally reaching out to take some morsel.

Beyond the harbour was the main shuttle port, from which rose the magnetic shuttle joining Thalatta to its Way Gate and thence to the rest of the Galaxy.

"Beer," said Paris, "cold beer."

"Wine for me," said Laurel.

". . . and for me," added her father.

The Beltane family made themselves comfortable in their favourite alcove at the end of the walkway above the harbour. Semyon Beltane was in the middle of a story. He was describing, for perhaps the hundredth time, some adventures that had befallen him when he was, for a time, a member of a touring circus. These were stories that Laurel and Paris had grown up with and, like good wine, they improved with age.

From performers, the conversation shifted to ways of cooking squid and from that to life on Lotus-and-Arcadia and finally to Pawl Paxwax.

"Does he really write songs?" asked Paris.

"Indeed he does. Bright, silly songs. I'd like to put his songs to music. I think a lot of people would like them."

"Tell us one," said the Master of Beltane. "By his verses ye shall know the man."

Laurel looked blank. "I've such a rotten memory. Oh. Here's

one I remember. It's not a song but it was one I liked. I can't remember why Pawl wrote it. Anyway, here goes."

> Who is that shadow with you,
> That dapple man with seaweed hair?

"Hey, does he mean me?" interrupted Paris.
"Of course not. Now shut up and listen. He's talking about the things we dream for ourselves." Laurel thought for a second and then continued.

> Is he your dream lover,
> The one who lives when eye-lids close,
> The lazy deadly lover who rolls in your dreams?
> Do you
> See his face on damp walls and catch
> His smile in the shadows of trees?
> Does he stare from the smoke that curls from your fire?
> Does he live in your cottage at twilight?
>
> I will blow in the face of the smoke man.
> I will stand in his sun
> And take his gleam from your eye.
> I will make me a coat from your darkness.
> Let him walk beside me if he can.

"Not bad," said Paris. "I liked the last line."
"He sounds a jealous lover," said Semyon. "Such can be difficult."
"He can be difficult. Sometimes he doesn't know which way to turn, like a dog with a new basket. But he is kind too, and silly, and I can usually make him laugh. It is when his father is in him that he is cruel. Then he is fierce, and you cannot tell what he is thinking. If you think it is difficult to be loved by such a man, think how wretched it would be not to be loved by such a one. There is an ancient fire burns in him. I sometimes think he is like one of our ancestors. A star-strider, one of the heroes. . . ." She broke off and laughed at herself in embarrassment, and then continued. "Sorry, father. When he entered my life it was as though every other man I had ever known had suddenly shrunk . . . No, I don't mean you or Paris . . . I mean lovers. They didn't matter any

more. Nothing mattered except him. The rules changed. Pawl made the rules and I obeyed them. The amazing thing is that he looked to me as the strong one. I didn't understand that for a while. But then I did. He needs me strong. I am the tenderness of the mother he never knew. I am the passion he needs to match. Poor man. He turns to words when life gets too much. I do not need to. My art is in my life and in my love."

"What is art?" asked Paris suddenly, and his words held a hint of derision.

Laurel sat back and sipped her wine. "It is a response," she said finally, "a response to life. Experience worked over and given shape. Experience made understandable. That's what I think."

Paris did not reply. He merely shrugged as if to say, "So what?" and that casual, mindless gesture angered Laurel, for she had taken time to work out her reply and knew what she meant. "And what does that shrugging of your shoulders mean, my fine brother? Any fool can say, 'So what?' That takes neither intelligence nor courage. The day you start asking questions is the day you'll understand why Pawl writes songs."

"Go on." The tone was still derisory, but defensive too. Paris had not expected to be taken so seriously.

"Pawl's songs help him to think and when I read them I begin to understand. Sometimes, not often but sometimes, he says something which makes me see the world differently. Well, when that happens I feel smaller and better somehow."

"Why better?"

"I don't know. Because less ignorant. Because I see more. And I want to see more. Smaller because the world, all the worlds, are so big and we understand so little. When next time you hear yourself saying, 'I understand', think to yourself, 'I understand that much only'." She held up her finger and thumb half an inch apart. "I mean, we crawl along, darkness before we are born, darkness after we are dead, pushed about by circumstances . . . well, songs such as Pawl writes, and paintings too, they help us see a bit more. That's all. They help with living. . . ."

"All right. All right. You don't have to shout."

"I'm not shouting."

"You two – " warned Semyon.

"So why can't I write songs, then? What's wrong with me?" Paris seemed suddenly angry, and his anger was in his crunched-up face.

The question stopped Laurel in her tracks, open-mouthed. "I . . . er . . . I don't know. Have you tried?"

"No."

"Well, then. . . ."

"Well, then nothing. And don't go saying to me, 'You don't know till you've tried', because I do know, I do know I can't write songs. And so do you. So save your sweetness for your boyfriend."

"Do you want to? Would you like to?"

"No. I don't know. No. I don't want to. Come on, let's stop talking about it."

"Why are you so upset?"

"I'm not upset. I just . . . I won't be made to feel inferior, that's all."

"No one is trying to make you feel inferior. If only you'd. . . ."

"Be quiet Laurel," said Semyon, joining the conversation properly for the first time. He turned his attention to Paris. "You are not inferior, and don't let me ever hear you talk that way again. Any more talk like that and I'll take you and drop you in the sea at the north pole and let you swim home."

Paris grinned. His mood was broken. "Sorry, Semyon. I didn't mean what I said. It didn't come out the right way. Sorry, Laurel."

"All right."

And there the conversation was interrupted by Milo who came shuffling along the pier bringing more beer and wine. He bent down and wiped the table, polishing away the ring marks. "I would appreciate a few words, Master Semyon. Some information," he whispered. "Join me in my office please, in a few moments." Then he was gone, head down, tray under his arm, shuffling; the image of a dejected and overworked innkeeper.

After a few minutes Semyon rose and stretched. "No more arguing, you two, while I'm gone," he said and slipped out of his gown. Then he dived into the bay and swam under the inn supports to the central building.

"Wonder what's up?" said Paris.

Laurel did not reply. Indeed, she had scarcely paid any attention to her father's departure. She was still thinking about Paris, trying to understand his attitude. His words had shocked her.

"Paris," she said, cautious and friendly. But he sat back, deliberately ignoring her, and stared out to sea where a small rowing boat had drawn round the headland and entered the bay.

"Do you resent Pawl?" she asked, her voice low and controlled.

"No, of course not. But . . . well, you are different now. You used to be fun. Now you talk differently. You're withdrawn. You don't treat me the same way."

"I'm sorry. I don't mean to be withdrawn, and I know I'm different. Listen. You'll like Pawl when you get to know him. He's a bit like you. Wild. Tough. He'll take you hunting, and you can teach him to swim."

"Swim?"

"Yes, he can't swim."

Paris looked at her with an expression of disbelief, and then he broke into a familiar boyish grin. "Swimming's easy."

"Sure."

The row boat which had come round the headland made erratic progress towards them. Seated in it were two young women wearing hydration suits. They were clearly from off-planet. The boat was being rowed by four men who had obviously never rowed before. It turned, swung in an arc. One man caught a crab and fell on his back. One of the others was dripping. A tentacle flipped out of the water and seized one of the oars and flipped it from the man's hands. The giant squid rose to the surface briefly and then sank again.

The six in the boat screamed and pointed, and the boat spun as they desperately tried to make shore.

Paris and Laurel laughed. Then Paris leaned forward. "Hey, that's them," he said and stood up and waved. The two women saw him and waved back. "Dive in and swim," he called. "The squid won't hurt you."

Their reply could not be heard. A light skiff, little more than a tapered and flattened log, darted from the harbour-side and made for the row boat. A squat dark Thalattan poled it through the water. The skiff came alongside and the Thalattan jumped over into the row boat, making it rock. Within seconds the boat was straightened up and heading for shore. The last they saw of it, the women were waving as it passed the jetty at the end of the Ferry Inn.

"Offworlders," said Paris, "comics. Think I'll go on the town again tonight. Have some fun."

"You were out last night."

"So? I'm not a child. I may not be all that smart, but I do have a man's body and I can do things."

Laurel smiled, refusing to be drawn. "So, one of those is your girl is it?"

"Both of them," said Paris. "They're sisters. They've come to see their grandmother. She's up at the San. They're staying for a few months. All right, eh?"

"Do they know who you are?"

"Hell, no. They think I'm a bit of a playboy."

"Well, father was asking about you this morning."

"I can look after myself."

Semyon bobbed out of the water close to them. He glanced round and climbed from the water.

"Problems?" asked Laurel as her father shook himself dry and slipped into his robe. He sat down.

"It seems we may have enemies here even at this moment. Milo has kept his eyes open and his ears flapping."

Semyon looked across the bay to where a fisherman stood up to his waist in the water casting a circular net with a sweep of his arm. Two other fishermen were working in a boat. Another sat on the harbour wall mending a net. Women stood behind stalls covered with fresh ice on which lay skinned eels, pepper fish, rice cakes. The ground about them was white with shed scales. Up in the town, a woman stood at a window testing washing against her cheek while another woman talked and children played. So many people. Most of them he knew vaguely. All of them knew him. All were Thalattans. All were alert, part of the vast family. "We are safe. There are plenty of people on guard. Milo has seen to that. I doubt if an offworlder can move without a pair of eyes on him."

"Who is causing trouble?" asked Paris.

"There is a woman at the Sanitarium called Milese din Corope. She is taking the rejuvenation course. She is joint ruler with her brother of the din Corope 730th. Have either of you heard of her?"

Both shook their heads.

"I think you may have, perhaps not by name. She has two granddaughters visiting her at present." Semyon looked hard at Paris, who stared back at him and finally shrugged as if to say, "Well what have I done wrong now?"

"Milo has told me a great deal," continued Semyon. "Anyway, the girls don't concern me nor does their grandmother, but their servants do. They have a full retinue. They have taken over an entire guest house on the south side. Milo has identified most of the servants. They are an Outlander Death Squad under licence to the Xerxes."

"What are they doing here?" asked Laurel.

"Spying on us."

"Why? What have we got to do with the Xerxes?"

"We have nothing to do with them. But the Paxwax do. Don't you remember the old song Laurel? You believe you can learn from poetry. Don't you remember the Big Chariot?

> Don't join the big chariot
> For its wheels are big and will crush you.
> Don't join the big chariot,
> For when it falls it will drag you down."

There was no hiding the bitterness in Semyon Beltane's voice. And Laurel did remember, a song from her childhood. "What shall we do?"

"Why don't we kill them?" said Paris. "It would be easy. We could even make it look like an accident."

"We will do nothing. We will leave here tonight in our houses. There is no way they can follow us once we are over the horizon."

"This is our Homeworld," protested Paris hotly. "Why should we be fugitives?"

"We are not fugitives," said Semyon. "Just prudent. Our guests are watched every second. Milo has them in check. We move away from an enemy we cannot fight. Never underestimate the power of the Great Families and never trust them. You see, size is everything. Here on our Homeworld, on Thalatta, we are safe because we are trusted and we are a threat to no one. We are a part of a small society. Ethical decisions are unavoidably linked to size. Beyond a certain size all you have is expediency."

"I don't understand," said Paris.

"You will. Come on, we're leaving now. Nice and gentle. No rush. But there'll be no wandering in the moonlight tonight for you, my son." He cuffed his son on the back of his shiny black head. "Fancy telling those poor girls you were a talent scout from Lotus-and-Arcadia," he laughed.

"Fancy them for believing it," said Paris. "Women are stupid sometimes."

38

ON BENNET

All Pawl had seen was a glimpse of Helium Bogdanovich rearing up out of his bath and nodding vigorously . . . then the communication had evaporated into a random pattern of sparks. Now Wynn was struggling to build a new communication bridge to Sable. The message, whatever it was, was undoubtedly important: the Shell-Bogdanovich Conspiracy did not use the Emergency-Imperative Code without good cause. But all Pawl could do was sit and wait. Some psychic storm deep in space was distorting all communications.

Images flickered above the black vivante plate. Images of what? Space was full of thought and emotion and the sensitive vivante aerial, lacking a precise focus, accepted what images it could. Most were meaningless, random showers of light, but occasionally a clear image formed. Once Pawl saw a baby which turned, thumb in mouth, and faced him with surprise showing in its eyes. Then it was gone. Moments later Pawl found himself watching a creature like a cockroach trying to climb out of a glass beaker. For an instant he saw the beaker as the cockroach saw it . . . but then it too spun away, throwing off splinters of light.

There was a great heaving of bright particles in the vivante blackness and then suddenly Helium Bogdanovich appeared. In his hand he was holding a human head.

"Seen this before?" he asked, holding the head up high. "Come on. Hurry up. I don't know how long this communication will last."

Overcoming his astonishment Pawl stepped close to the vivante image. "That's Songteller's head. What the hell is going on?"

"Wrong," said Helium. "Not Songteller's head but a very credible reproduction. It was recovered by one of my agents on Portal Reclusi. It was lodged in a trash chute. Songteller put it there."

"Songteller? But Songteller is dead. I saw his remains. A boating accident."

"Sorry, but you didn't. I have been doing some checking. Your man Songteller passed through Portal Reclusi a few days ago. For some reason best known to himself he entered a puppet-maker and had this facsimile made. Then he entered the Xerxes sector. It was there that he abandoned this head. One of my agents identified him. There can be no doubt. Your dead man walked."

"Entered the Xerxes sector?"

"That was what I said."

"Then whose body did I see on – "

Helium interrupted. "That is a matter of complete irrelevance. The fact you have to grasp is that your creature Songteller was a traitor. Start working out what damage he has done. Anticipate the worst; then you won't be disappointed."

"But why?" said Pawl. The magnitude of the defection was finally beginning to sink in. "Why? What could the Xerxes offer that the Paxwax couldn't?"

"Ask the Xerxes. One thing is certain, you won't be able to ask Songteller. If I know the Xerxes ladies, that man is now just a bundle of rubbish floating out there." He gestured vaguely. "That is their normal way with informers. They keep a death squad on duty at all hours. Now, what would you like me to do with this?" He lifted the head.

"Send it to the Xerxes," said Pawl. "I don't know. Destroy it."

"Very well. Good luck, Pawl. Be thorough. If I can help without endangering the Conspiracy I will." Helium broke contact and he and the head vanished.

Pawl sat for many minutes staring at the empty vivante space. Lacking any further instructions the vivante console folded in on itself and retracted into the ceiling. Songteller a traitor. It was hard to think of any news that could be worse. In fact, the tidings were so bad they were almost comic. But Pawl didn't laugh. He felt betrayed, not just by Songteller, but by life itself. *Typical*, thought Pawl, *typical. Just when I thought things were starting to go well, wham.* Slowly he began to uncoil his hair. *That's it, isn't it? There's always something waiting. The moment you start to feel happy you discover that a friend is dying of cancer or your house burns down or you find out that you've been betrayed. It's unrelenting. It never fails. Bloody Songteller, wizened little witch-man!* Pawl hoped the Xerxes had boxed him and flung him out into space. But what would Pawl have given at that moment just to have Songteller between his hands?

He imagined Songteller's dry gloating and the glee of the Xerxes ladies as they gobbled up information. He could imagine their laughter as they thought about the Paxwax and the young boy who called himself Master. Probably Helium was laughing too . . . and the Sith . . . and the rest of them. Pawl thought of the Great Families and wondered at the bitterness he felt. Neddelia was right: they were cockroaches and he, Pawl Paxwax, if he had the chance, would set the bloody box alight.

And what had his father been doing all this time? That silly bigoted old man . . . Pawl strode out on to his balcony and, despite the darkness and the cold and the wind, climbed up on to the very roof of his tower. He stared up into the sky and hoped some vestiges of the spirit of his father yet remained. He wanted to shout a curse to end all curses, to pin and nail his father for all eternity. He stood with his mouth opening and closing and could think of nothing. It was all so futile.

A cold wind blew, and Pawl shivered and finally went back inside. One thing was certain in his mind, one thing was decided beyond any question: if the Xerxes were coming hunting the Paxwax, then the Paxwax would fight with tooth and nail and claw.

Pawl saw his reflection in the window of his tower. He looked tall and hunched and dangerous. He smiled at his reflection.

The first task was to discover how much damage Songteller could have done. There were limits to his power and Pawl knew that his father was cautious and suspicious. Even so, best assume the worst, as Helium had said.

Pawl thought back to his last conversation with Songteller, the morning after his father had died. He remembered the conversation about Lapis . . . was there something about Laurel?

For a moment Pawl's blood ran cold. He had a sickening certainty that Toby had told Songteller about Laurel . . . in which case the Xerxes now knew about. . . .

Pawl was on his feet and running. He dived into the communication egg, shouting for Wynn to get him a bridge to Thalatta, to the Beltane Homeworld.

"Sorry, Pawl," said Wynn. "There is nothing I can do. The psychic storm is worse than ever. I am just able to hold contact with Veritas. I can't link with the Beltane at all."

"Is there any way I can get a message through?"

"Well, we can shunt it via the Way Gates. They are still in operation. They are more resilient than the vivantes."

"We'll do it," said Pawl.

"Of course, the message will take longer and the communication can be intercepted."

"Set it up. Don't worry about interception, I'll take care of that."

"Ready, Master Pawl."

"This message is for Thalatta, Beltane Homeworld. Message reads: 'PAY CLOSE REGARD TO THE WISDOM OF THE CARPETAL TREE'. End message. Now send that message direct to Laurel Beltane. Shunt it through the Pocket."

"Done."

"When will it arrive?"

"Don't worry about the 'when', worry about the 'if'. Things are bad out there."

That gave Pawl no comfort. He just hoped that Laurel would understand his code.

And she did.

The message found its way to the Beltane Homeworld and was re-set in words by the Way Gate Guardian. It was then broadcast directly to Laurel. The line came from one of Pawl's songs.

Laurel quickly found the song and remembered the day it was written. She and Pawl were at a picnic on Lotus-and-Arcadia. They saw a troop of the Proctors coming with their servants and animals. Together Pawl and Laurel scooped up their things and crawled under the heavy red foliage of a Carpetal tree. It was like being in a beautiful glowing tent, and the air was still and mysterious and heavy.

They had made love stealthily while the Proctors played the fool outside. Then Laurel had dozed, and when she awoke she found that Pawl had scribbled these words.

> I'm here, a whole-in-one,
> A sleeping girl beside,
> Gazing up this sun-splashed tree . . .
> And I notice the wise Carpetal.
>
> How bold its red leaves!
> Blood and wine offered
> To the crushing sun.

But yet,
But yet see there,
Tucked behind each blazing leaf,
The fruit of the tree.
It hides its secret well.
(It hides us well)
And we who lie in its shade,
We are part of its secret now.

Hush. The tree is speaking.
"Show fierce. Show fair.
But that which you hold dear,
Hide well.
Lest the questing snout of the beast,
Or keen knife or clattering tongue,
Destroy your composure."

That is the wisdom of the Carpetal tree.

The warning was clear. Laurel thought of the assassins who even now were staked out on her Homeworld. She and her father and brother moved their houses high, and joined them and sealed them against the thin cold of space.

Pawl Paxwax was studying. He was trying to think like Songteller. He had to discover where the Paxwax were weak. The answer was not difficult. The Way Gates. The most protected and most jealously-guarded contracts among all the Families concerned the Way Gates.

"Wynn, have you been able to follow the events of the past few hours?"

"I have followed them. I do not understand them."

"We are in trouble. Deep trouble. How deep, I don't know as yet. I want you to run an analysis. Go back through ten years. Pluck out all the Way contracts. I want to see the distribution through the Eleven Families. See if you can find anything strange."

"Strange?"

"An imbalance. A bias. Discover the pattern in my father's dealings. You know the way we work."

"Give me a few minutes."

*

Pawl sat back. A stillness seemed to have fallen over his world. He hardly dared look out of his windows in case the sky turned red and he heard the clamour of alarm bells and felt the shutters going up. Although he had no firm evidence as yet, he had a deep foreboding.

"Ready, Master Pawl. I think it would be best if I were to take you through this material. It is very complex and quite vast." Numbers and names and coded references began to flicker a ghostly blue above the vivante plate. "First, there are many patterns in your father's negotiations. He appears to have been quite a brilliant strategist, very subtle in his arrangements. He favoured the Shell-Bogdanovich Conspiracy and helped them on several occasions in negotiations with the Outer Families. He appears to have engaged in a protracted economic war with the Xerxes de la Tour Souvent. On the whole I would say that they came out equal. He scored some triumphs but he fell into their traps too. He seems to have baited the Lamprey Sixth and managed to involve them in a small war with the Longstock Eighth. He made gains from both parties. He was surprisingly generous with the Felice Eleventh and several times favoured them over the stronger Sith Tenth. But on the whole what I have found is little more than the static of Empires rubbing against one another. I would say that during the past ten years your family's status has hardly changed. The Paxwax are a competitor among equals."

"There's got to be something."

"Not from the data that I have available. Not from the contracts which relate to dealings with the Eleven Great Families."

"What does that mean?" said Pawl, detecting something in Wynn's guarded, neutral voice.

"A great number of contracts were negotiated with smaller families, even down to single-system families."

This was news to Pawl. He sat forward. "We are still talking about Way Gate Contracts, right?"

"Of course. That was what you asked me to check."

"Show me one. Pick one at random."

The vivante space became fully alive and the ghostly outline image of a man formed. "Now here is Rimij Appel, patriarch of the Appel family. Have you ever heard of him?"

"No," said Pawl.

"Well, the Appel family own one planet and seven moons. Nine years ago they negotiated to own a one-thousandth part in a Way

Gate that would link them with Portal Reclusi. They were granted
limited access. Songteller has added a note that he suspects the
Appel family are planning to ship merchandise into Portal Reclusi
though they did not apply for commercial clearance. Two years
after it was signed, the contract was monitored by the Paxwax. It
was found that the Appel were indeed dealing in contraband and
the contract was terminated." The patriarch faded.

"This is trivial," said Pawl.

"You asked me to pick one of the minor contracts at random.
Most of them are like that. Inconsequential."

"Why did Toby bother with such things?"

"Toby did not authorize that particular contract. It comes under
a broad policy directive to Songteller to establish more influence
close to the Lamprey."

"Then why was the contract terminated? It doesn't make sense.
You let a little family have a smell of the big time and then, when
they try to prosper, snub them out."

Wynn was silent, having nothing to add to Pawl's observations.
"Tell me, Wynn: this is just a shot in the dark, but are there many
Way contracts which relate to Elliott's Pocket?"

"Some. Here are the names."

A roll-call of names appeared above the vivante and began to
process. Most of the names were new to Pawl. Then he saw one he
did recognize. "Hey. Hey. Hold up. Go back. Find the Family
called Tyger. They're a subsidiary of the Lamprey, aren't they?
Why would father negotiate Way contracts with them in the
Pocket?" The question was rhetorical but Wynn answered it.

"Limited concession mining rights. And . . . that's interesting."

"What?"

"It is another blanket contract. Your father authorized the whole
package but not the individual parts."

"So Songteller could have slipped that through?"

"He could. It looks that way."

Pawl thought about that. He was beginning to get the feel of the
way that Songteller had operated. Under normal circumstances
there might be nothing strange. But Songteller was a traitor,
Helium had proved that, and so now his every move needed to be
questioned. "Wynn?"

"Yes, Pawl."

"Forget about the Great Families. Concentrate only on the
smaller Families. Look for Way contracts that my father did not

personally authorize. I don't care for how short a time span the contracts were supposed to operate, study them. I shall want to see them in relation to the Paxwax domain. Can you do that?"

"Yes. The contracts are not referential. I shall have to study each one."

"Take your time. Go back over thirty years."

"I shall need to speak with the main computer on Veritas."

"Do it. Do it. We may have stumbled on to something. We may not. But be very thorough. How is space between us and Veritas?"

"Still a bit stormy, but clearing."

"Good. I am going for a walk. I shall return in an hour."

It was a long hour. Pawl spent part of his time down in the new greenhouses, seeing how some exotic trees he had brought into the Homeworld were faring. They were Saprosma trees, a surprise for Laurel.

When he returned to his room in the tower Wynn was humming like bees in a hive. "Sit down, Master Pawl. I believe I have bad news for you."

It was not like Wynn to be dramatic and Pawl sat down. The mantra for calm began to whisper in his mind.

> See the leaves of autumn falling,
> See the hand that stirs. . . .

Wynn spoke calmly, in a matter-of-fact voice. "I have spent some considerable computer time in communication with your old computer on Veritas. I believe the memory of that computer has been tampered with."

"That is impossible. . . ."

"It is not. Let me explain. You have a very fine computer on Veritas, slow after the way of the old, but very dependable, very thorough, very honest."

"So?"

"So, I found certain gaps in its knowledge, certain non-sequiturs, inexplicable shifts . . . the imprint of erasure. Your computer could tell me nothing directly, of course, but the gaps in its knowledge drew attention to themselves. Perhaps that was its way of telling us."

"Erasures?"

"Correct. I have verified that Songteller had the authority to use the total erasure code O. . . ."

"Do you mean there is no record of what was erased?"

"That is exactly what I mean."

"Surely. . . ."

"None. There is just an untidy hole, where the bolting horse left the stable gate open."

"For God's sake. Let me get this straight. You are telling me that there are some contracts, negotiated presumably by my father or Songteller, and that we now have no idea what they were."

"Correct."

"They could be anything."

"Correct."

"And presumably, if they were erased by Songteller, he must have regarded them as important and damaging."

"Presumably. The man was a traitor."

"And is there no way we can recover them?"

"No way. I have every memory cell on Veritas working on the problem. We are cross-referencing everything. We are bound to discover anomalies, but we cannot recover the memory."

"Good God. We could be attacked from anywhere."

"May I suggest you contact your friends on Sable."

"We're facing death in the eye."

"Be calm."

"Calm and polite, is that it?"

"You must remain so. You are a Master. Speak to your friends on Sable. I am making the bridge now. . . ."

"No," said Pawl. "Hold off. Wait." He gulped down a glass of Seppel juice and waited while that fine liquor found his stomach and spread. "I am the Master here, and I will decide the action." The mantra whispered in his mind.

> See the leaves of Autumn falling,
> See the hand that stirs the stars,
> Both the quiet beast that stamps in the meadow
> And the abomination that holds to its lair
> Know dread;
> What then is your trouble,
>   running man?

"So we are vulnerable. That is nothing new. Let me see the pattern made by the Songteller contracts."

The room darkened as the vivante space came alive. Wynn's

voice, calm and thoughtful, spoke. "Here, first, is a standard projection of the Paxwax domain as seen from Proctor Central."

A hazy cloud of blue sparks appeared in the vivante space. It had roughly the shape of an hourglass tipped on its side. Within the total shape there were pockets of darkness. These were the areas in space occupied by other Great Families and by the myriad small Families. The shape of Pawl's empire began to revolve, revealing its lateral contours. Just as a sculpture changes as you walk round it, so Pawl's empire became a saucer, a flared bottle, kidneys on a string, and an hourglass again. At the narrow neck of the hourglass was Elliott's Pocket.

"That is your domain as it was at the moment of Toby's death. I will now present the contract locations. Remember that many of these contracts were for only a limited duration."

"Let them stand. Even one wrong transit through a Way Gate can spell trouble." Pawl watched as red sparks began to appear round the blue cloud. Some appeared within it. There was a marked concentration round Elliott's Pocket. Pawl's empire began to look like a pin cushion. "Turn the image again," said Pawl. It began to revolve. At all times there was a network of red dots round his empire. "Let us assume," said Pawl, "that only half those contract locations are dangerous. It still means that we are pretty comprehensively boxed in. Let us remember also that there are key contracts that we don't know about. Whichever way one looks at it we are meat on the block." He stared at the revolving pattern for many minutes. In his mind's eye he saw each of the red sparks as a Way station primed and ready. At the same time he knew that the true situation was probably far more complex and inscrutable. New Gates could have been built and coded and be waiting up there. They would not have been used yet or their presence would have been revealed. But they could be brought into commission within minutes.

"Wynn, fill in the Xerxes domain. Use the same red. Let's see what happens."

Pawl's empire shrank and a new shape appeared. It was like a rearing horse. It joined with all the existing red dots and became a hydra with long red fingers locked round Pawl's empire. And there it was, revealed in its starkest simplicity, the entrapment of the Paxwax.

"Would you like me to add the Lamprey?"

"Why not? Use a different colour."

Again the empires shrank, and a green dragon's tail appeared which wound about and through the Xerxes and Paxwax.

"Well now, given their obvious advantage, the question is, why have they not attacked already?" asked Pawl.

"Delay is rarely to the advantage of the aggressor. They must have their reason," stated Wynn.

"Mmmm. I think I *will* speak with Helium Bogdanovich. Perhaps he can make more sense of this."

The image of Helium Bogdanovich when it finally appeared was sharp and vivid, as though space had been cleansed of its impurities during the recent storm. He looked grumpy and sleepy.

"Found something, have you? Want to ask my advice, eh? Well, fire away."

Pawl took his time. He was careful not to sound alarmist. He explained about the Way contracts that Songteller had negotiated with the hordes of small Families and his fear that these might have been manipulated by the Xerxes. He showed Helium the vivante of his empire wrapped about by the Xerxes and Lamprey. During all of this Helium lay back in his bath and puffed on his pipe. But when Pawl mentioned the lacunae in his computer's memory, Helium sat up with such speed that he caused a great tidal wave that swilled round his bath.

"You are doomed, boy."

"Not yet. They haven't attacked yet."

Helium accepted this and ruminated. "Hmm. Good point. If I were them I wouldn't have waited. I'd have moved in as soon as I heard that Toby was dead. So why haven't they attacked?"

"I was hoping you could tell me."

"Dame Clarissa has an elegant mind. She will have her reasons." Helium studied the intertwined empires. "I don't like that concentration of Way Points between Elliott's Pocket and Portal Reclusi. All those gates are hard against the Conspiracy domain. It suggests they may have designs on us. But you know, Pawl, if this attack formation . . . let us call it that . . . if it is true, then it means that the Xerxes are planning to use a phased attack."

"What is a phased attack?"

"Didn't they teach you anything on Terpsichore?"

"I learned how to shoot down a Sennet bat."

"If we were being attacked by Sennet bats I would sleep easily. But we are dealing with the Xerxes. That family has remained

powerful for so long because they are shrewd and ruthless. And
you must learn to be like them. A phased attack is one that comes
in synchronized waves. How many people can a Way Gate take at
one time?"

"Six as a rule. Four on some of the smaller ones."

"Right. So a basic attack team consists of six people.

"Imagine a Way Gate. Six people enter and lie down together.
They are in teams of two – three teams therefore – and in each
team there is a Killer and a Way Technician.

"You have never seen a Xerxes assassination team, have you?
The Killers are always women. I don't know why; they seem to
have the will-power, the reflexes and the necessary intensity. The
Way Technicians are invariably men. Dreamy men.

"Anyway, three teams enter. At the end of the first gate, one
team takes its time getting changed. They will have special,
impeccable credentials and the local Way Computer will not suspect
them. The remaining two teams move on. After the next jump,
one team remains while the last team moves on. It *is* as simple as
dominoes. And when the final team is in position, at a specified
time . . . bang . . . the Killers do their job. They kill everyone at
the Way Station. They usually use gas. Sometimes a particle spray.
With that part of the operation completed, the Way Technicians
get to work. They crack open the Way Computer and alter the co-
ordinates so that the Gates can only be used in one direction and
probably from only one boarding place. Some of the Gates will
break down, for they are very sensitive, but enough will remain
active.

"Now is when the flow starts. It will be like cancer. One cell will
be contaminated after another . . . until your Empire dies. You
will have no retaliation. The Lamprey will swarm like vermin
round a carcase.

"You will capitulate, if only to spare the innocent lives, right?
And within an hour of the attack beginning, you will meet Dame
Clarissa, or perhaps Jettatura, for she has a mean streak, riding
down on your shuttle to take possession of your tiny, wild
Homeworld."

"The Lamprey?" said Pawl. "Are you sure that the Lamprey
will be part of it?"

Helium nodded, "Ah yes, the Lamprey will be there. Clarissa
has been cultivating them for years. The Xerxes will manipulate
the Way Gates and control the flow, but the Lamprey will do the

dirty work. Anyway, I am sure *that* is the Xerxes plan. It is simple, elegant and bold, just like Clarissa."

"How can I stop them?"

"Yes, that is the question. That needs thought. We must first discover why they have delayed. I think I shall swim for a while. I find it easier to think about such things when I am swimming. I believe Clover has something she wants to say to you now."

Helium paddled to the end of his bath and then drew his grey bulk out of the water. He shook himself like a great bear and then reared up on to his hind legs and walked out of Pawl's view.

Pawl was left staring at the rippling brown water of Helium's tank. *Now what?* he thought.

The water rose and fell and the pretty bright face of Clover Shell broke the surface.

"Hello, Pawl. Sorry to hear about your worries. Glad you contacted us. Helium will sort things out. I want to talk to you about something much nicer. Dama Longstock. Now, I know you won't mind me asking, but your father did get to talk to you about Dama before he died, didn't he?"

Pawl had trouble pulling his concentration round. Here was he staring the end of his family's fortunes in the eye and Clover Shell wanted to talk about Dama! "Well, we talked. Argued mainly. He wanted me to marry Dama."

Pawl saw the relief on Clover's face and the way she began to smile. "Well, that is wonderful. I just wanted to be certain. You know, it was going to be a toss-up between you and Lapis. But I'm glad it is you. I know that Dama wants you. She. . . ."

"Just a minute," said Pawl, holding up his hand and stopping Clover in mid-flow. "Toby and I argued. I told him I didn't want to marry Dama. I have made my own choice."

Clover Shell's face set. The shape was still that of a smile, but her eyes had lost their sparkle. "I'm sorry, Pawl. I don't think I understand. Livil Longstock spoke to your father only hours before you returned home. She made the position quite clear. He agreed. Told her there were no problems."

"Well, he never told me."

Clover Shell eyed Pawl coolly. There was not even the shape of a smile now. "Well, perhaps there is no harm done. You are now Master so I shall make the position quite plain to you. We of the Conspiracy consider it a matter of some importance that you should make an attachment with Dama Longstock. We wish to see the

Longstock rise, and naturally we would support your interest in very tangible ways . . . such as helping you in your present predicament, helping to squeeze the Xerxes . . . other ways too. Say yes now, Pawl. It is very simple. *I* will take matters from there."

Perhaps if Pawl had been more experienced in diplomacy, perhaps if he had had longer to accustom himself to being Master of the Paxwax, he would have handled this situation better. As it was, he let himself be irritated by Clover Shell's tone and his reply sounded rude, though that was not his intention. "I will not be dictated to. I will marry whom I choose, and my father had no right to make commitments on my behalf."

Clover Shell's face went pale. It was a frightening sight, for with the paleness went a look of revulsion such as Pawl had never seen. She paddled back from him. "How dare you speak to me like that!"

Pawl tried to make amends. "I'm sorry. I didn't mean . . . Look, I like Dama and I know she likes me . . . But when I returned to Bennet Homeworld, I made my position clear. I intend to marry Laurel Beltane. . . ."

"Silence. I should have known better than to trust the Paxwax. Helium shall hear of this, and do not look to the Conspiracy for help." Abruptly she struck her hands together and her image disappeared. Pawl found himself again alone. He immediately ordered Wynn to try and contact the Shell-Bogdanovich Conspiracy, but when the computer did so, it found that the Paxwax call sign was rejected.

Pawl made his way out on to his balcony and looked up at the stars and felt them weigh down on him. He breathed deeply, drawing in the night air, and then returned indoors. Nothing had changed. In the brief time he had spent on his balcony nothing had happened. All his decisions lay before him.

"How can we protect the Paxwax?" He asked the question aloud, not expecting any answer, but Wynn took up the challenge.

"We must protect the Way Gates."

"How?"

"That is for you to decide."

Pawl thought for a few moments and several possibilities began to suggest themselves. "All right, so we protect our Way Gates. We still don't know when they will attack."

"True, but I think Helium Bogdanovich has given us the clue. He was very helpful without knowing it."

"Ah. The phased attack."

"Exactly. If he is right we shall be able to spot the onset of an attack by the synchronized movement of six individuals through your Way Gates. Did you know that on average only 3.8 people use your Way Gates for any one jump, so six people moving together should be easily recognizable."

"So long as they use established Way Gates."

"True. I am only trying to help."

Pawl pondered this. "Tell me, Wynn, given the information we now have, could you run some sort of probability survey to show which Gates might be attacked?"

"Yes."

"Then leave the protection to me. Just tell me which gates to protect."

"It will be a statistical projection."

"Meaning?"

"It will be wrong in particular instances."

"Use your best stealth."

Wynn had prodigious capability. But even so, its deliberations took time. It surveyed every Way Gate (and there were tens of thousands) which led into the Paxwax. It sought the most likely paths which an attacking force might take.

While Wynn flickered to itself, Pawl thought about particle screens. He wondered if a Way Guardian could be adapted to trigger a particle screen? He was sure it could. The plan hardened in his mind. He would mine his own Way Gates. When groups of six moved together he would fire blind, cutting down whoever was travelling. Such a move might blunt the attack and buy him some time. At least the Xerxes did not know that he had guessed their plans; that was his one advantage.

"I think I can see the most strategic routes into your Empire, Master Pawl." Wynn's voice was soft. "Shall I begin to roll call?"

"Go ahead."

"Lenten Tri-Way, Blue Roger, Portal Reclusi, Forge. . . ."

The list went on, enumerating the main-line Gates into the Paxwax. Halfway through its catalogue Wynn stopped. "There is a call from the Shell-Bogdanovich Conspiracy. Helium Bogdanovich would speak with you."

*

The blubbery Master of the Shell-Bogdanovich stared steadily out at Pawl. "Well, you made a mess of things, didn't you? In all my years with Clover I don't think I have ever seen her so angry before. A dangerous woman when she is roused is Clover. . . ."

"Have you contacted me to gloat or. . . ."

Helium shook his head. "Don't be rude to me, Pawl. You need every friend you can muster. I've contacted you merely to tell you that I know why the Xerxes have delayed, and to tell you that you have very little time. It's very simple. If there is one thing that Clarissa likes more than preening it is a moral advantage. She is waiting until you defy the Code. Then the Xerxes will pounce. But they will not wait long. At the most a few more days, perhaps a week, then suddenly, *poof*, her patience will disappear. She is like that. I have watched her for a very long time."

"Why have you decided to tell me this?"

"Self-interest. The Conspiracy would suffer if the Paxwax fell."

"Is that the only reason?"

"I like your cheek even though I disagree with you."

"Will you help me further?"

"Possibly. That rather depends on Clover Shell. She is speaking to the Longstock at this moment. Have you made any plans?"

"Some."

"Tell me. Let me see if I can pick holes in them."

Pawl and Helium talked on through the night. At one point Clover Shell interrupted them. Her manner was brittle and dry but she confirmed that the Longstock had no claim over Pawl. With that she left them, wishing Pawl neither well nor ill.

For the rest of that long night Helium and Pawl sat in conference. When they parted they had a plan and a programme.

That day Helium was to spread the rumour that a cooling of relations had taken place between the Paxwax Fifth and the Shell-Bogdanovich Conspiracy. This would alert the Xerxes that something was happening, for these two Great Families were traditional allies. They hoped it would dull the Xerxes suspicions. As Helium put it, "If they think you are alone, they will be that much the bolder." At the same time Helium was to prepare a select task force. Helium himself was contemplating taking part in the action. This task force would be ready to move at the first hint of trouble.

The Beltane were to be protected, and the only safe course was for them to evacuate. "This must be done with care," said Helium. "They must leave their planet in secret. They would be safest if they lingered in space, perhaps aboard an old Vanburgh."

A Vanburgh was a miniature planet, no more than five miles in diameter, enclosed in a shell. They could wheel like a satellite round any great mass or be equipped with transformation generators and make their own slow way. They were used to make the short hops from a Way Gate station to a neighbouring planet.

"I doubt if the Beltane have any Vanburghs. They have a small domain but it is well serviced with Way Gates," said Pawl.

"Let us have a look at it."

They called up a star glyph of the section of the galaxy where the Beltane Empire lay.

"See how close they are to the Xerxes," said Pawl.

"Yes, but see down here. That narrow cone. That's part of the Sith Tenth. They did some fancy trading with the Xerxes years ago to get that. Where's the nearest Sith Way Gate?"

A point began to blink brightly in the middle of the cone.

"Now look, that's not too far from the Beltane Homeworld. And the Sith are sure to have a Vanburgh or two in that area. Look, there aren't any other Way Gates. Worth a word with the Sith, my boy."

Pawl arranged to begin negotiations with Singular Sith as quickly as possible.

"Do you begin to feel time moving quickly?" said Helium. "Because it will. It will. Now you must concentrate on getting the particle screens into place. Move with care. Remember, the Xerxes have eyes everywhere. A random pattern would be best. And after all, it is reasonable that a new Master would want the pathways into his domain to be as attractive as possible, perhaps a bit of decorating, some running repairs. You might even contrive to have a couple of Gates break down and that will affect a whole sequence. They'll have to be repaired. Use your imagination, you're supposed to have plenty of that, but don't be too long about it. We don't want the Xerxes to get trigger-happy. I hope you get the Beltane girl safe. I like the Beltanes. One of my younger brothers once spent some time on their Homeworld. . . . But I want you to know that I shall do all in my power to convince Semyon Beltane to forbid the match between you and Laurel, and I shall continue to try and convince you of its foolishness."

Helium moved to break contact. But before he did so he turned
to Pawl. He stirred the water with his large hand so that it formed
brown, frothy whirlpools.

"One other thing, Pawl. Are there any of the Inner Circle still
with you?"

Pawl hesitated for a second.

"Ah. I see there are. How many?"

"Just one."

"Is he trying to be friendly?"

"Yes."

"Mmm. Well, watch out. What does he look like?"

"They all look pretty much the. . . ."

"Is he big or little?"

"Very short."

"Mmm. Walks with a sort of glide?"

"Yes."

"I've heard of such. Alien. Does he ask many questions?"

"I've never heard him speak."

"Just watches, eh?"

"Mainly."

"Yes, well. You be careful round him. Could be a telepath.
Some of the Inner Circle are very strange. Whatever you do, don't
let him know what is going on. Perhaps his presence is to our
advantage. I doubt if the Inner Circle want a full-scale war. He's
probably just keeping an eye on you."

"That was my guess."

"Mmm. Well, watch him."

Helium waved and the circuit was broken. The vivante space
became opaque and then the original image of the Paxwax Empire
trapped by the Xerxes and Lamprey sprang back into focus.

Singular Sith had obviously taken pains to get ready for the
meeting. His great bull horns were polished and shone a deep
brown. The steel-capped ends were burnished. His black coarse
hair was parted in the middle and he wore a pale blue moonstone
in the centre of his forehead. His loose singlet emphasized the
muscular weight of his shoulders.

His obvious strength, added to his eagerness to please, made
him seem a fool. Pawl was on his guard.

After standard pleasantries they got down to business.

"In your sector 707–3RL, do you have a Vanburgh?" asked Pawl.

Singular, surprised at the request, consulted an advisor off-screen. "We have three in that sector. Outer Families are not allowed to have more than one Way Gate within any local solar system . . . you may be aware of the ruling."

"No, I was not aware," said Pawl. "It sounds rather restrictive. Especially if you have perishable merchandise which you hope to vend to some of the Inner Families."

"It is indeed a restriction, but would you like us to transport something in one of our Vanburghs?"

"No. I wish to hire one."

"I see." His broad nose wrinkled as he stared at Pawl. "Each Vanburgh has a specified run. The timetable is linked to crops. If we missed a run we could miss a harvest. That would mean. . . ."

"How if I were to offer you Paxwax Way Rights for your produce from that sector through to the Shell-Bogdanovich and the Wong, through Elliott's Pocket?"

"Well, er. . . ."

"I understand you are in competition with the Felice. With a Way concession like that you could beat the Felice hands down."

"We could." Still he ruminated. "Exclusive rights?"

"Meaning?"

"Not the Felice, or the Paragon."

"Of course."

"Done." Singular slapped his hands together. "When will you require the Vanburgh?"

"Now."

Singular took hold of his horns, one in each hand, and ran his hand up their curve. "Well, that's. . . ." He looked at Pawl. "Urgent. Right."

Again Singular Sith spoke off-screen. His nostrils were flared as he gave orders. A loud voice answered him. Singular shouted back and beat his fist on the front of the vivante plate. He turned to Pawl. "A moment please, Master of Paxwax. A negotiation – " He stepped out of vivante range and Pawl heard a furious argument break out accompanied by thumps and swearing in the thick dialect of the Outer Families. When Singular reappeared he was panting and rubbing one of his fists. "You have the Vanburgh. It is called the *George a'Green*. It is waiting at our Way Station Rosa Luxemburg. Will you require crew, services?"

"Nothing. A Paxwax team will Gate through. And no communication with anyone, agreed?"

"Agreed. When can the Way Right be granted?"

"One standard week from today."

"Accepted."

The communication ended. Pawl reflected. He knew that he had sounded confident but he was well aware of Helium's words. Time *was* moving quickly. Who knew if he would have an empire in one standard week's time?

"I want you to leave here," said Pawl, speaking directly into the moving mass of red worms. "I want you to travel far, outside the Paxwax domain, back to the Inner Circle if need be, and discover what movements there are against me."

Odin did not speak. He lay very small in Pawl's mind and Pawl could gather no flavour of him.

"Do you hear me? Can you understand?"

"I understand." How distant and small the voice was. Only a fragment of Odin's consciousness was with Pawl. Most of his concentration was inwards. He was experiencing a chafing of his stone. It was burning because Odin was being torn apart. Here was a man whose spirit he had come to know but whom he must, later, somehow, betray. That was the way it would be.

We are the movement that is against you, thought Odin. *I am your enemy*. But the thought never reached Pawl. It rang like a bell in a vacuum, Odin held it close. And it hurt.

"Will you help me?"

"Of course. I will return to the Homeworld of the Inner Circle. Much news is gathered there. When shall I leave?"

"Now would be best."

Odin did not reply.

Pawl reached forward and placed the flat of his hand against the coiling tendrils. Immediately several of them swarmed round his hand. Their grip was surprisingly strong. And then he was released. Odin glided away.

"You will return?" asked Pawl.

"When the battle is lost and won," replied Odin.

The small creature entered the vacuum chute, the doors closed, and it was gone.

Pawl felt Odin withdraw slowly from his mind. There was a sadness like music, a sighing of wind over cold marshes, a tumbling of pebbles as the sea retreats and gathers: it became a memory, a memory of a memory, fading, smaller . . . gone.

In that moment Pawl felt lonely. He had become so used to Odin's presence that he hardly realized how much the small creature gave him strength.

Tiredness.

Tiredness that left half his face numb as though punched, and his eyes closing.

Pawl fought. Briefly he closed his eyes. He pressed his fingers to his temples and worked the pressure points. In his mind he imagined a red carnation. It became a red fountain. A fountain of blood. Bright and cheerful and full of fun, bubbling inside him, carrying strength to tired fingers, dropping cheeks and tense shoulder muscles. Pawl waited and felt the hypnotic injection take effect. It drove the barriers of tiredness back. It would hold for a time. Meanwhile . . . Semyon Beltane was waiting.

Semyon sat, dressed in green, his arms bare and resting along the sides of his chair and his squat black face unsmiling. Pawl wondered if Helium had already spoken to him.

"Semyon Beltane, I salute you. We have not had an opportunity to get to know one another. That is a shame . . . If I had any choice in the matter . . . but, well, I don't. Let me speak simply." Semyon raised his head but beyond that gave no sign that he had heard Pawl's words. "I want to take your daughter as my wife, to be with me in the management of the Paxwax. This means that I must oppose the Code which guides the Eleven. This I will do. But it means danger for you. There are powerful groups within the Eleven who would like to see me fail.

"Semyon, Master of Beltane, I have arranged for a Vanburgh to wait at your Way Gate. You will be safe in space. All of you."

Semyon stirred and drew his green gown closer about him. "Are you asking me to leave my Homeworld, Master of Paxwax?"

"I am. For safety. Just for a while. Until the danger is passed."

"I see. And is the danger imminent?"

"I believe it is. Please, take action now. When I know that you and Laurel and the members of your family are safe I will breathe more easily. I would not call like this without good reason."

"I am sure you would not. Do you wish to speak to Laurel? She is very near."

"Yes," said Pawl, surprised. "I thought you all had separate houses."

"We do. But for the time being we are together."

The wall behind Semyon cleared as the particle charge dispersed. Laurel stepped through. She was restrained in the presence of her father. "I understood your message," she said. "A Xerxes killer squad is already here. We have them watched."

"Where are you now?"

"High above the polar seas. No one can find us."

"There is a Vanburgh waiting at. . . ."

"I heard."

"Please go to it. I cannot protect you at this distance."

"Are you in danger, Pawl?"

"We are all in danger." Pawl directed his attention to Semyon, who had sat unmoving while his daughter was speaking. "Please, Master of Beltane. Move quickly. Helium Bogdanovich knows of this plan. I know he is a friend of yours."

"Set your mind at rest. Laurel will depart shortly. I have already spoken with Helium. We are rising now and will shortly meet with the Vanburgh. Good luck, Master Pawl. I wish all our Homeworlds well."

39

ON MORROW

Standing together, the two sisters looked down at the sweating face of Dame Rose, confined before her time. The quills on the back of Dame Clarissa's head stood stiff and straight. Jettatura's face was paler than usual, so that her pink eyes seemed to glow.

"It is dead," whispered Rose.

"No it isn't, Rose dear. Its heart is still beating. We can see it. Your child is alive." There was a quality of pleading in Dame Clarissa's voice.

"Dead. I know. I am alive."

The attending doctor leaned over and directed a flow of tranquillizing gas across Rose's face. It dulled her pain and consciousness. She breathed deeply, her mouth slack and open, and her neck arched back as she gazed, large-eyed, vacantly, at the ceiling.

"There is nothing we can do here," said Jettatura. "All may yet be well."

The two sisters left the room and a team of doctors and nurses replaced them.

Walking down the corridor, Clarissa raged in a whisper. "Why now? Why now, when everything was just coming right?"

Jettatura paced on, her face white and set. "Rose lacks confidence in her life," she said. "She has no resilience in her spirit. If it were you or I that were carrying that child it would live . . . But we are barren."

The two sisters paced on in silence. They entered the conference chamber, which was now being converted into a battle HQ. A new vivante had been installed in the centre.

Brightly-coloured charts hung on the walls. In one corner a long low machine mumbled to itself. It was scanning the spaceways, picking up whatever intelligence it could. At present it was surveying all communications going into and from Sable.

Clarissa sat down heavily in the control seat in front of the vivante. Her brilliant red plumes shifted as though stroked by an invisible hand. "Do you ever feel weary?" she asked, smoothing her brow with a jewelled hand, "I do."

The athletic Jettatura did not reply. She walked round the room, clasping and unclasping her hands. Her lips were tightly pressed. She seemed to be struggling with some turbulent emotion which threatened her normally glacial composure. She tossed her head like a horse teased with flies, and her fine white hair fanned out and swirled round her shoulders.

Finally she sat down opposite Clarissa. "We all need a rest. When all this is over we shall take a holiday. We will travel. We will go to Lotus-and-Arcadia and refresh ourselves. You can go to balls and I will hunt. You would like that. There will be peace." She paused, and a rare smile quickened her pink eyes. "You'll see. Peace. That is a glorious thought."

Clarissa nodded. "A glorious thought." She reached out her hand and the two sisters sat with hands linked over the dark vivante plate.

"But for the moment, Clarissa, we have business afoot that demands all our attention. Be of good cheer. Do not waver now, Clarissa. Pull your clothes about you. Concentrate. We are close to victory."

"Yes. If the Paxwax boy does not make a move within the next few days I believe we should strike. The strain is killing me."

Jettatura stood and came round the vivante and sat down next to Clarissa. From her sleeve she produced two despatches. "These arrived just before we were called to Rose. There is something happening between the Paxwax and the Conspiracy. I cannot read the true meaning. Helium Bogdanovich has let it be known that he is renegotiating primary Way rights with the Paxwax."

"He wants to restrict him."

"Perhaps."

"Maybe he has news of the Beltane girl. He has spies everywhere."

"Maybe."

"You do not sound certain."

"What is certainty? I just have doubts. It is all too easy. Either they are falling out or they are conspiring against us."

Clarissa pondered this for a moment. "On balance," she said, "I think that the Paxwax boy will irritate Helium. He is too idealistic. What was the other piece of intelligence?"

"The member of the Inner Circle has left the Paxwax Homeworld."

"Aha. That is good. Well, at least we know why he was there. The Inner Circle like their spies. Now he has gone, and that means he has found out all he wants to know."

"You think he has found out about the Beltane woman and is now carrying the news to the Inner Circle?"

"It is a fair assumption."

"Indeed it is. And an even stronger reason why we should act quickly. I will contact the Lamprey and bring them to full – "

Her further words were interrupted by a message which came through one of the large speakers in the roof, summoning both sisters to go to Dame Rose's chamber immediately.

They met the stricken face of the doctor. Her mask was off and her hair had worked loose from her cap. Beyond her lay the still body of Rose lying on a white survival bed. Beside Rose, in an incubator, lay the still, dark body of her baby.

In the room no one moved.

40

ON BENNET

Now events were moving quickly.

After the tension, action brought release.

Pawl listened to the whistle and crackle of space as the charges built between his Homeworld and Proctor Central.

Pawl was contacting Lar Proctor. He intended to announce his matching with Laurel Beltane. He was as ready as he could ever be. Delay would be fatal.

An androgynous voice spoke from the darkness. "Lar Proctor regrets that he cannot be available for some time. Is your business urgent?"

"Very urgent."

"I see."

The absurdity of the situation struck Pawl. Here he was, a solitary man pushed into prominence, waiting to speak to a vain old man with false teeth and tell him a story as old as time but which would now precipitate a war.

"Lar Proctor will speak to you presently. We will hold this contact." The voice faded.

Pawl had received the news that the Beltanes were safe. The Vanburgh had drifted silently away from the Way Gate and now held position, undetectable, amid a belt of asteroids. He had also received confirmation that the most vulnerable Way Gates in his domain were protected with particle screens.

He had done what he could, buying information, trading with the Wong and the Felice, running logic tests. He had discovered seven colonies that were not registered and a mining settlement on a rogue asteroid cluster. An attack could have been launched from any of these.

Odin had sent news of a great build-up of Lamprey forces

close to Portal Reclusi, and Helium Bogdanovich now had them monitored.

During their last conversation, Helium was very friendly. "You have an ally in Dama," he said. "She and Clover have been talking. She said just what you said, so now Clover is coming back round to your side. That makes my position easier. But she is still unhappy about your tampering with the Code."

The seconds dragged past and became minutes.

How silly, thought Pawl, *how silly if the Xerxes were to attack now, before I can light the fuse.*

The black vivante plate in front of him became charged and a milky vapour like ectoplasm began to gather.

"Lar Proctor on vision," said the indeterminate voice and in an instant he was there. Lar Proctor appeared, seated on a small throne. Above him was a vast window, through which poured shafts of blue and gold light. He was obviously in conference and something in his manner, a certain smirkiness of face, revealed that he didn't mind being interrupted at all.

"Yes, Pawl. Can I help?"

"Lar Proctor. I have thought about the advice you gave me. I wish to strengthen my position by announcing an alliance, a marriage."

"Aha." Lar Proctor looked crafty. "You *have* acted quickly. May I know . . . ?"

"Someone you will not expect. But I am very happy, and so is she, and we shall all be the stronger for it. I now ask for the traditional Master's right to make the announcement personally through Central."

It was the tradition. The Master on the male side of the alliance made the announcement.

"Of course, my boy. Nothing would give us greater pleasure. It will only take me a minute to clear the lines and get the call signals out." Lar Proctor stepped away from the vivante.

Though he could not see them, Pawl could hear the tumult of voices, as his news was digested by the Proctor councillors. One, a bearded Proctor with long curving black tusks, peeped into the vivante space, saw Pawl looking at him, and bobbed out of the way again. Then Lar Proctor was back.

"Everything is ready. The call signs are going out now. All the Families are joining. I'm using the Paxwax anthem so they know it concerns you. Nearly there. . . ." Lar Proctor nodded to someone away from the vivante plate and then cleared his throat. He was broadcasting live. "I, Lar Proctor of the Proctor First, take great pleasure in introducing Master Pawl Paxwax of the Paxwax Fifth who has his own, important announcement to make."

Then he was smiling like an uncle at Pawl and Pawl found his perspective change as his own vivante linked with the giant image-casters of Central. The eyes of all the Families were on him.

"I AM PAWL PAXWAX. I WISH TO MAKE A DECLARATION. HEREAFTER THE FORTUNES OF THE PAXWAX FIFTH AND THE BELTANE FIFTY-SIXTH ARE JOINED. LAUREL BELTANE WILL MARRY ME. IN MY HAPPINESS I ASK FOR THE SUPPORT AND GOOD WISHES AND WISE COUNSEL OF ALL THE GREAT FAMILIES."

And that was that. Pawl broke contact, and even as Central faded he saw Lar Proctor staring at him in dumbfoundment, his mouth sagging open.

The message was broadcast and recorded. Already, on the Homeworlds of the Great Families, frowns were being exchanged, looks of amazement. Already the catalogues were being consulted to discover the whereabouts of the Beltane and their lineage. Frowns became a gathering of anger as the news sank in. Space was cleared between the Homeworlds and then became flickeringly alive as messages danced between the worlds. The tone of the messages was outrage. Who was this pert young man, this insolent who felt he could flout the Code of the Eleven with impunity? He would learn.

Lar Proctor was on the receiving end of his senior brother's anger.

"Weren't you supposed to be looking after the boy . . . ?"

"I didn't know," said Lar Proctor weakly.

"Didn't know? Didn't know! It was your job to know. You should have climbed into his mind if necessary." The senior brother raged and his great golden tusks cut the air.

For Pawl there was nothing to do but wait. The message had been carefully timed. All communication channels leading into his Homeworld were open, waiting for word of disturbance or the all-important, telltale synchronized use of the Paxwax Way Gates.

*

It was early afternoon on Bennet and the day was warm. Through the curved windows of his tower Pawl could see the rolling plains leading to the Mendel Hills and distant Frautus. Smoke was rising from the small village hidden in the hills. Along the road which led to the village, a team of men and women were clearing out the ditches and throwing the rich sodden humus up on to the road, where it steamed.

Pawl walked round the glass walls of his tower, looking down at the roofs and sloping walls, the bushy tops of trees and brilliant creepers, the shaded walkways and open courtyards.

Throughout the small island, life was transforming the sad Homeworld into a place of activity. The atmosphere spoke of steady optimism. People, all the new arrivals, were building towards a future.

With all his heart Pawl hoped that their faith was not misplaced.

Any further speculation was cut short by the voice of Wynn. "Master Pawl, I have a confused report. There is disturbance at a distant Way Gate. There is synchronized movement. Clear all vivante circuits, we have action. Repeat. . . ."

41

ON MORROW

The headless body of Rose lay stiff as a statue, rigid with balmcrete. The body lay beneath a battery of white lights on the central slab in the Taxidermy Hall. Here her mother had rested, and her grandmother and great-grandmother and so on back to the early generations of the Xerxes, when the practice of preserving the ruling matrons first began. It was an honoured place.

A sterile breeze issued from vents in the slab, keeping the body dry and wafting away the faint, sweet odour of the balmcrete which seeped through the skin. Silently the body rose several inches, and the underside rippled as though bathed in light reflected from water. These were the feather lights of the anti-gravity units which raised her. A team of sister-surgeons worked round the body, checking the skin for blemishes. The internal organs were already out and replaced with a springy, inert fibrous material.

To one side, the senior surgeon and her team worked on the head. It was painstaking work, carried out as tradition demanded. They were mending the face, making hairline incisions, easing out small rolls of fat, and then cutting and tucking and glueing the skin. When their work on the face was finished Rose would look dignified and alive, a woman arrested for eternity at the moment of her prime. The body beneath the clothes would hint at firm muscles. There would be a merriness about the face, and the eyes would be smaller.

The final posture of the body had not been decided. Events had moved too quickly for that, and Clarissa was now engaged in sifting through designs prepared by the embalmers. They worked from life, from pictures and vivantes, and the aim was to create a perfected image of what had actually existed.

The design room was a cubicle just to one side of the Taxidermy Hall. It was pleasantly cool, being deep in the stone tree, and Clarissa was relaxed as she leafed through the designs.

She paused at one picture. It showed an elegant Rose, standing on tiptoe as though about to run or dance, and with the wind behind her blowing free her magnificent dark hair. Clarissa shook her head at the conceit. Rose, who could not run without puffing, who caught a cold if she walked through a draught, whose hair was always greasy . . . Rose would have shied away from such an image as from something that mocked her. Where was the design that spoke of the Inner woman, not something dressed up merely for show?

She leafed on.

Most of the designs depicted Rose in movement. Only one showed Rose seated and this Clarissa set aside as too stylized. But then she turned to it again. There was something . . . (she held it at arm's length) . . . a boldness of line and colour, a pleasing simplicity. With a start she realized that this was the only design which included the baby. She studied it closely.

Rose was seated, her hair parted in the middle and falling in waves down the sides of her face. *Well, so it could have if she'd taken the trouble to grow it*. The face was crisply symmetrical and stared out at the viewer with radiance. In her arms nestled the

infant, one arm thrown back as though just turning from the
breast, its attention caught by the onlooker. Even its eyes were
alive. *What joy is here?* The gown was formal, dark blue and red,
and the full fabric rested easily on the bare shoulders and lap. It
was Rose as she might have been, as she should have been. The
likeness was not forced. The grace was a human grace. The image
spoke of . . . spoke of . . . Clarissa could not find the word . . .
but it *was* Rose and her baby, and showed the joy that should have
been and was not.

Clarissa knew she had found the right image.

She hurried through to the Taxidermy Hall, brushing aside two
small bald men who tried to carry the design for her. She waved to
the senior surgeon. That lady paused in her work on an eyebrow
and joined Clarissa.

"This is the final image I want you to achieve. A bit different, I
grant you, but then Rose was different."

The senior surgeon studied the design. She looked at it with a
technician's eye. "The face we can do easily. I'll raise the hairline
and open the lips a fraction. Mmmm. Shoulders are fine, we have
plenty of spare skin. I'll have to soften the pelvis. I'll run an
armature down from the neck to the chair so we can get that slight
lean forward. Attractive, isn't it? As though she was saying, 'Look,
see my child.' That's why the lips must be open. Mmmm. The legs
worry me. We may have to do some building there. At least
they're covered." She set the design down. "Well, there is only
one real difficulty, that I can see."

"And what is that?"

"The baby."

"The baby is essential."

"We have so little experience with babies. . . ." She realized she
had said something tactless. "Their flesh does not react like adult
tissue."

"The baby is essential, as in this design."

"We shall need time."

"Ah yes. Time." Clarissa relaxed. "Take plenty of time. We
have not yet announced poor Rose's death and do not intend to do
so for some weeks. Then we have the ceremony to arrange."

The senior surgeon nodded. She remembered well the pomp and
circumstance that had surrounded the funeral of Clarissa's mother.

"So *you* have plenty of time." Clarissa smiled suddenly, mischiev-
ously. She touched the curling feathers at her throat and the long

quills which dressed behind her ears. "If you think this is difficult,"
she said, indicating the design of Rose, "Wait until you have *me*
down here."

Clarissa left the Taxidermy Hall. She felt cheerful. She had often
studied her moods and come to the conclusion that she did not
understand herself. Why should she feel cheerful after visiting that
place of rouge and death?

She decided to walk through the tree, and without any conscious
thought guiding her, found herself heading downwards towards the
Corridor of the Ancestors. The air in this part of the tree was very
still.

"Ah, but she will look beautiful. We all will in time. Three
sisters. Rose and her baby. Jettatura on her silly trapeze. And me,
regal and still, my hand resting on the book of the Family, my
feathers like flames rising."

Clarissa came to a place where four corridors met. She was close
to the chambers deep within the roots of the tree where the worker
families of Morrow lived. She did not want to be near them. She
wanted silence.

The Guardians came to attention as she passed. Fine fighters,
fine women, ready should any disturbance break out on Morrow.
She thought of that filthy Spideret and shuddered. She thought of
Latani Rama as she stood bathed in blood; Latani Rama, now
many light years away from Morrow, waiting on a secret asteroid.
Latani Rama, who rarely spoke but who was an embodiment of
strength and courage. Clarissa missed her.

Clarissa was close to the Corridor of the Ancestors now. The
chatter of the little men who accompanied her began to irritate her
and she sent them away with a wave of her hand. "Stupid and
useless! Part of the baggage of tradition. Perhaps when this business
with the Paxwax is over we will have a real clear-out. Reassess all
the traditions. Get rid of the silly little men with their squeaky
voices. Rethink the fertility strategy. Perhaps find new sperm. Get
the wheels of the Xerxes women turning again. Yes, that is what is
needed, a shake-up."

She stopped in front of the glass case behind which the bead-
eyed face of Dame Rex stared out at her. Automatic lights filled
the case with a gentle glow as Clarissa settled herself on to her
stool.

"Well, we are about it, my dear," she said. "Action will be easy.

It is the waiting that is hard. The teams are all ready. They just are waiting the word. I've used your name. Rex. A good code word." She paused and sighed. Not for the first time she wished that queenly lady could reply. "I've just seen Rose. She will look different. Different but beautiful. Softer than most of us, I think. But softness does not mean weakness, does it?"

Again she paused. Her thoughts were not coming easily. Some days she could chatter to Dame Rex and it was as though that lady heard her and her eyes glimmered with understanding. But today . . . Clarissa realized that it was her own unsettled state. Gone was the brightness of humour with which she had left the Taxidermy Hall. Now her mind was filled with dark concern about her family. In her worst moments she feared the Xerxes were dying. They trod a narrow and diminishing corridor of humanity. Clarissa felt her limitations. She tried to be comprehensive; she studied history and music, but in her darkest moments she saw life as shape without substance and knew that beyond all vanities, such a state was derelict. Rose, poor Rose, who lacked that one ingredient of a successful life, the will to live – Rose had been the most comprehensive of them all, with her silly ideas about the future. Poor Rose, what was the value of interesting ideas without the will to make them actual? Where in her was the fierce driving energy which flushed the faces of the long-dead Xerxes? "A family is more than its inheritance. We will be strong again, and in being strong we will be different. When the Paxwax are under heel, the Xerxes will come into their own. It is the work you started, my dear Dame Rex, and it is the work I shall finish. We are poised."

Behind Clarissa in the corridor someone moved, her shape reflected palely in the glass panels. Clarissa did not see her.

"Our most capable fighters will lead the attack. My girl, Latani Rama, will drive like a spear to the Paxwax Homeworld. She will hold the Way Gate when I choose to descend. Oh, Rex, so much rides in the balance. If only you could speak, a sign. . . ."

A hand touched Clarissa's arm and she jumped. She spun round in her seat and found herself staring into the pale, cool face of Jettatura. The grip on her arm tightened. Clarissa could see perspiration standing on Jettatura's forehead. Her pink eyes were bright. She licked her lips.

"I knew I would find you here. I felt a need to tell you in person. Just a moment ago . . . I came as fast as I could . . . an announcement from the Paxwax."

"What!"

"I thought you would like to hear it from my lips. The boy has just spoken. He used the marriage formula. He declared himself for the Beltane girl."

"Just now?"

"Yes."

"Come on. We must . . . There must be no delay."

"Calm yourself, Clarissa. We have time on our side now. Now, more than ever, we must be firm and careful. We must not rush. Bid Dame Rex a gracious farewell."

There he was, the Paxwax boy, insolent in his humility.

"I AM PAWL PAXWAX. I WISH TO MAKE A DECLARATION. HEREAFTER THE FORTUNES OF THE PAXWAX FIFTH AND THE BELTANE FIFTY-SIXTH ARE JOINED. LAUREL BELTANE WILL MARRY ME. IN MY HAPPINESS I ASK FOR THE SUPPORT AND GOOD WISHES AND WISE COUNSEL OF ALL THE GREAT FAMILIES."

That was new, that phrase *In my happiness*, and Dame Clarissa sensed a contemptuousness in the mind of Pawl Paxwax as he uttered those words. Others would have noted it too.

Already the main vivante computer was registering alarm at the number of incoming signals which were being logged with the Xerxes. Clarissa could feel the outrage. As the Fourth Family, the Xerxes would be expected to take a leading part in the debate which was brewing. "Have the Shell-Bogdanovich Conspiracy lodged a call with us?" she asked Jettatura.

"Indeed they have, immediately after the Proctor."

Clarissa smiled. "Then, my dear Jetty, you must now take charge of the debate. Be amazed. Be angry. Stir the brew. But before you open contact with the Great Families take my hand and watch me."

Jettatura joined Clarissa at the main vivante console. She took Clarissa's left hand between her palms. With great deliberation Clarissa tapped out the letters R.E.X.

As a code of letters it flashed from the planet at the speed of light. Transformed into its symbolic equivalent it bit through space, reaching the farthest outposts of the Xerxes empire.

The dice were bouncing on the table.

"To work, Jettatura. Whip up a storm."

"And what do you plan to do?"

"I intend to dress. I have promised myself these few hours.

There is nothing I can do until the teams are in position. I estimate
– " she glanced at the chronometer above the vivante – "I estimate
the attack will begin in a little over two hours."

Rex. Simply decoded the word means, "Report immediately to
your team section. Identify yourself. Await instruction."

The network of people and organizations tuned to respond to
this injunction is vast.

On Ampersand, amid the ancient petrified bones of a great land
crab, a tour guide pauses. She listens to a woman who has
interrupted her and who now whispers in her ear. Briefly she
explains to the tourists that for family reasons she must leave them.
She hands over to the woman who interrupted her. She hurries
down the petrified shell, through the claws and out to a waiting
transporter which carries her first to her apartment, where she
collects a simple Way sack, and thence to the shuttle port. Within
the hour she is rising above the jungles of Ampersand to join the
other members of her team. She is an assassin.

Rex. The word finds its way to Primus, the planet of ice. There it
rings in the head of a man who sleeps in an insulated crucible with
the rest of his family. Quietly he wakes and dresses. His wife stirs
and he quietens her with a kiss. Minutes later he is shooting under
the ice aboard a small lane-craft. It glides to a halt at the shuttle
port, where the sea is like jelly. Soon he is aloft, the tools of his
Way Technician craft in a bag over his shoulder.

Rex. Sandringham hears the call. She has known it was coming for
days. She breaks a phial and draws the liquid into a hypodermic
needle. She injects her mother.

"Rest now," says Sandringham, tucking the covers round her
mother's neck and making sure that she is comfortable. "I have
work for a day. Sleep sweet. When I return we will visit the golden
desert."

She joins the crowd waiting to board the shuttle. A man jostles
her arm. She hears him mutter the call words and gives the reply.
Together they push through the crowd.

Rex. The signal is received and mashed by the vast gravity fluctu-
ations of Cochburn. Two bulky spheres bump and lock.

"Where's Porpi 127?"

"He was here a while ago. We drank together."

"Look. He hasn't even placed his A–G sphere on gravity feed."

"He must have left in a hurry."

Rex. A woman, shopping barefoot by the shore, hears the call. For a moment she pauses, enjoying the lemon sea and the pale green waves for perhaps the last time. She returns to her cave home, scribbles a note to her husband, and then screws it up and throws it away. She removes a Way sack from under their bed and hurries out through the cave mouth and down to the beach. A boat is waiting. But she slips and twists her leg to an ugly angle. Her bag spills open, showering a trigger mechanism and a small particle generator on to the sand.

The man in the boat splashes through the yellow sea. He scoops up the pieces from the sand. He offers his hand to the woman but she cannot take it. Her leg is white and swelling. Deliberately the man shoots her through the head and quickly climbs back into his boat. He escapes in a plume of spray.

On a distant continent a woman in furs, a replacement, shakes snow from her hair. She hears the call, checks the contents of her handbag and calls a snow taxi.

She sees the yellow ice slip by below her as the shuttle rises.

Rex. Within a hermetic pod on a lost asteroid Latani Rama assembles her particle gun with her eyes closed. Her movements are deft as a conjurer. She has done this many hundreds of times before.

Under the white dome and facing her are the members of her team: two other women and three dreamy men.

Beyond the dome is the bleakness and blackness of space. The stars that wheel are not known to Latani Rama. As a warrior she has accepted her orders, though she would rather be at home on Morrow. As a warrior she has accepted that she will lead the main assault force which will drive to the very Homeworld of Pawl Paxwax. It is an honour.

The asteroid is unlisted. It is a Way Gate loose in space.

Thus it is, all around the Paxwax Empire: teams join, exchange their discreet welcome signs and send a brief confirmation back to Morrow. Then they wait. There is nothing suspicious. An onlooker

would discover nothing irregular in the gatherings. The killers and
the clever Way Technicians wear the same bored get-my-journey-
over-as-soon-as-possible expression.

Then one of them is called. They begin to move. One by one
they present their Way passes to the Way Computer and are
cleared for transit. Here is a farmer travelling home, here a wife, a
translator, a surgeon, a father, a senior son of a minor family, all
going about their business. They do not tell any lies . . . they just
do not tell the whole truth.

On a thousand Way Stations the teams enter the Way Gates
like strangers. Once inside their manners change. The assassins
assemble their weapons from innocent materials. A toothbrush
contains a trigger. A block of soap or a box of pills contains a
generator. The Way Technicians begin the complicated hypnotic
sequence which will allow them to handle the Way Computers on
other stations.

Their preparations complete, the teams settle down in the mirror
chamber. One Way Technician lingers in the particle shower,
delaying the action of the Gate until the pre-determined time is
reached. Then he takes his place.

At a thousand places across the wide bowl of the galaxy,
wherever the Paxwax Empire touches its neighbours, Way Lights
begin to whirl. They hurl the attack team like darts, deep into the
Paxwax.

In silence Dame Clarissa watched as the attack teams registered.
Only a few teams were incomplete.

She looked magnificent. The flame of her dress matched the
flame of her feathers. The fine down at her neck was fluffed,
revealing a turquoise iridescence. Her primary and secondary
plumes were gathered close to her head like an elf cap. The face
was white, with the eyebrows penned in black.

She looked like a great hawk, and her eyes held a bright certainty
of prey.

For a few minutes she joined the impromptu debate that had
broken out among the Great Families. The debate was angry.
Jettatura was playing a leading role, advancing the argument that
the whole established economic order was threatened by Pawl's
action. "If we allow the Beltane to water our ranks, what other
opportunists will follow?"

Clarissa was pleased to see that Clover Shell was railing against

Pawl. She denounced him for his deceit. She called on the council
to take concerted action against Pawl. Clarissa smiled at this. She
half-wondered if the perfidious Shell-Bogdanovich Conspiracy were
planning to move against Pawl themselves.

Even Old Man Wong was belligerent. He held up the white
coiled balls of his fingernails as proof of his age. "Never till now,"
he whispered, "have I called for the two edged sword that kills
both life and spirit. Let the Families unite."

Clarissa was well pleased. She saw that the tide was running
against Pawl Paxwax, and left the debate and returned to her vigil.

She sat at the great vivante console in the main communications
hall.

It would be about an hour before word of the first attack came
through.

That was the longest hour of Clarissa's life.

42

ON BENNET

"Give me visual," said Pawl.

"The disturbance is distant, beyond the Pocket. I will gather . . .
but much is happening."

Pawl found himself staring into a Way Station many thousands
of light years away. He did not know its name or recognize it.
Close in front of him lay the still-bleeding remains of human
beings. The Gate was red. He could see right through to the mirror
chamber and that too was stained red with blood. The people had
been scissored at the moment they left the Gate.

"I have this recorded," said Wynn. "Shall I replay so you can
see what happened?"

"Replay."

The bodies jerked and began to reassemble. An arm stopped
bleeding and joined a shoulder. A face that had been sliced like

bacon knitted together. Red stains disappeared. A stomach closed like a rose and the flesh became white and then was hidden beneath grey clothes. Men and women pulled together and stepped jauntily backwards through the doorway and the Gate closed.

There was a moment's blackness and then the Gate opened and the same men and women stepped forward. They did not even have time to express surprise as the particle beam sliced them. The blood spouted and spattered. It was a thick tide on the floor. Pawl wondered that a human being could hold so much fluid, and then the image froze.

"There is action at other Gates," said Wynn. "Wherever six are passing I have stopped them. Do you wish to see?"

"No," said Pawl. "Just warn me if something happens that is not according to plan. Now is the most dangerous time."

43

ON PORTAL RECLUSI

Portal Reclusi jabbered and bartered, all unaware of the peril in which it stood. The Saints of the Lamprey poured through the Xerxes Gates. Some formed into sections and stealthily occupied the transit lanes.

Others, dressed in motley, mingled with the shoppers, hucksters, pickpockets, prostitutes, moneylenders, mask-makers and charm vendors who plied their trade in the great concourse. But where the eyes of the rogues were bright as they cheated and gulled, the eyes of the Saints were dull.

The Saints took up positions at the corners of alleyways. They gathered in the small central park and round the wide rim which surrounded the whole of the concourse. They waited.

High above, on the carved domed roof, a lone Spideret toiled. It was cleaning, rubbing the burnished relief work with its bristled abdomen. It held its position by anchoring its feet into holes drilled at regular intervals into the roof. From the floor of the concourse these holes were invisible, disguised by the complex design which swirled across the roof.

Beyond the holes was stealthy movement. Men and women climbed among the trusses. Their heads were bottle-shaped due to the gas masks they wore. Across their shoulders they carried the needle poles of fine-line particle generators. These could project a coherent particle beam that was only a few microns wide.

They swung into position, anchoring their gear to the steel trusses with magnetic clamps. They stared down through the small holes and the light from the concourse shone on their green masks. Each of them had a target. They watched as the Saints emerged from the Xerxes Gates and they followed them, keeping the heads of the Saints in the fine cross-sights of the particle generators. There was a soft whispering as they conferred with colleagues on the ground below.

A shape like a large, soft-sided black balloon drifted through the trusses, bumping gently against the cross-pieces and contracting to squeeze through. This was Helium Bogdanovich, safe within what he called his "dirigible". Inside the balloon he enjoyed the foetid atmosphere of his own Homeworld. He was contained within a complete ecosystem, though there was scarcely enough room inside the balloon for Helium to turn round. From this HQ he controlled everything. He monitored activity in the concourse from a camera hidden in the sting of the mechanical Hammer. He watched as some of his fighters, disguised as wizened Way travellers, dogged the path of those Saints who were occupying the transit lanes.

He did not know when the attack would begin, but he was as ready as he could be.

Now he waited, drifting gently, a creature with a thousand eyes, waiting to pounce.

He did not have to wait long.

Came a moment when all the Saints were clear of the Xerxes Gates. A clanging alarm started. The steps in front of the Xerxes jerked like a concertina and then lifted and flattened to become an impregnable wall. An unfortunate peddler who was standing on the steps when they rose was cast to the floor of the concourse along with his tray of soft fruits and sweetmeats.

On cue, the Saints threw off their disguises to reveal the glazed

grey micromesh of their combat suits. They raised the stumpy
nozzles of their particle guns. Some began firing, scouring the
alleys and walkways of the concourse.

When he saw the Xerxes steps move, Helium gave the order to
fire. The particle generators began to glow.

Some Saints collapsed, the beam having severed their spinal
cord. Others stood vacantly, their costumes hanging about them
and their weapons half-revealed, parts of their brains excavated by
the invisible beams. Some moved just at the moment when the
beams struck and found holes drilled through the bone and marrow
of their arms and chests. On one man's face a tear opened as
though he had been flicked by the flail of a whip.

Many escaped and continued firing. They began to burn the
roof.

Then came the gas.

It poured as a green liquid which vaporized as it fell to become a
grey drifting mist. By the time it reached the ground it was as pale
as the air. The gas was benign. Those who smelled it stumbled as
their sense of balance deserted them. They fell to the ground, their
eyes clenched shut as their universe wheeled. But they did not die
and the effect lasted only ten minutes or so. This was long enough
for Helium's men to swarm into Portal Reclusi and take charge.

Only one non-human creature died and that was the Spideret
that was crawling on the dome. It received the gas in its liquid
form, which burned. The Spideret contracted, then released and
fell. It turned like a falling glove and crashed to the ground in the
courtyard of a small brightly lit cafe.

Finally, when there was no more firing from below, a section of
the domed ceiling slid open and the vast, sagging black balloon
eased through and began a slow descent. Helium was marshalling
his men. The Shell-Bogdanovich Way Gates began to run at full
pace, ferrying in technicians and weapon-masters from a hundred
worlds in the Conspiracy domain. Helium had not told Pawl
everything. What he was assembling at Portal Reclusi was an
assault force. He was going hunting the Xerxes.

44

THE XERXES ATTACK

Latani Rama became aware of herself as she lay beneath the spinning mirror lights. She felt that first breath, as her body changed from coded particles to living tissue. Her body knitted as her heart took up its beat and her blood flowed and memories returned.

She sat up as the lights slowed and shifted from violet to white. Nausea gripped her stomach and bile burned the back of her throat. Two breaths and it was gone.

She checked her companions and was relieved to find them well and aware. One man's eyes had changed colour. Another had gained curly hair. Latani Rama was disconcerted for a moment to discover that she now had freckles on the backs of her arms and on her face.

But there was no time for wonder.

The first and longest leap was over. They were now deep in Paxwax territory.

While one assassin removed weapons from the Way sack, Latani Rama and her team dressed. There was no time for a particle shower.

When they were ready, one of the Way Technicians used magnetic probes to distress the Way Computer, forcing it to release the Way door without formal entry requirements.

The door slid open and Latani Rama, her particle gun raised, stepped through. She entered a dismal Way Station. It was in the middle of a host of asteroids. It served a mining station and the Way Platform was purely functional, a terminal for cargo.

She heard a singing. It came from behind some packing cases which were stacked ready for the shuttle. It was a man's voice and he was obviously unaware of her arrival.

She signalled for her companions to hold their place and then she crossed the Way Platform silently.

The man was seated with his back to her. He was eating a red-fleshed fruit like a watermelon.

At his feet was a baby Spideret. It was little more than a foot across its back. It was devouring a rat, pulling at the furry flesh with its mandibles. A small harness was strapped to the Spideret's back and its leash was tied to a table leg.

The sight of the Spideret stopped Latani Rama with a gasp.

The man heard, began to turn with surprise. His face, burned by deep space, was the colour of a ripe raspberry. She killed him quickly and then burned the Spideret as it bounded, held by its leash. She dragged and kicked the bodies into a corner.

There was no more life on the Platform.

Swiftly a technician and a fighter took up their positions, while Latani Rama and her three companions made ready for the next jump. So far there had been no problems.

They settled down side-by-side on the Way Table and the lights above them began to flicker and spin and dull to violet.

When they were gone and the bright Way Chamber was still again, the technician broke into the Way Guardian and began to alter the Gate's co-ordinates. He made a one-way linkage direct to the Lamprey Gates on Portal Reclusi.

It was now ready for the pale army of the Saints.

45

ON BENNET

"What do you mean, you can't make contact?" Pawl was starting to shout. "It is one of our Gates. I thought it was protected. It can't just have disappeared. If it is there you can contact it."

Wynn replied slowly and calmly. "Yes, the Gate is there but its co-ordinates have been realigned. It no longer speaks the Paxwax language. It is deaf to us."

"How? *How?*"

"It must have been surprised."

The pattern was becoming familiar. It meant quite simply that the Xerxes were making inroads into the Paxwax and the Paxwax did not know where they were. Any of the thousands of Gates within the Paxwax domain could be the next to fall.

"Trace that Gate," said Pawl. "Check every link we have. Most of them have limited terminals. Close every terminal. I don't care how important they are. Just pull the plug. Is that understood?"

"I am already acting on your advice. The Gates are dying."

Wynn was not inaccurate. Gates did die. Their ability to disseminate and construct life gave them a near sentience. What Wynn transmitted through space was an imperative. It was perceived as a symbolic statement: a ball breaking a sheet of glass, the closing of a shark's jaws, a trillion-volt discharge vaporizing rock. All the symbolic messages meant the same thing; only their imagery changed to suit the receiver.

Gates buckled like stunned oxen. Mirror chambers slowed while still receiving. Gruesome monstrosities of diseased and incomplete thought flopped and slid in the mirror chambers, and gasped and died. Things which should have been human came and went. Here was a hand the size of a man. Here a head, closed in a stomach, gained consciousness and screamed.

There was much screaming, for all life screams in its own way when threatened, and the screams echoed in the spaceways between Gates. The screaming infected other Gates. Gates within the Lamprey and the Longstock and the Freilander-Porterhouse wavered and became sick. The Proctor Gates heard the crying and faltered.

And still the danger was not stopped. Pawl could not close every Gate in his domain, for had he done so no information could have reached him.

He tried to contact Helium Bogdanovich and found that Portal Reclusi was closed and silent.

46

THE XERXES ATTACK

Latani Rama was well pleased. She relaxed in a Xerxes Gate. *How*, she wondered, *did Dame Clarissa manage to place a Xerxes Gate within striking distance of the Paxwax Homeworld?*

She enjoyed the familiar odours of Morrow and ate some of the food. Her Way Technician, who was not of the Xerxes, sat in a corner and mused. He had no idea where he was.

The Gate was like a sphere of glass. It hung, independent of any sun, in its own darkness. Looking out through the walls, Latani Rama saw a patch of space which glowed a misty green and blue and glittered with red and yellow suns. Elliott's Pocket. How often she had heard of this! It looked dangerous and attractive. Already, she knew, the attack would have entered the Pocket. Perhaps there was fighting there. Perhaps the battle was already won. Perhaps there had never been a battle.

Latani Rama had seen no problems. So far as she was aware the attack was proceeding without interruption. Her next task was clear: to capture the Way Gate above Pawl's world.

It was time for the last jump. Latani Rama sent a coded signal back to Morrow so that Clarissa would know what was happening, and then she entered the Way Chamber.

47

ON MORROW

Clarissa stared at the column of white sparks above her vivante plate. The vivante was running hot. This was the fourth time she had tried to contact Portal Reclusi. Her vivante grappled to make connections but there were no outgoing signals. Portal Reclusi had closed like a clam.

Clarissa reminded herself, and tried to believe, that no news was good news and that she had not arranged to contact Portal Reclusi, but even so. . . .

She sat, staring at the shower of sparks, feeling foolish and impotent.

Had something gone wrong? Were the Lamprey playing games? By God, if they had tried a double-cross, she would skin them alive and broil their tender parts over a slow fire . . . But no, they wouldn't double-cross. What had they to gain? Clarissa resigned herself to patience.

The voice of her vivante spoke. "We have a transmission from Thalatta standing by. Will you receive?"

"Yes. Put them on, but if you get word from Portal Reclusi, anything . . . you understand . . . anything, interrupt. I want to hear."

"Understand." The tower of white exploded silently and was replaced by the solid presence of a woman. She was dressed in a Xerxes Way suit and wore a helmet with the visor back.

The vivante transmission was from the Way Platform above Thalatta and Clarissa could see, behind the warrior, the slowly-moving blue and speckled brown of the planet's surface.

"We have captured Thalatta," said the warrior, without preamble. "There was no resistance. We have Semyon Beltane in his house. He wants to speak to you."

"What about Laurel Beltane? She is on the planet, I know that."

"There is no sign of her. We found her house drifting. Her house and her brother's house. . . ."

"And . . . ?"

"They are not there."

"What does Semyon Beltane have to say? Does he know where they are? Of course he does."

"He won't say. . . ."

"Then make him. Move. We don't have all day."

Before the Xerxes warrior could speak, her image froze and the vivante controller cut in. "We have a transmission from Portal Reclusi . . . signal is weak . . . we will augment."

The image of the Xerxes warrior became translucent and vanished. In her stead there appeared one of the Lamprey Saints.

It was a sorry sight. It was crushed in one of the small vivante cubicles on Portal Reclusi, crouched down and whispering. The face was burned and the hair wispy and frizzled.

"Portal Reclusi. Bogdanovich surprise. All gone. No one now. Me in station calling. Bring in any strength you have." In obvious pain the figure slumped. Clarissa was able to see beyond it to where the beautiful ornate carved dome spread above the concourse. Something was moving there. Something ridiculous. Clarissa watched as a big sagging balloon slowly drifted downwards. She had never seen anything like it.

She was about to ask if this were some new alien form when there was a sudden crackle of particle fire. A figure jumped down by the cubicle and fired at point-blank range. The Lamprey warrior exploded like something hit by a propeller. Then the vivante went dead.

But Clarissa had seen all she needed to. She had observed the bottle-shaped head of the attacker, noted the style of its movements and seen the insignia of the Shell-Bogdanovich Conspiracy.

So there was battle on Portal Reclusi. The Shell-Bogdanovich were involved. The Lamprey had been caught flat-footed. What was the next move?

Believing that it was anticipating Clarissa's wish the vivante controller re-established the link with Thalatta. Clarissa looked down on to the blue sea and the brown and green islands. Her warrior leader was there, awaiting instructions.

"Burn the planet," breathed Clarissa. "Burn it. I don't want to hear Semyon's lies. Tell him we'll find his girl. But burn his planet. Burn him with it."

The Xerxes warrior saluted and departed.

"Now get me the Lamprey," called Clarissa to the vivante controller. "I want to know what is going on."

48

ON BENNET

And suddenly Pawl understood.

Wynn had printed for him a three-dimensional plan showing the activity at all his Gates. He could track the invasion, noting where one attack group disappeared and, within minutes, re-emerged. Information was beginning to flow freely and he knew where the Lamprey had attacked, what worlds he had lost, and where he had stopped the attack. There was a pattern. The attacks, after an initial stealthiness, became flashy. They drew attention to themselves. And when Pawl noticed this he understood.

Somewhere hidden in his empire, was a secret Way Chain that led directly to his Homeworld. Everything else was flim-flam. He, Pawl, was the prize. The strike was not just for territory; that would come later. They wanted him. They had counted on surprise. They had almost succeeded.

"Connect me to the Way Gate above Homeworld," said Pawl and the pattern of Pawl's empire faded as Wynn made the connections.

The Way attendant appeared. He was a red-haired youth, newly arrived, just settling into his new routine and his new responsibility. He stood to attention when he spoke to Pawl.

"All quiet?" asked Pawl.

"All quiet, Master Pawl. I have advance warning of a consignment of honey bees due in from Raphael and a troupe of actors is due to arrive anytime from Rigveda. They hope to establish here on Homeworld. Advance papers say you know of them. In a few hours I expect to receive. . . ."

"Yes. Yes. Now, listen carefully. How many people have you up
there on the Way Platform."

"Fifteen, not including the shuttle staff. The usual complement."

"Good. I want you all to leave. Take the shuttle down to the
surface now. I want everyone out of there."

"But – " began the Way attendant. And then something in
Pawl's face or manner must have stopped him. "Straight away,
Master Pawl." He stepped away from the vivante stand. Pawl had
a clear view right through to the exit door from the Gate. It was
through here that any enemy would have to pass.

Pawl watched as the Way crew ran across to the escalator which
led down to the shuttle.

"All safe and ready to descend," said the red-haired Way
attendant.

"Good, can you see me clearly?"

"As if you were here in the flesh, Master Pawl."

"Life-size?"

"Close."

"Adjust your receiver to make me taller."

The red-haired boy did as he was bid. Pawl could judge the
height of his simulacrum by the way the boy looked up. "Now get
out of there," he said. "Come down to the surface."

"Yes, Master Pawl." The boy ran. Moments later Pawl heard
the whoosh as the air stabilizers came on to compensate for the
departure of the shuttle.

Methodically Pawl took charge of the Way Platform.

Latani Rama came to consciousness gently, like bubbles rising
slowly up through the sea to the silver surface. Her Way Technician
was leaning over her, whispering the hypnotic words that would
return her to herself. In her mind she had travelled to Pawl's
Homeworld as a six-year-old child. Now, as the bubbles rose, she
came to herself.

The Xerxes had learned. After their assassins had been disseminated at the Gate, they learned. To the Way Computer that
received her thought-patterns high above Pawl's Homeworld,
Latani Rama was an innocent but wilful child. Her ability to kill
without conscience was masked behind a desire for order and
cleanliness. That she was a fully-developed woman was merely a
matter of volume as far as the Way Computer was concerned.

The mirrors stopped moving and she slid off the smooth bench.

The freckles had gone from her arms. Her breasts felt larger and more wholesome. She was aware of their weight as she leaned forward. She discovered gold lights in her hair and the dry redness of eczema behind her knees. But she was aware of herself as herself, and of a tingling excitement. This had been the last jump.

The Way Technician gathered the Way sack and began to assemble the deflection unit which, when linked to the power of the Way Platform, would give them protection. In place, this unit would reflect all incoming energy. Next he began to assemble the particle cannon which would reshape the energy of Homeworld's sun into a narrow-focus beam that could vaporize Pawl's tiny island.

The steady work of assembly took several minutes. Latani Rama enjoyed a particle shower. She felt sensuous. She wondered about making love (as a warrior she could know no other state than virginity) and was amazed at herself. She began to suspect that passage through the Way Gate had transformed her in mysterious ways. But her mind was clear and sharp. She knew her duty. In a few moments she would step out above the Paxwax Homeworld, take the Way Gate, establish her weaponry and after an opening salvo to demonstrate her strength, demand immediate surrender.

The Way Technician was ready. His eyes were dull with trance as he established contact with the Way Computer and pre-empted its will.

A bell was ringing as Latani Rama stepped through and on to the Way Platform above the Paxwax Homeworld.

That same bell warned Pawl. He watched the Way door slide open and was surprised to see the slim, well-shaped woman who slipped through. She held a gas canister which she did not throw. She held it, her thumb white, when she saw that the Way Platform was deserted. That fact seemed to disconcert her. She had obviously expected people. Their absence was a warning to her. She crouched and ran with a dancer's grace across the small entrance foyer to the balcony which looked down on to Pawl's planet.

The blood-red reflection of Pawl's seas made her face glow. Then she crossed to the central armature column and, with one burst of her particle pistol, burned open the door leading to the power cells.

A man appeared through the Way door. In his arms he carried

some apparatus. Pawl realized it was time to act. He allowed his vivante image to build.

"Welcome to my Homeworld. I am Pawl Paxwax, Master of Paxwax."

The man glanced up at the giant figure which seemed suddenly to have materialized before him. In his astonishment he dropped the apparatus he was carrying, which spilled some of its contents on to the floor.

Latani Rama fired from where she stood. The bright blue beam of her particle pistol cut through Pawl's neck and caused a ripple of static before the beam dissipated its energy against the wall of the Way Platform.

Pawl acted quickly. He opened prophylactic vents at the base of the shuttle which began, methodically, to pump the air from the Way Platform into the void of space. It was a pressure reaction which, once begun, accelerated.

In sudden vacuum the blood of Latani Rama and her Way Technician boiled.

Before she died, Latani Rama fired a final shot. She had seen the giant figure of Pawl with his wild hair and yellow eyes, and knew it for what it was, a vivante image. *What vanity*, she wondered, *makes a man wish to appear as a giant?* Her final shot destroyed the vivante transmitter. Pawl vanished.

Pawl understood. What creature wants to have its death observed?

After five minutes of complete vacuum he closed the vents and stopped the pumps and allowed the atmosphere to build up. He ordered the shuttle crew, which had barely reached the ground, aloft again.

Later, a bell announced the arrival of new visitors to Pawl's Homeworld. The atmosphere had returned to normal. Pawl allowed them to enter. Though he could not see them he could hear and he followed their conversation with interest.

"Quiet isn't it . . . ?"

"I expected someone to meet us. I did contact them."

"Thank God we don't have a performance tonight. That Way Gate has made my sinuses burn."

"What's that?"

"Good God. What's happened to its face? It looks like sponge. And there's another. What's been going on here?"

"I feel sick."

"But look, will you. Look. You may need that face sometime."

"Is that blood? It looks like burn marks."

"Such a sight as this becomes the field, but here shows much amiss."

"Spare us. Do you mind?"

49

ON MORROW

Everett of the Lamprey Sixth is speaking to Dame Clarissa of the Xerxes de la Tour Souvent Fourth.

"You betrayed us."

"Of course I didn't . . . we didn't."

"You must have. Our Saints were ready. They were an elite. An elite. Fighting machines. They were irresistible except for deceit. You have betrayed us."

"We haven't. Where were your warriors, your Saints, when we needed them? Where are they now? You didn't commit them, did you? Not the way we planned. Not like a claw. You were mean. You tried to be too clever."

"Clever. Clever." It seemed that Everett Lamprey was about to have a heart attack. His blind, closed eyes stretched and closed like wrinkles on an elephant's trunk. "We were never clever. You were clever. Wanting to wait. You should have dragged the body of the Paxwax boy in front of his brother while you had the chance. You should have crushed him before he had any advantage. Now look where we are."

"You have made gains."

"Gains. Ha. We wanted to tear the whole empire into bits. But all we have is scraps. Elliott's Pocket is closed. No one can get in there. Portal Reclusi is silent as the grave. All we have are bits of empire. A world called Mako. Who has ever heard of a world called Mako? But we now hold Mako. We are grateful to the Xerxes. They have let us take a place called Mako."

"You are raving."

"Raving am I not. We are not fools. We trusted your stratagem and you are fools. The Xerxes sisters are fools. Now we see you slipping down the slope and we will stone you. Look for no joy from us. Stare into your mirror, Clarissa with the bright eyes; the face you see is the only friendly face."

Any reply which Clarissa might have made was stopped by a sudden clarion call. It was an emergency demanding immediate attention. It came from the Way Platform high above Morrow.

Clarissa let the communication build.

She saw a black balloon. Somehow it had squeezed through the Xerxes Way Gate and now hung there, disgusting, above her planet. She remembered the same alien shape on Portal Reclusi.

Before her eyes the balloon contracted. A seam appeared in its skin and then the balloon began to open.

A maggot shape . . . no, a great soft-sided creature . . . slid like a foetus into view. Dame Clarissa recognized Helium Bogdanovich.

Her fingers flew, tapping out co-ordinates which should have resulted in the destruction of the Xerxes Way Gate. But nothing happened. The power which leaped from the surface of Morrow and which should have shaken the Way Platform to fragments was absorbed and then spat back down to Morrow.

"Sue for peace, Clarissa," said the voice of Helium Bogdanovich. "I've outguessed you. Don't make me use force."

"How did you – ?" began Clarissa, but her voice clogged in her throat. She could not speak. Her stomach churned. Unable to help herself she pitched forward and vomited across the face of the vivante.

50

AT A POINT IN SPACE

The council summoned to condemn Pawl was in chaos. The Masters of the Great Families remained joined, but throughout their empires Gates closed, defences sprang up, and the rhetoric of war was heard.

All eyes were on Jettatura. She sat, white and pink and seemingly indifferent, as reports came in detailing the attack of the Xerxes and Lamprey upon the Paxwax. The council watched the battle swell and then fade inconclusively. They knew nothing of Pawl's lonely battle above his Homeworld, but they were aware of the battles at his Gates and the sudden ferrying of the Lamprey Saints. The abrupt silence of Portal Reclusi was frightening, and then came word that Helium Bogdanovich was above Morrow. Only when that news was announced did Jettatura raise her head. Then she stood up, excused herself, and after a brief, fathomless look at the daisy-bright face of Clover Shell, departed.

Moments later there was a stretching and bending in space as a new vivante presence sought to establish itself. It came to wavering focus and the great face of Helium Bogdanovich, usually benign and sleepy, stared savagely out at the assembly. "The war is ended," he said. "The Xerxes have capitulated." He looked round, staring into the face of each of the Masters in turn. "Pawl Paxwax, our youngest Master, was attacked without warning by the Xerxes and the Lamprey. I see that Everett Lamprey is not present. That is perhaps as well. There is a great reckoning to be made between the Paxwax and the Lamprey. I call upon the Council of Eleven to act together and censure the Lamprey."

The Senior Proctor stirred himself. "I think in this instance we will take it upon ourselves to carry out disciplinary action. I think it would be unwise to involve any more forces than are necessary." He turned his attention to the younger Lamprey, who sat shrouded, his face averted. "Our first request is that you cease all military activity immediately and return to your former boundaries. Failure to comply will result in action by us. Convey that message now."

The Lamprey representative stood, and with a formal incline of his head, dissolved his vivante image.

The Senior Proctor sat back. He felt rather pleased with himself. He thought he had spoken with dignity. However, his threat needed to be backed by action. It would not do for the smaller Families to observe what a shambles lay behind the Proctors' strict bureaucratic facade.

Wong Lungli indicated that he wished to speak with a slight movement of his fan. His voice was like dry leaves rubbing. Every phrase was translated distinctly. "We have a new Master to greet. I would like to see him. I want to see the man who can step aside from tradition. Such men are rare."

"Is that the wish of the Council?"

Daag Longstock raised his hand. "I have never seen the man," he said softly. Singular Sith rumbled his agreement. All the other families joined in giving their assent.

Pawl was not sure what was happening. Everything had stopped. About him was a great silence. He felt like a man who is deafened by an explosion and then sees buildings topple in complete silence.

It seemed that movement through the Gates had stopped. There was a suggestion that Gates were being abandoned. Wynn was struggling to hold connections, but the Way Gate system was so shocked as to be unstable. It would be a long time before confidence returned to it.

He knew that whole sections of his empire had been occupied by the Lamprey. He feared, knowing their mentality, that reprisals had already been taken. But there was no word from the Lamprey. He had tried to contact them, prepared to barter. And where were the Xerxes and the Shell-Bogdanovich? Of all the Great Families only the Wong acknowledged his signal, but then they politely refused to speak with him.

Was he being ostracized? Is that what was happening? Didn't they know there was a war on?

But then there came a message of blinding clarity. And Pawl, alone in his tower, looking down at his Homeworld basking in the late afternoon sunshine, was glad. It was a summons from the Council of the Eleven, demanding to speak with him immediately.

Wynn aligned the vivante beam into coherence with the incoming beam, and magically Pawl appeared as one of eleven glowing bodies, alive with that more-than-living brilliance characteristic of the vivante transmission. They were in no-place, and the darkness about them was not the darkness of space. They were at a mathematical point, or, to put it another way, they were at a confluence of symbols.

Pawl stared at the other Masters of the Eleven Families and they stared back at him. There was the Proctor, whose golden tusks coiled and whose mane shimmered.

Old Man Wong, with a face like crumpled paper. It was impossible to see his eyes.

Helium Bogdanovich, grey and sagging and uncomfortable out of water. Clover Shell, her face bright above her fat, unwholesome body.

The Lamprey, cowed and dirty. Pawl was reminded of a cast-off damp sock.

The Freilander-Porterhouse, bland and grinning.

The Longstock, still as a white mantis and with an insect's blank eyes.

Cicero Paragon, fat as a maggot.

Singular Sith, bull-faced, breathing through his nose.

Laverna Felice, a painted doll with purple eyes and bubbly white hair.

That was them. The power of the galaxy.

They looked at him. They saw a crookbacked figure with awkward legs and long dank hair and yellow eyes that blazed as though lit from within.

"Welcome to the Council of the Eleven, Master of Paxwax."

Pawl stood as straight as he could. "Well, despite everything I haven't changed my mind. I still will marry the Beltane."

The fan in the hands of Old Man Wong twitched and his head rocked. The old man was laughing.

51

ON BENNET

Laurel Beltane faced him. Her face was pale but her eyes were dry. The vivante image was clear.

"My father is dead."

Pawl stared at her. It was late in the evening and high above his tower the stars were twinkling. A night for love and healing, he had thought. He had not expected this news.

"But surely he was with you . . . I mean, I thought he was aboard the Vanburgh with you and Paris and anyone else you wanted to take along."

"My father would not leave. He insisted that his world was his and that he would die with it if need be. That was how he felt about things. He was a good man and now he is dead." The tears came, and with them anger. "He was a good man. Damn your Families and your squabbles. They have cost me a world where I felt at home and a father that I loved. Nothing can ever replace that."

"This war was not of my making."

"No, but you fought it. You could have given up your name. You could have given the Xerxes all they wanted and more. You could have come to us. We would not have loved you less and my father would still be alive and our Homeworld would still be a place of . . . He kissed me when we parted . . . he was not a very demonstrative man but his emotion ran deep. I think he knew . . . I think he had seen the future. When I got into the Vanburgh he said, 'Be happy.'"

Behind Laurel appeared the sad face of her brother Paris. He put his arms round her shoulders and stood looking at Pawl. "I am now Master of Beltane, a family of gypsies. My sister is Queen of the Gypsies."

"My love. My love," said Pawl. He tried to crush his soul into the words. "Please look at me."

Laurel Beltane lifted her eyes and looked at him through her tears. "Oh Pawl. Who could have dreamed that our hopes would begin this way. Look at us, all of us."

"We will be happy," said Pawl. "Believe me." Something began to stir in him. Something of his anger. Something of the feeling that drove him to his notebook. "Believe me, if it lives within my power we will be happy. I love you. Take strength from me."

"Oh Pawl." Her eyes held a touch of warmth. "Comfort me."

"Come to me now. Now. This very instant. Some of the Way Gates are open. Use the Proctor Gates. Our way is clear. I need you by me. I love you."

"Oh Pawl. Thank God, at least you are safe." She stepped away from the vivante.

Pawl found himself facing the sad, dark, otter face of Paris. He was just a boy. "Can I come too?" he said.

52

ON SANCTUM

Sanctum is roaring.

A million species, none of them human, have followed the events in the human world. They have rejoiced in the burning. They have longed to join in the battles, but have held back, watching the order of the Families shift and the balance of power adjust. Their time is not yet. But soon . . . soon.

Now they are busy under the guise of the Inner Circle, organizing the repair of the Way Gate system, easing relationships, being helpful.

But in every alien consciousness there is hope. The Paxwax boy is safe. Now he has power. Soon that power will be turned against the Families themselves. The Tree has told them.

Far beneath the surface of Sanctum, the small Gerbes called Odin is standing before the giant silver Tree. The two entities are alone.

Their thoughts drift together like smoke.

The Gerbes waits. Almost all that he is, is spread out.

HAVE I DONE WELL? the Gerbes asks.

VERY WELL, answers the voice of the Tree. YOU SEEM TO HAVE A WAY WITH HUMANS. BUT THE ORDEAL HAS TIRED YOU. NOW YOU MUST RETURN TO YOUR HOMEWORLD FOR A TIME AND GATHER YOUR STRENGTH. LATER WE SHALL CALL ON YOU AND YOU WILL JOURNEY FOR THE LAST TIME TO THE HOMEWORLD OF PAWL PAXWAX. THIS BATTLE WAS JUST THE BEGINNING. SOON WE SHALL MOVE TO VICTORY.

SO BE IT, says Odin, and slumps.

THE END

THE STORY OF PAWL PAXWAX, THE GARDENER,
IS CONTINUED AND CONCLUDED IN
"THE FALL OF THE FAMILIES"